Transformation of the French Demographic Landscape
1806–1906

Transformation of the French Demographic Landscape 1806–1906

Noël Bonneuil

CLARENDON PRESS · OXFORD

1997

Oxford University Press, Great Clarendon Street, Oxford OX2 6DP

Oxford New York
Athens Auckland Bangkok Bogota Bombay
Buenos Aires Calcutta Cape Town Dar es Salaam
Delhi Florence Hong Kong Istanbul Karachi
Kuala Lumpur Madras Madrid Melbourne
Mexico City Nairobi Paris Singapore
Taipei Tokyo Toronto
and associated companies in
Berlin Ibadan

Oxford is a trade mark of Oxford University Press

Published in the United States by
Oxford University Press Inc., New York

Copyright © Noël Bonneuil, 1997

British Library Cataloguing in Publication Data
Data available

Library of Congress Cataloging-in-Publication Data
Data available

ISBN 0–19–823340–X

1 3 5 7 9 10 8 6 4 2

Typeset by the author
Printed and bound in Great Britain by
Bookcraft (Bath) Ltd., Midsomer Norton, Somerset

to Maya and my son Willy

Acknowledgments

For their most constructive criticism, advice and encouragement, I wish to thank professors Ronald D. Lee, Kenneth W. Wachter, and Robert Chung from UC Berkeley, Ted W. Margadant and G. W. Skinner from UC Davis, David R. Weir from Yale University, as well as Nicolas Brouard from the Institut National des Etudes Démographiques (INED).

My gratitude also goes out to Catherine Doz, Jean-Marc Germain, and Françoise Maurel (Ministère des Finances and Institut National de la Statistique et des Etudes Economiques, Paris), for their heartful and ready willingness to discuss the manuscript with me.

I am indebted to my former students from the Ecole Nationale de la Statistique et de l'Administration Economique (ENSAE) and from the Ecole des Hautes Etudes en Sciences Sociales (EHESS), who continuously motivated me with their infectious enthusiasm.

I would also like to express my gratitude to the anonymous reviewers of Oxford University Press for their comments, which contributed toward improving the original version of the manuscript.

The final preparation of this book has been very much facilitated by the kind and competent help provided by Sylvain Baudry, Arnaud Bringé, and Nicole Berthoux (INED), and I wish to thank them for this.

Finally, for their friendly support on which I could always rely, my appreciation is extended to Nadia Auriat (UNESCO), Xavier Bry, Paul-André Rosental (EHESS), and the PhD students of the Laboratoire de Démographie Historique: Juliette Hontebeyrie, Morgane Labbé, Carmen B. Losa, Odile Macchi, and Anne-Christine Voelckel.

Maya and our son Willy were and are my constant source of love and optimism.

Contents

viii   *Contents*

II   Results and Dynamics

Figures

Tables

1

Introduction

1.1 Population Dynamics from Historical Data

The study of populations is increasingly focused on dynamics. Population dynamics are characterized by the evolution of certain attributes, such as the size of the population, its age structure, or its geographical distribution. Governing these attributes are three forces that evolve through time and space: fertility, mortality, and migration.

These are basic elements in population studies, be it for animals or for humans. Historical demography is the scientific study of population which provides the temporal dimension essential to imagining human societies in the process of development. But this discipline conceals a specific enrolment fee for the analyst, because our knowledge of populations is very often confused by the quality of data. Data for nineteenth-century France include censuses and vital statistics, the unreliability of which has been known to demographers at least since Van de Walle (1974).

Hence, anyone willing to explore past populations has to overcome the obstacle of flawed data, and to construct rigorous correction methods, so as to extract valid information and interpret underlying processes. The first intention of this work, therefore, is to provide a methodological renewal in the domain of population reconstruction.

In this work, I present in detail a methodology adapted to the historical case of the feminine population in nineteenth-century France. Although the technical detail is rather dry, demographers should recognize the value of building an analysis on solid foundations. It is always a pity to see enlightening results compromised by misconceptions or vague adjustments in the reconstruction process. Therefore, I shall try to make every step of this enterprise explicit.

Our lack of confidence in historical records should also warn us about neglecting information. Available material should be incorporated into the puzzle to piece together a whole. This is why the term *coherence* is regularly considered and accorded a precise meaning defined later in this text. Following investigation into the accuracy of my basic data, I

intend to build as specific a model as possible in the given context. I
invite the reader to discard common and incorrect approximations, such
as estimating net migration flows through subtracting the deaths from the
intercensal cohort differences. I prefer writing equations expressing the
process at work, and trying to solve the system through introducing the
weakest hypothesis possible. Some readers may find it more complex, but
it is also better controlled from the mathematical point of view. This
approach is not new, and even routine in mathematical demography.

Once demographic forces are revealed, I shall study their evolution over
time and space, and put special emphasis on examining whether a synergy
emerges between these forces. In addition to the description of trends,
short-term fluctuations, which have become a common theme in historical
demography, can be related from one region to another and help portray
the French demographic transition. Carlsson (1969) classified explanations
of the fertility transition into one of two categories: innovation/diffusion
or adaptation. In the innovation hypothesis, the adoption of fertility control represents a new behaviour. In the adaptation hypothesis, on the
other hand, fertility control reflects the adaptation of couples to changing
economic and social circumstances. It will be possible to illustrate innova-
tion/diffusion processes shaping the long-term alteration of behaviours.

As noted by A. Fine and J. C. Sangoï (1991), French demography is
better known in the eighteenth than in the nineteenth century. One reason
for this is the more intensive exploitation of parish registers than of civil
statistics, although there are plenty of the latter.[1]

As early as the mid-eighteenth century, France experienced the beginning of a sustained decline in its fertility, a decline which began in other
countries only after the middle of the nineteenth century, such as Sweden
after 1860 or England and Wales after 1880 (see Coale and Watkins, 1969).
The dynamics of the decline over time and space, however, still remains an
interesting research topic, since it is difficult to explain a collective attitude
when family formation depends on the individual will (see Le Bras, 1988).
As for mortality, France experienced the health transition, with, among
others, the Pasteur discoveries, in spite of several mortality crises (1832:
cholera caused 102,000 deaths in Paris; 1834: cholera in the south and in-
fluenza; 1847–1849: bad harvest, commercial, industrial and financial crisis,
revolution and cholera in 1848; 1853–1854: 143,000 deaths from cholera;
1870–1871: Franco-Prussian war, smallpox (200,000 victims), measles, and
dysentry (see Fine and Sangoï 1991, or Dupâquier editor, 1988b).

However, the study of the relationship between fertility and mortality
during the nineteenth century is often limited to the diagram of crude
birth rate versus crude death rate (Coale and Watkins (1969), Woods and
Rees (1986), Wrigley and Schofield (1981)). It is even rarer to see migration

[1] Important work has been done in *Histoire de la population française*, volume 3,
showing the specificity of the French demographic transition.

rates as the third dimension in the explanation.

It can thus be useful to attempt a further analysis, where the three dimensions would appear in an intricate empirical framework, capable of highlighting a possible synergy amongst the three. This could assess the importance of change and depict how mutations occurred throughout the century, which is the principal aim of this book.

The intended readership is interdisciplinary among social scientists with an interest in the introduction of measure and modellization into past population studies across space and time. These scientists may be concerned with better understanding the evolution of mortality levels and demographic behaviours during the transition, forming temporal patterns, and drawing a specific human geography. Historical time and space are thus presented here as the framework for demographical dynamic systems, and emphasis will be placed on testing and validating them.

1.2 Limiting the Study to the Female Gender

The subject is limited to the feminine population, as in Van de Walle (1974). Statistics do exist for males, but the additional difficulty for males relative to females should not be underestimated. Census under-registration is likely to be even more important than for women in these periods of militarism (Napoleonic campaigns until 1815, two revolutions (1830 and 1848), wars abroad (Mexican campaign, Crimea campaign, the war of 1870–1871), and migration is likely to be heavier than for women. As an example, the 1861 census missed 125,000 soldiers (*SGF*, volume 1866, Introduction)! A study for males could be done, but I cannot guarantee that the smoothing methods employed here for females would be efficient. This question could deserve attention in a future volume.

Female age pyramids could be cloned into male ones with the help of sex ratios estimated in statistics of 'deaths from a certain cause' with no gender difference. Kuagbenou (1992) has developed this idea for Paris from 1832 to 1849 to obtain the Parisian male age pyramid with its confidence interval from the female age pyramid as reconstructed in the present book. Unfortunately, such statistics are hard to find for each *département* throughout the nineteenth century and need extensive time to be collected.

The study of the feminine population brings to light a considerable amount of information, particularly on migration patterns and fertility/mortality dynamics. The main additional problematic a two-gender study could introduce is specifically the relationship between the genders in term of total numbers. Extensive information on military mobility would probably be essential before undertaking such an analysis.

1.3   On the Tracks of Etienne Van de Walle

Published in 1974, Van de Walle's book entitled *The Female Population of France in the Nineteenth Century* (subtitled *A reconstruction of 82 départements*) represents a major step in furthering our knowledge of the French demographic transition (see for example the review by Henry and Blayo, 1975). The work has numerous merits. Not only does the author highlight the qualities of the nineteenth-century census data and vital statistics, but more significantly, he identifies numerous flaws in these data. Van de Walle suggests useful methods for reconstructing the French population by *département* in a manner that is consistent from a demographic viewpoint. He draws upon a series of *départemental* indicators of mortality and legitimate, illegitimate, and overall fertility, which have subsequently been used in research by numerous scholars.

My purpose is neither to undermine nor to displace this work, but rather to offer a sort of 'companion book' which re-examines, using different methodological approaches, a number of delicate questions which Van de Walle had appropriately simplified. Given the important foundations laid by Van de Walle, I will make sporadic references to and comparisons with his work.

Specifically, my reassessment of the nineteenth-century demographic data focuses on the modelling of migrations. Van de Walle had to content himself with a simple approach to this issue, a priori independent of time and identical for all *départements*. Here, one important contribution of my work is the systematic treatment of migrations, which makes it possible to reconstitute the very urbanized *départements* which Van de Walle had to ignore; thus, I shall be capable of completing the *départemental* analysis by making it compatible with the national analysis after adding up numbers from *départements*. It is the first time that mobility between *départements* will have been figured out, whereas previous analysis relied solely on migration toward Paris. The maps of migration intensities are new, and show the importance of urban centres as well as a dichotomy between a mobile part of France and a stagnating one. The consequences of the Franco-Prussian war of 1871 are visible, as well as the rhythm of life cycles.

A second difficulty confronting Van de Walle was the occurence of misreporting in census declarations and the under-registration of births and deaths. He cautioned against the scarcity of reliable data and nevertheless managed to reconstruct a coherent whole which enabled him subsequently to correct the biases in the data. Here, I suggest a new method based on adjusting model life tables to directly estimated life tables. This situates the smoothing operation at the very heart of the demographic process and has the advantage of imposing a coherent demographic structure capable of correcting the original data with rigour. One weakness of this method is the heavy reliance on model life tables, which are not infallible, especially for younger ages, where uncertainty remains in distinguishing between mortality and fertility in under-registrations of births. However, in accordance with my choice to work with Ledermann model life tables, I shall estimate under-registration of births and deaths over time and space. Then, I will show a strong similarity between maps of fertility and maps of mortality. Notably, mortality is shown to be higher after 1840 than was estimated by Van de Walle, which raises new questions concerning the impact of social hygiene. The diminishing difference between cities and countryside is another new result, as well as the higher mortality level compared to Van de Walle's estimation in less developed regions such as Brittany or Limousin.

To summarize, the first part of this work addresses the two difficulties of correction of extant flawed data and estimation of demographic intensities, including migration. The second part gathers results in synthetic maps which show historical regions known for the specificity of their customs and certain noteworthy regularities.

I deliberately will not distinguish between legitimate and illegitimate fertility. To obtain age distributions of married women, on the subject of which 'the censuses err also', Van de Walle (1974, p. 99) had to 'rely most on the vital registration, which may not share the biases of the censuses'. He suggested a way 'to allocate women within each age by marital status'. Contrary to Van de Walle, I shall try to prove that vital registration was not that good, thus further developing and improving Van de Walle's procedure to reconstruct the birth and death statistics. Moreover, under-registration at birth has a doubly deleterious effect: when Van de Walle, banking on a very high quality of vital statistics, could both reconstruct the population of married women by age and calculate the legitimate Coale index I_g, by using the total number of recorded legitimate births, important biases in birth registration raise a serious obstacle. Evaluating age distributions of married women becomes hazardous, while the total number of legitimate births entering into the estimation of I_g is completely unknown, since it is groundless to assume that under-registration affected only one marital state. I shall endeavour to illustrate that the knowledge produced by the overall fertility index can enlighten and contribute to current debates on the nature and pace of the fertility transition, and reveal otherwise hidden patterns in time and space.

1.4 The Data

References for the census data used in the analysis are presented in Table B.1 and vital statistics are referenced in Table B.2 (in Appendix B).

The knowledge of demographic facts of 1789 to 1914 was the focus of an entire chapter in *Histoire de la population française* (Dupâquier and Le

Mée, 1988). This thorough work is recommended to readers interested in learning about the origins and emergence of the *Stastistique Générale de la France* (*SGF*). In addition, Van de Walle (1974) detailed the quality of the French statistics in the nineteenth century. I am similarly interested in population statistics by age, by gender, and by *département*. Unlike Van de Walle, however, I disregard civil information.

The major points of Van de Walle's critique of French nineteenth-century statistics are reviewed in the following section.

1.4.1   Selection of the Censuses

The year 1851 demarcates the era of the first exhaustive censuses. The population by age and by *département* was published for the first time in France. Van de Walle noted a considerable bias already resulting from a tendency by respondents to round off their age to a number ending with a zero.

Prior to 1851, census data is barely usable. According to Van de Walle (1974), the first two real censuses, conducted in 1801 and 1806, are mainly estimates rather than enumerations in the exact sense of the term (p. 17). He details the reasons. No census was carried out in 1811, nor in 1816. The census allegedly of 1821 was actually conducted at different dates varying from 1817 to 1821. Methods employed were still largely questionable. The census of 1826 was simply inferred from the preceding enumeration of 1821. The 1831 census marks the beginning of a quinquennial series, followed by the census of 1841. Nevertheless, neither of these censuses are sufficiently reliable. Van de Walle recalls that under-reporting in censuses could be related to the widespread contemporary belief that they were linked to fiscal investigations.

Although the census of 1846 was conducted under improved conditions, it did not contain detailed information about the distribution of the population by age. As explained by Moreau de Jonnès (cited by Van de Walle), 'il est presque impossible de connaître l'âge des gens avec précision, parce que certains l'ignorent, d'autres le dissimulent' [it is almost impossible to ascertain the age of respondents with any degree of precision, because certain people disregard their age, while others intentionally cover it up]. Around 1851, an effort was made by the French administration to improve the quality of the census. The 1901 census inaugurated the use of Hollerith machines, which enabled the adding and classifying of data, and considerably reduced the amount of error.

This résumé of Van de Walle's analysis leads us to be wary of censuses prior to 1851, despite the fact that this author used them in his reconstruction. For the missing censuses (1811, 1816, 1826), Van de Walle resorts to interpolated values. Despite his corrections, I believe that the data is too inexact to be included in this subsequent reconstruction. I will therefore only employ censuses from 1851 to 1906.

As demonstrated by Van de Walle, however, I must examine the demographic coherence of these censuses, before manipulation of the data. This will be the focus of Chapter 4. Since census dates varied in this second half of the nineteenth century, I furthermore suggest a method of calibration.

1.4.2 Vital Statistics

It is worthwhile to begin by reviewing Van de Walle's analysis (1974).

The responsibility of recording vital statistics was shifted from clergymen to mayors by a law decreed on 20 September 1792. It took several years for this new organization to function efficiently, and as a result, usable data was available only at the beginning of the 1800s. Van de Walle (1974) notes that the poor quality of the data was not only caused by under-registration, but could also result from incomplete centralization or counting errors.

He remarks in particular on the issue of stillborn babies. Throughout the entire century, the term 'stillborn' was used to designate both babies who were actually born dead, and those babies who came into the world living, but who died before registration had taken place. The total number of live births was therefore contaminated by this systematic under-registration.

Furthermore, he showed foresight in noting that as the century progressed, there was a gradual decrease in the number of *départements* which had an abnormal sex ratio generally superior to 105 (Van de Walle, 1974, p. 51). He concluded an under-registration of the female population, which progressively evened out over time (p. 52). From a geographical perspective, he noted that the quality of the data was generally better in the north than in the south of France.

Finally, the sequences of recorded births suffered from an obvious under-registration, which varied by region and progressively diminished over time.

Van de Walle (1974) mentioned no other defect in death statistics other than false 'stillborns'. In *Histoire de la population française* (Dupâquier and Le Mée, 1988), there is also mention of 'double counts of foundlings', as well as populations completely unaccounted for both in civil records and in census data.

As did Van de Walle, I employ death statistics from 1800 to 1855 in addition to the birth and stillborn series from 1800 to 1906 by *département*. The *SGF* had published deaths by age, gender, and *département* from 1856 to 1906. Although the data is most likely biased by age heaping and perhaps also by under-registration, I have incorporated the information into my analysis, whereas Van de Walle had chosen to ignore the data and worked only with the total number of deaths from 1856 to 1906. I will see how the information on deaths by age contributes to the reconstruction, which in reverse, will enable the correction of this data.

1.5   Organization of the Book

My topic is to reconstitute the demographic evolution of the system constituted by 89 French *départements* throughout the nineteenth century. Three difficulties are in store for such a task: the cleanliness of the original data, or book-keeping coherence; the demographic coherence, or whether data are internally coherent with demographic processes; and the crossed effects of mortality, fertility, and migration.

The first part of this book is devoted to the population reconstruction. Chapter 2 is a brief review of methods in this field, with special emphasis on Van de Walle's approach, which was specifically conceived for the same set of data that I examine.

Before entering into the actual reconstruction algorithm, I shall devote Chapter 3 to a clean up of the original data issuing from the official publications, the *SGF* volumes (*Statistique Générale de la France*). I have indeed detected over 500 errors in the *SGF* tables, most of them minor, but important to correct since the tables form the basic material for the analysis. It turns out that copying errors cluster on certain digits, and certain regular types of errors can be characterized. I hope the reader will enjoy observing the history of calculus, of statistics, and even of France, whose statistical errors offer a sort of barometer, through the analysis of a microscopic and fortuitous phenomenon.

This cleaning up done, the major experiment begins in Chapters 4 and 5. The demographic coherence raises a formidable difficulty. Sorting out regular patterns of numbers from those that are accidental is a complex task. Therefore, a series of smoothing operations are applied successively, piecemeal, to different parts of the demographic system. Incrementally, the technical steps I shall present in this chapter amount to an overall procedure.

In Chapter 4, a preliminary treatment of the data is necessary. First, months when censuses were conducted and elapsed time between censuses vary throughout the century. Thus, the location of successive birth cohorts throughout the censuses is an important step, in order to dispose of homogeneous and comparable sets of people.

Unfortunately, once located, cohorts appear to fluctuate abnormally along with age, essentially because of age heaping. Methods have been developed to handle this question, but they are not intended to be applied to a whole series of censuses. Therefore, I shall present an original technique to treat age heaping specifically throughout cohorts. This set of adjustments constitutes only a preliminary treatment of the censuses. The final one will be done by the reconstruction itself in Chapter 5.

Vital statistics are also biased, be they total numbers of births, deaths, or deaths by age. The correction will also come from the reconstruction, but deaths by age must first be treated so as to identify them by each birth cohort. Therefore, I shall develop an original method based on two-dimensional smooth interpolants on the cumulated distribution of deaths by age and months of the year. This technique produces total numbers of deaths for each cohort and each age (triangles in the Lexis diagram) without altering observed values of total number of deaths for a given age class. In other words, this smoothing operation does not modify existent information, but restores missing information.

Chapter 5 presents the general algorithm of the reconstruction. Two periods can be distinguished: from 1801 to 1855, where only the total number of deaths is published in the *SGF*, with no distinction of age; and from 1856 to 1906, where statistics of death by age are available. In this latter period, I shall reconstruct the French population successively period by period, going from the more recent census of 1906 to the oldest one of 1856. At each time step, a life table and a distribution of net migration by age for each *département* is produced. The estimated life table is then smoothed by fitting the best Ledermann model life table for some carefully chosen distance. This correction of age-specific probabilities of dying enables the correction of censuses in return. It also helps in correcting the total number of births and of deaths.

Thus, the original demographic *SGF* series will have been superseded by a coherent system, resembling as closely as possible the basic data. The sequence of the five operations: adjustments for dates of censuses, identification of deaths by age to corresponding cohorts, preliminary smoothing of the cohorts, smoothing of the life tables to the closest model life tables and reconstruction on the basis of this adjusted model life table constitutes a global correction process, consisting in finding demographic structures that are coherent (equations are verified), plausible (thanks to the Ledermann model life tables), and as close as possible to actual raw figures (least squares smoothing of cohorts and of life tables).

The distributions of net migration rates by age and the correction of vital statistics, notably the adjustment from estimated to model life tables, are further included in the reconstruction of the population from 1806 to 1856. This reconstruction is more simple, but still has the benefit of taking *département*-specific distributions of net migration rates by age.

The second part is devoted to the analysis of the results obtained from the reconstruction, especially to the study of the dynamic relationship between mortality, fertility, and net migration.

In Chapter 6, I gather the results obtained for each *département* and compare the sum of these results to other studies on a national scale. This is the first time since Van de Walle that national results will have been obtained by aggregating *départemental* results. This author avoided urbanized *départements* and had to content himself with approximations of the national age distribution. Population sizes can be added up, yielding age pyramids for the whole of France. From these pyramids, mortality and fertility indicators can be calculated and compared to other estimates made directly at the national level. Also in Chapter 6, a European perspective is brought to light by comparing France to other countries.

In Chapters 7 and 8, I shall present the spatio-temporal evolution of mortality, fertility, and the distribution of net migration rates by age. Instead of publishing plenty of maps for each variable and each date, I have systematically classified *départements* according to the temporal evolution of each variable. This allows me to divide the French territory into geographical types of more or less homogeneous evolution for the variable concerned. There is no reason for the classification based on one variable, fertility for example, to be similar to that of another variable, for example mortality, but it would be interesting to observe overlaps. For net migration, the age distribution as a whole has been considered in the classification, so that typical distribution patterns emerge. Maps will reflect a good agreement between geographic distributions of mortality and fertility at the beginning of the nineteenth century. Moreover, the higher estimates of mortality will be an important result, which raises new questions about the influence of social hygiene.

The study of a possible interaction between mortality, fertility, and net migration of young women is the topic of Chapter 9. First, a classification according to these three variables leads to a division of French territory into geographical types of relatively homogeneous temporal behaviour. Once again, these classifications do not necessarily resemble those obtained when *départements* are classified according to any single variable. The landscape of the demographic transition will then turn out to be arranged around three diffusing poles and ordered along an urbanization hierarchy. To my knowledge, this is the first time that such a dynamic structure of the demographic transition is illuminated in this way.

This organization of French space throughout the nineteenth century can be used to study the diffusion of short-term temporal fluctuations of fertility. Short-term demographic changes have been treated on historical time series (Lee, 1981; Eckstein et al., 1985; Galloway, 1988, 1992), but rarely on space-time series like here. The statistical model I present is a step toward short-term dynamic analysis of the transition. The techniques I shall use are derived from state-space models (Aoki, 1990), space-time models (see Cressie, 1991), or co-integration models in the study of trends (Engle and Granger, 1987). I shall neither use nor recommend a technique in use by some authors consisting in comparing descriptive clusters of demographic behaviour calculated separately at each period as if they were independent. Space-time models are more accurate, since 'they are characterized by linear dependence lagged in both space and time' (Cressie, 1991, p. 449). Here, these models will help emphasize the importance of the structure of the territory, both in terms of geographical and cultural distance and in terms of urban hierarchy.

I hope that this voyage through the intricate web of French demography will help shed light on the recent history of European countries, and will provide the reader with a more unified view of the ensemble of changes over a determined territory throughout the nineteenth century.

Figure 1.1 Regions of France.

Figure 1.2 *Départements* of France.

Part I

Reconstruction

2

Reconstruction Methods: A Brief Review

2.1 Reconstruction from Parish Registers

Wrigley and Schofield (1981) have produced long annual series of baptisms, burials, and marriages for England from 1541 to 1871. This material was the basis for various reconstruction methods which I will just touch on here, to give the reader a glimpse of the reconstructions catalogue. I wish to point out that, in spite of a superficial resemblance, my own project is very different. Wrigley and Schofield (1981) or Lee (1974) were reconstructing time periods where there were no or few censuses. Moreover, they were working with data in which there was no breakdown of deaths by age. This differs from my project which has a far richer amount of raw data as explained in Chapter 4.

2.1.1 Lee's Inverse Projection

Lee's inverse projection (1974) aims at producing annual (or quinquennial) age pyramids, and series of mortality and fertility indicators. This method requires baptism and burial series and an initial census. Intermediate censuses are not essential, but can be incorporated into the reconstruction and help give a rough idea of migration flows (Lee, 1985).[1]

For a closed population, starting from an age pyramid $p_x(t)$ the 1st of January, year t, mortality conditions of year t are summed up by an indicator e_t such that:

$$\sum_x p_x(t) {}_1q_x(e_t) = D(t)$$

where $({}_1q_x(e_t))_{x=0,\cdots,90}$ denotes the model life table of parameter e_t, $D(t)$ is the total number of deaths. Model life tables are taken in usual net-

---

[1] R. McCaa (1989) has implemented the inverse projection algorithm on a software called 'Populate'.

works such as Ledermann's or Coale and Demeny's. For Ledermann's, the parameter e_t is the life expectancy at birth at year t.

This equation yields a single solution e_t. The next age pyramid at 1st of January of year $t+1$ is obtained by equations representing the aging of the population:

$$p_{x+1}(t+1) = p_x(t)(1 - {}_1q_x(e_t)) \quad x = 0, \infty$$

From an initial census, a simple iteration based on these two latter equations yields population by age $(p_x(t+1))_x$ and life expectancy e_t (t=1541, ..., 1871 in the English case for example).

Instead of having an initial census, if the population is closed and the registration of good quality, the initial population size can be calculated from the final one by subtracting births and adding deaths. The initial age structure is generally taken as stable, since a theorem by Wachter (1986) guarantees the ergodicity of the inverse projection, that is to say the oblivion of the initial age structure. Note that if baptisms or burials are badly recorded, or if the population is not really closed to migrations, determining the initial population size, which is very important in the reconstruction, can become a hazardous matter.

2.1.2 Wrigley-Schofield-Oeppen's Back-Projection

With the back-projection method, Wrigley and Schofield (1981) suggested the reconstruction not only of fertility and mortality indicators, but also of net migration rates.

I will not expand here on the back-projection and refer the reader to the critical paper of Lee (1985) and to Bonneuil (1992) for more detailed discussion. This method has been superseded by J. Oeppen's new version, which I present briefly below.

2.1.3 Oeppen's Generalized Inverse Projection

This method suggested by Oeppen (1992) applies to birth and death series, as well as to a terminal census. It produces age pyramids, fertility, mortality, and net migration indicators.

The method works with a terminal census $(\hat{p}_x(T))$ at date T (x is age, $x = 1, \cdots, K$), death series $(\hat{D}_t)$, and birth series $\hat{B}_t$, $t = 1, \cdots, T$. Model life tables have a single parameter a_t:

$$ {}_5q_x(t) = {}_5q_x(a_t) $$

age-specific net migration rates $m_x(t)$ have a single parameter b_t:

$$ m_x(t) = m_x(b_t) $$

The open age class $p_K(t)$ for cohorts born before the beginning of the death series are filled with the assumption of stable population. Parameters a_t and b_t are obtained through approaching the raw data on all ages and dates:

$$\min_{a_t, b_t} \left(\sum_0^T (1 - \frac{\hat{D}_t}{D_t(a_t, b_t)})^2 + \sum_0^K (1 - \frac{\hat{p}_x(T)}{p_x(T; a_t, b_t)})^2 + \lambda \sum_0^{T-1} (b_{t+1} - b_t)^2 \right)$$

where λ is a parameter giving more or less importance to the smoothing of migrations.

This method seems to work. However, it is not clear whether it produces the best solution or only an approximate one.

2.2   Reconstruction from Censuses and Vital Statistics

2.2.1   Van de Walle's Method

When censuses are regularly conducted and vital statistics available, one danger is to take the data for granted. If the data were accurate with consistent age categories and geographical boundaries, it would be easy to approximate net migration, fertility, and mortality indicators. The difficulty in the case of nineteenth-century French statistics consists in the correction of extant flawed information.

To correct births and total population sizes in the censuses, Van de Walle relied on the ratio 'R/E' = '*Recorded/Estimated*' or 'R/CB' = 'Recorded/Computed by balance' between the declared number and the number estimated by him.

To correct the births, in following a same cohort g, he compiled the list of the $(R/E, a)$, where R/E is the ratio of the recorded age class a, cohort g (published from 1856 onwards) divided by its estimation. He then corrected the total number of births at $t = g$ by multiplying by the inverse of the mean of R/E's. This enables him to narrow the gap between the reconstruction and the published censuses. For instance, he was led to re-evaluate births of 1811–1815 of 5.1 per cent in Calvados. He admitted that it is sometimes difficult to adjust births, using only 'R/E', which can oscillate around the reference value equal to 1.

The intrinsic rate of Lotka considered in the initial stable population is estimated on the basis of births and deaths between 1800 and 1805. However, on examining the list of 'R/E's for the three generations, which were respectively 0–4 years, 5–9 years, and 10–14 years of age in 1801, in the most reliable censuses (from 1851 to 1866), we detect distortions, which can be corrected by modifying the value of the rate of Lotka in the initial age pyramid.

Finally, to avoid too large distortions in migrations, Van de Walle smoothed the population size series P_t, which can suffer from a significant under-evaluation. He then calculated a list of ratios 'R/CB(t)' of the population size R declared at date t over the population size CB deducted from the 1846 census through births and deaths, following which he regressed $R/CB(t) = \alpha t + \beta + \epsilon_t$ and corrected the numbers P_t by $\hat{P}_t = P_t(\hat{\alpha}t + \hat{\beta})^{-1}$. It is on these smoothed series $\hat{P}_t$ that the migrations $M_{t \to t+5} = \hat{P}_{t+5} - \sum_a p_t(a)(1 - {}_5q_a(t))$ are calculated, to be redistributed by age according to a fixed schedule ${}_5w_a$:

$$p_{t+5}(a+5) = p_t(a)(1 - {}_5q_a(t)) + {}_5w_a \left(\hat{P}_{t+5} - \sum_a p_t(a)(1 - {}_5q_a(t)) \right)$$

As admitted by Van de Walle, these manipulations are based on the assumption that migratory flows are stable and that they represent a constant proportion of the population. On page 92 of his book, he even cautioned the reader that the estimations of the numbers he proposed were not worth much more than the published numbers, aside from the fact that they could assure a certain demographic coherence for the whole of France throughout the century. Nevertheless, the reconstruction is useful for assessing the validity of published censuses (p. 66 of his book).

2.2.2 Weak Points of Van de Walle's Reconstruction

Van de Walle discussed in length the hypotheses he chose to investigate. His choice of Coale and Demeny north or west model life tables, although different from mine, is well defended in his book. In this book, I selected Ledermann model life tables in order to guarantee a certain demographical coherence. This different choice of model life tables does not make any methodological difference in the reconstruction.

Van de Walle also raised the question of under-registration of deaths, above all for 0 to 5 year olds. He did not make any correction on the declared total numbers by *département*, but he recognized that a deficiency in deaths could not be distinguished from a deficiency in births. I shall later discuss a re-evaluation of deaths.

In my opinion, the most fragile hypothesis is that regarding migrations. Van de Walle clearly showed that it was inconceivable to ignore inter-*départemental* migrations (example of Hautes-Pyrénées Figure 3.4 p. 80 of Van de Walle, 1974). However, he had to develop a standard schedule for the age distribution of net migrants, a technique later used in the reconstruction of the English population by Wrigley and Schofield (1981). Furthermore, he had to refine the series of total numbers, in order to produce plausible migratory flows.

To develop this schedule, Van de Walle projected the population of *département* of the Seine, which absorbed the largest proportion of internal migrations, from 1861 to 1866. In comparing the population projected in 1866 to that recorded at the same date, he deduced the migratory standard schedule. He proceeded in the same way for the Seine between 1896 and 1901, and then calculated the average of the two profiles. Finally, he attributed a value of 0 to the migrations of the 0–5 year olds, under the pretext that such migrations often mask children who are actually being nursed.

There are difficulties associated with this calculation: the censuses used have been accused of being distorted by age heaping or by under-registration; the application of a schedule constant in time and place, even though calculated for the key *département* of the Seine, implies an approximation of effects that are badly controlled. Finally, this procedure ignores migratory dynamics between *départements*, which we know are clearly structured in the twentieth century (Poussou et al., 1988).

Similarly, the total number of migrants depends too heavily on the (smoothed) population size of the census, and should result more from global inter-*départemental* dynamics.

3

Book-keeping Coherence

3.1 Correction of Tables

Before proceeding, as did Van de Walle, to examine the demographic reliability of the *SGF* statistics, the 'book-keeping' reliability of this data must
first be assessed.

The statistical tables of the *Statistique Générale de la France*, and in particular the censuses and vital statistics of the population, give the illusion
of first-rate data to anyone who studies nineteenth-century demography
(for instance Van de Walle, 1974). An examination of the quality of these
published figures however seems necessary, but is rendered difficult by the
considerable amount of data. Contemporary informatics enables us to in-
spect, correct, and augment the figures with a certain measure of reliability.

I should clarify here that I am criticizing neither the coherence nor the
credibility of the demographic statistics of the *SGF* in the nineteenth century, a task already undertaken by Van de Walle (1974). Rather, I initially
want to precede this type of analysis, with the goal of having at my disposal
tables that are correct from a numerical perspective. Only in an ulterior
study (Chapters 4 and 5) can I discuss the 'demographic' validity of these
tables.

3.2 Principles of Correction

3.2.1 Book-keeping Coherence and Demographic Coherence of SGF Tables

In the censuses and the statistics of deaths by age, the rows of the tables
represent the *départements*, while the columns are the age groups. The
two columns on the statistics of births and stillborns are, respectively,
legitimate and natural.

I would say that a table is 'coherent on the book-keeping level' when, on
the one hand, the sums following the rows or the columns correspond to
the written totals and on the other hand, when a table declared as a combination of other published tables is effectively the stated combination—for

example, the table for the population by age for both genders ('les deux sexes réunis') is equal to the sum of the table for men and that for women, or again, the table for women is equal to the sum of the tables for women classified by civil status.

It is according to these simplistic criteria that I have made some corrections to the *SGF* statistics from 1801 to 1906. A priori, these are errors either of calculation or of printing and transcribing. This cleaning operation is considerably laborious, considering the mass of numbers involved, and also rather superficial, since the operation does not correct inconsistencies of a demographic nature. Nevertheless, it is an aim not totally without interest, in so far as it permits us to tackle precisely the true demographic calibration. In passing, it reveals some curious traits in the relationship between those digits or numbers and the men who printed them.

3.2.2   Pursuing the Error

The Tables of Population by Age   Caution is the rule: two or more wrongly corrected numbers in the same table quickly camouflage the true errors. Thus, when an inadequacy between the sum written in the book and the calculated sum is detected, its origin must be located: is it due to a miscalculation or to an erroneous number in the cell? If the same shifting is found in the line (*département*) and the column (age class) summations, I initially suspect the cell. In this case, either the error is obvious in comparison to the adjacent numbers [1] and the profiles of distribution apparent in the other rows, or else I must pursue the error in the more detailed tables. For example, if in the records of population by age, I find a four digit number when the adjacent age classes are two digits, and that partial sums add up in the presence of an error, I would conclude that the cell is wrong. If the general surrounding level does not render the inscribed value unusual when the partial sums are wrong, I try to identify the error by adding the potentially more detailed tables: population by gender, age, and civil status, and population by age classified according to rural or urban residence. When the table for both genders by age exists, the agreement with the tables by gender has to be assured.

When only one of the two partial sums calculated differ from the partial sums inscribed, I doubt the summation in itself. Following all the verifications indicated in the other tables, I can suggest that it is the total which is wrong, and not one of the cells.

However, this correcting scheme may not always be appropriate. Consider the following three examples: a first case could arise where a particular cell is correct and the two marginal totals contain the same error. A second possibility may be when a particular cell is wrong and only one of the

---

[1] e.g. in a series of numbers '250 200 310 2000 220 ...', it is obvious that '2000' is erroneous.

marginal totals contains an error, thereby rendering the other apparently wrong. A third example of when the correcting scheme may fail is when all three of the numbers in question are wrong. After a certain overflow of inaccuracy, one has to give up. I have basically been able to correct the series of censuses from 1851 to 1906 with a certain assurance due to the relative richness of the volumes in the tables which tend to review each other.

These guidelines based simply on common sense can today be applied in a systematic and exhaustive fashion with the help of computers. However, certain censuses are 'clean', such as those from 1861, 1866, or 1872 as well as those from 1901 and 1906, notably dates in which statisticians received help through 'mechanical means', such as the Hollerith machines.[2]

Département of Origin versus Département of Residence   The tables classifying the population between *département* of residence and *département* of origin have only the total sums for verification. Thus the correction for this type of table from 1891 and 1896 was very limited, and many inadequacies are still present. I have, nevertheless, eliminated the most visible. Luckily, the table from 1901 is almost free of error.

Tables of Deaths by Age   Few guidelines are available for cleaning up the tables of deaths by age: the partial sums remain the foremost measure of reference; the comparison with the numbers of the adjacent age classes, with the profiles of the *départements* of the same numerical level and with the numbers published in neighbouring years; at times the confrontation with the partial intermediate sums, like the deaths of the '5–10 years old', '5–20 years old', '20–60 years old', or the '60 years old and above' are confirmed efficient tools, yet fallible. Subsequently certain numeric incoherencies have remained undetected. An example of such a fallacy would be an error of +10 in the column of the 10–14 years old counterbalanced by a minus 10 in that of the 35–39 years old, with nothing to draw attention to the combination of the rows. Where is the error situated? In the marginal totals for the whole of France, or in a specific but unknown *département*? Although error location is unknown, this type of residual error is rare and practically insignificant: for example, an error in the magnitude of 10 is present in a numerical row of figures in the hundreds.

The Tables for Births, Marriages, Total Deaths and 'Stillborns'   Until 1851 exclusive, the tables for deaths without age distinction consist of three columns, one for men, the other for women, the third for both. The total

[2]See 'Lettre à M. le Ministre du Commerce, de l'Industrie, des Postes et des Télégraphes' signed by C. Moron, in the 'Recensement des Industries et des Professions' of 1896.

of the first two rarely differs from the third; when it does, the correction is often evident.

The tables for births and stillborns may reflect the rough appearance of the tables for deaths without age distinction, but more often, the distinction is made between births by gender and by legitimate or natural status, with the sums in the margins. In this case, the correction made holds more validity.

Finally, the tables of the total number of marriages are often detailed according to gender, age, civil status (boy, widow, divorcee), and are easy to correct.

3.3   Analysis of Errors

I have carefully withdrawn from the present analysis the 'errors' obtained from the total errors already uncovered—generally, those found on the row *France* or *Totaux*, which are a result of errors made in one or more *départements*.

The psychological relationship between man and numbers has recently received renewed interest in medical research (Grafman 1988). In this study, the figures examined are derived not from the ill, but from professionals dealing with numbers. It may therefore be useless to want to compare the errors of one with those of another. Nevertheless, a comparison illustrates that the mode of confusion in the arithmetic or the inscription of the figures by professionals of the *SGF* in the nineteenth century reveals a certain mental structure.

3.3.1   Errors by Substitution

I discuss 'error by substitution' when the corrected number differs from the written number by only one digit —for example, 59 instead of 57. This type occurs in 83.5 per cent of the 516 errors analyzed.

The process of choosing the wrong number may not be arbitrary. This is shown in Figure 3.1.

I have represented each Arabic number in function of:

- in ordinate, the estimated probability of writing the given digit instead of another is the degree of attraction held by the digit;
- in abscissa, the estimated probability of writing the given digit (which is the correct digit) as another digit is the degree of ambiguity possessed by the digit.

I ascertain that the digit 7 is the least ambiguous in written form as well as the least attractive: the digit 7 read in the *SGF* has the best chance

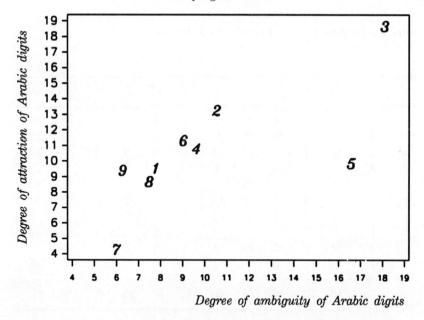

Figure 3.1 Ambiguity and degree of attraction of Arabic numbers.

of indeed being a 7; if a digit is badly written, it has a minimal chance of being a 7. The digit 7 is therefore a stable sign.[3]

On the contrary, the digit 3 is unstable: when it is found written in books, it is possible that in reality it is another digit; reciprocally, another digit written has more of a chance of being in reality a 3. The digit 3 is therefore very attractive as well as very ambiguous.

Between the two, the digit 5 is poorly attractive, but ambiguous. This digit is therefore under-represented in the *SGF* tables, relative to how it should be. The digits 9, 1, and 8 are however more attractive than ambiguous, and are subsequently somewhat over-represented.

Deloche and Seron (1987b, p 164) broach the subject of the coding of digits and the errors made in the process of restitution of the linguistic stimulus into the numeric digit. For them, this aspect of the transmission of numeric information cannot be avoided: it is an integral part of the cognitive process and of the individual relationship with numbers. They indicate that their patients confuse similar digits such as a 5 and a 3 in

---

[3]Note that generally in France, the digit 7 is handwritten as '7' with a cross on the vertical axis. This can be said to differ from North-American handwriting, where the digit is not barred and is therefore more easily confused with the digit 1. Although *SGF* volumes are published without the cross on the axis, we suspect that potential confusion was diminished because of the particular form of the handwritten digit.

Reconstruction

Table 3.1 Frequency table of errors by substitution

		corrected										
		'0'	'1'	'2'	'3'	'4'	'5'	'6'	'7'	'8'	'9'	total
	'0'		7	1	2	0	2	9	0	0	8	29
i	'1'	4		13	2	11	1	4	3	1	0	39
n	'2'	7	9		22	3	3	3	3	4	3	57
s	'3'	2	3	16		9	33	3	1	10	2	79
c	'4'	1	5	4	15		11	4	2	1	0	43
r	'5'	4	4	1	8	13		6	2	0	3	41
i	'6'	7	1	1	3	2	20		7	2	2	45
b	'7'	0	3	3	2	0	0	6		4	1	19
e	'8'	2	0	3	20	1	1	2	0		7	36
d	'9'	16	0	3	1	1	0	1	7	10		39
	total	43	32	45	75	40	71	38	25	32	26	427

459 written as 439, or a 6 and a 9 in 1246 written as 1249. They have unfortunately renounced a more intricate study due to the restrained frame of their data, judging that the patients did not manifest too evident a problem in this type of confusion. With the *SGF* statistics covering more than a century and representing a considerable wealth of numbers, I am perhaps in an adequate position to suggest several hypotheses. Let us examine in detail the correspondence between the written digits and the corrected digits in Table 3.1. Two types of confusion are evident:

- the first seems very much related to the physical form of the digits. The round forms can be more easily confused with each other: 0 was written especially in place of a 6 or 9, and 6 or 9 in place of an 0; the angular forms of the digits with each other: 1 written in place of 4, 4 in place of 1; the double looped forms: 3 in place of 2, 5 or 8; 5 in place of 3 and 8 in place of 3;

- the second is related to the similarity between the correct digit and the mistaken digit, which is reflected by a stressed sub-diagonal and super-diagonal.

  Gonzalez and Kolers (1987) discuss the effect of symbolic distance: in their experiments, the subjects are quicker to decide that 7 is larger in the (2, 7) pair than in the (5, 7) pair. This demonstrates a confusion between adjacent values and numbers having closer positions, a confusion that Deloche and Seron (1987b) have also discovered with aphasic persons. They indicate that the error in position at minimal

distance has been compared by other authors to symptoms of para-
phasia. Spiers (1987) also categorizes this type of error as 'simple
substitution', and ranges it under the diagnosis of paralexia, para-
phasia or paragraphia.

I have examined here the role of the digit in itself. However, in Arabic
notation, unique in the history of numbers (Hollender and Peereman, 1987),
digits are attributed different symbolic values according to their position
in the number. To be mistaken on a 1 in a position of a unit, a tenth, a
hundredth, or a thousandth is not meaningless either on a formal level or
on the linguistic level which can also interfere. Deloche and Seron (1987b)
have treated the subject in depth. Amongst the multitude of cases they
present, let us mention the violations of the left right direction: 500 as
105 (*cinq cent* as *cent cinq*) or morphological types of confusions: *cent*
transcoded as 5 (*cinq*) or as 20 (*vingt*).

I have tackled this question for the *SGF* by, on the one hand, comparing
each orally read pair (corrected number, erroneous number), which has
not produced results and, on the other hand, by crossing the position of
the error (unit, tenth, hundredth, thousandth etc.) with the length of the
number where the error was made.

3.3.2   Position of Error in the Number

The general table without distinction of the particular substitution turns
out to be equidistributed at 1 per cent level, which militates in favour of
the independence between the position of the error and its length, and
therefore in favour of an absence of mental transcoding of the linguistic
type.

If I distinguish according to the erroneous number, it seems that the 0 is
placed preferentially in the unit position, which would indicate a tendency
to round off the numbers. I find nothing significant for the other values of
the erroneous number. It is true that the numbers are weak. The same
pattern applies to the correct number: no phenomenon appears significant,
except for the 0, which seems to be modified as another number when it
occupies the unitary position. It would come from a kind of fear of rounding
the numbers, one compensating for the other. However the few observed
numbers make it difficult to draw conclusions. The notion of a linguistic
type interference could therefore be discarded.

Another aspect inducing the apparition of errors is the actual length of
the number, which goes in hand with the quantity expressed. Gonzalez and
Kolers (1987) call to mind how large numbers (from a psychological point
of view) can perturb the attitude of a subject and how the quantitative
variation can exert an influence on the result.

Table 3.2 Length of numbers and appearance of errors

Length of the number	Census of 1876 male	Census of 1876 female	Census of 1881 male	Census of 1881 female	corrected numbers, 1876, 1881 both sexes.
1	204	111	185	154	0
2	127	116	132	139	2
3	175	181	168	186	1
4	2690	2709	2719	2721	61
5	602	520	517	522	9
6	202	189	106	105	0
7	2	2	1	1	0

3.3.3 Influence of the Length of the Number

To test the influence of the length of the number in the error making process, one needs to line up comparable and relevant *SGF* statistics. The censuses from 1876 and 1881 are comparable for the length of the numbers used and their closeness in time, while the lists of respective errors are relatively long and concern the total numbers of age classes, males, and females. These censuses are thus comparable. Not counting France as a whole, I obtain Table 3.2. A Kolmogorov test permits acceptance of the hypothesis of no difference between empirical distributions at the 1 per cent level: the influence of the length of the number in the error-making process in book-keeping is therefore denied.

3.3.4 Error by Permutation

I refer to 'error by permutation' when the corrected number can be obtained by the permutation of digits in the written number. This case covers 3 per cent of the errors. Among the 16 cases identified, 14 are transpositions of digits.

Table 3.3 has been drawn up to illustrate that in 7 out of 9 possible cases, the permutation took place in the middle of the number.

Spiers (1987) calls this problem, which consists in reversing a sequence of numbers 'Mirror reversal', or 'Partial reversal'—e.g. 564 instead of 654.

3.3.5 Errors by Omission or Addition

Table 3.4 consists of 3 per cent of the total number of errors. In 6 out of 12 cases, the digit 1 was omitted in the position at the far left, meaning

Table 3.3 Errors by permutation

département	year	written	corrected
Alpes-Basses	1886	73	37
Saône-et-Loire	1890	251	215
Calvados	1892	187	178
Maine-et-Loire	1892	956	596
Rhône	1900	301	310
Oise	1841	4702	4072
Meuse	1842	3374	3734
Meurthe	1875	9950	9590
Meuse	1875	6590	6950
Gironde	1851	4382	4832
Yonne	1851	3497	3479
Ardèche	1861	9853	9583
Sarthe	1861	37147	37174
Ille-et-Vilaine	1896	310418	301418
Marne	1877	712	127
Charente	1874	3954	3495

at the beginning of the written number. Other digits may sometimes be omitted, and their positions varied.

This observation follows Spiers's (1987) who includes the pathology of being incapable of recognizing a digit under the name of 'omission'. He indicates that it often consists of the number to the far left (as in the case of Figure 3.4), which suggests an error stemming from negligence.

In addition to this, I have noted of three 'additions', concerning only a 1 put by mistake at the beginning of the numbers. This kind of mistake is not commented on by Spiers.

In globally observing all the omissions and additions, there seems to be a certain fragility with regard to the position at the far left of the term.

3.3.6 Other Errors

Of the 518 errors analyzed, 58 cannot be classified under any of the categories discussed to date. They potentially consist of errors of calculation more difficult to comprehend in our limited context.

None of the errors listed by Deloche and Seron (1987b) seem to be applicable here, except, perhaps, the tendency for the subject to distort the far right of the number, while conserving the proper length of the numeric form. In fact, I note that the units column is the preferential position of

Table 3.4 Errors by omission or addition

département	year	written	corrected
Hautes-Pyrénées	1890	4	14
Eure-et-Loire	1900	1	10
Saône-et-Loire	1875	89	189
Loire	1889	84	184
Aisne	1891	21	218
Marne(Haute)	1903	55	555
Nord	1867	352	1352
Ain	1898	129	1293
Seine	1867	435	1435
Haute-Saône	1900	124	1249
Côtes-du-Nord	1867	6908	16908
Dordogne	1866	1883	16883
Meuse	1897	19	9
Côte-d'Or	1891	193	93
Manche	1901	192	92

the error, at least for numbers which are four digits long (Table 3.5).

3.3.7 Influence of the Nature of Digits

I have additionally tested whether the corrected numbers differ from the other numbers of the same table by the nature of the digits they contain. One may speculate whether the presence of a given digit or the combination of certain digits preferentially induce an error of transcription. I have therefore counted the frequency of digits 0, 1, ..., 9 in the corrected numbers in the censuses of males, then in the female ones from 1876 and from 1881. I then compared the totals to the distribution of the same digits in these two censuses taken together. It seems that there is no influence at the 1 per cent level.

I have reiterated this type of manipulation by limiting myself to the digits neighbouring the erroneous digits. The digit preceding the error is skewed by the general level of numbers. The digit following the error, when it exists, should be, in absence of influence, tested as equidistributed between 0 and 9. After statistical computations, this hypothesis of equidistribution (on the 274 numbers examined), is rejected neither for wrongly written digits nor for digits corrected by myself.

Table 3.5 Position of the error in the numbers not previously classified

length	position				
	unit	tenth	hundredth	thousandth	not determined
2	2	0	0	0	1
3	4	4	0	0	2
4	16	1	5	0	8
5	0	0	0	0	2
6	0	0	1	2	8

3.3.8 Book-keeping Standing by Département throughout the Century

In vital statistics or in a census, errors are relatively well divided among the rows of the various *départements*. No one *département* conceals errors systematically throughout the course of time, and at one given period, there is no one *département* that is particularly erroneous. *départements* with similar names—for instance, Vienne and Vienne(Haute-)—do not share the same errors even for the same periods of time.

Nevertheless, it is noteworthy that Loire-inférieure and Lot-et-Garonne contain erroneous digits at the successive censuses from 1881, 1886, 1891, and 1896; this remains limited however and does not call into question a certain neutrality concerning the *département* nor its name.

3.3.9 Book-keeping Standing by Year

A rich commentary can be found in Dupâquier and Le Mée (1988) on the establishment of population statistics between 1789 and 1914. The quality of the published works can be evaluated through an in-depth look: for instance, we learn how certain segments of the population, especially at the beginning of the century, did not figure in any statistical document, or which obstacles the census-takers ran into at the time, etc.

The concern in this preceding process of correction was simply the book-keeping coherence of the *SGF* tables. Based on this process, I posit that vital statistics are almost without error from 1801 to 1835. This data belongs to a single publication entitled 'Territoire et Population', published in 1837 under the responsibility of Moreau de Jonnès .

According to Dupâquier and Le Mée (1988), the census launched in 1851 makes us 'enter resolutely into the statistical era' due to the reorganization of the *SGF*, under the direction of Alfred Legoyt.

The statistics of births, deaths, and stillborns from 1836 to 1850 are published in volume II from 1851. Although during the century errors are generally not very numerous and are spread out in a more uniform manner, they have accumulated during the brief period of 1846 to 1850 with a peak in 1848. To explain this, we can invoke, as suggested by Dupâquier and Le Mée (1988), the rivalry during these years between Alexandre Moreau de Jonnès, then head of what became the 'Bureau de la Statistique Générale', and Alfred Legoyt, initially a member, and then head of the Statistics section of the Ministry of the Interior. Could arithmetic troubles reflect conflicts between men?

From 1851 to 1865, the tables of vital statistics including deaths by age were better maintained, whereas the censuses from 1851 and 1856 left much to be desired. Those from 1861, 1866, and 1872 are relatively correct. Of course, this does not prevent these censuses from being faulty on the level of demographic correction, like that of 1872, firmly criticized by Van de Walle (1974), who actually judged it inferior to those preceding and those following. The censuses from 1861 and 1866, correct on the book-keeping level, interest us because they cover the same territory as today.

Vital statistics (births, stillborns, and deaths by age), from 1867 onwards, do not have a comparable book-keeping quality as the statistics prior to 1865, especially during the post-war period, 1871 for births, from 1872 to 1877 for deaths by age.

The census from 1876 also suggests neglect (51 errors), and here again, human movements can be spotted behind the negligence: A. Legoyt was revoked at the time of the fall of the Second Empire; the *SGF* had again become 'a simple office attached to the general secretariat', directed as of 1875 by Toussaint Loua. The transitional years therefore seem to have left their mark.

The statistics of births and stillborns from 1873 onwards are quite acceptable, counting only one or two errors per year, with the exception of the 1891 census which contains 5 errors. From 1895 on, they are without reproach.

We have seen that the post-war 1872 census was correct, but that that of 1876 was particularly bad. The 1881 census is not much better (29 errors); that of 1886 shows some improvement (11 errors).

Toussaint Loua retired in 1887, and was replaced by Victor Turquan until 1896. This transfer of power was perhaps the origin of the absence of *départemental* statistics from 1887. The directorship of Turquan corresponded to a notable carelessness: the 1891 and 1896 censuses are mediocre statistics on population by age (53 and 39 errors respectively), and also for the tables combining the *département* of residence with the *département* of birth (numerous errors). The quality of the tables for deaths by age, which had improved as of 1877 (on average 4 errors per year), also deteriorated between 1886 and 1892 (between 11 and 16 errors).

In the transition of power in 1897, the table recording deaths by age is equally bad with 19 errors. From 1899 on, things stabilized with 4 to 9 errors per year. Blancheville was the new director from 1896 onwards.

The 1901 and 1906 censuses are practically flawless. One can therefore see the mark left by the beginning of the full-scale mecanographic exploitation which is at this time brought into effect by the aid of the classifier-counter-printers invented by Lucien March ('l'exploitation mécanographique intégrale, qui serait effectuée cette fois à l'aide des classi-compteurs-imprimeurs inventés par Lucien March') (Dupâquier and Le Mée, 1988). The statistics for births already showed no error from 1895 onwards; those for deaths by age annually show some errors until 1906.

Although lacking any form of proof, the above analysis summarizes how simple arithmetic may document and elucidate periods of time, men and their rivalries, their changing careers, and the advent of mechanical progress.

3.4   Book-keeping Coherence: Conclusion

From this point on, I have at my disposition tables coherent from a book-keeping perspective. Complete tables of corrections are published in Bonneuil (1989). In analyzing the errors, I often found a certain structure already highlighted by neuropsychologists of numeric and arithmetic processes. On the whole, errors were made by substitution through a process of dynamics that resembles a 'game of exchange'.

Additionally, I have observed other types of error, such as omissions, permutations, or others not classified which have certain similarities to arithmetic errors.

At last, curiously so, throughout the century, the *SGF* tables and their book-keeping coherence carry the imprint of career events or of the various personalities of the directors of the statistics services.

To paraphrase Gonzalez and Kolers (1982), I could conclude that the information is not totally separable from its incarnation as a symbolic system (p. 319), nor, let me add, from the men who serve it; that the manipulation of numbers as they are, with their individual forms in Arabic notation governed by the decimal system, introduces *de facto*, in borrowing the personalities of the actors of the moment, a bias which we may consider in any situation concerning the exploitation of digits.

4

Demographic Coherence of *SGF* Tables

4.1 Census Dates

4.1.1 Months Differ and Elapsed Time Varies between Censuses Throughout the Century

Census dates are presented and assessed in Dupâquier and Le Mée (1988), who stated: 'in 1851, mayors received instructions to begin the operation on 1 April of that year' (p. 37); in 1856, the census was launched from 1 May to 30 May; in 1861, 'sometime during the month of May'; in 1866, it 'occurred in May'; the war postponed the next one to the following year, from 15 April to 15 May 1872; that of 1876 was postponed to the end of the year, from the 1 November to 31 December; that of 1881 took place precisely on 18 December. In 1886, 'we return to the principle of the spring census: all of the population is censused on 30 May'; in 1891, it was 12 April; in 1896, on 29 March; in 1901, on 24 March; and finally, in 1906, on 4 March'.

For practical purposes, Van de Walle assumes, despite the variance in the dates, that censuses were conducted on 1 January from 1801 to 1906: 'We have assumed, despite the variability of dates at which censuses were actually taken, that the figure was valid for 1 January 1801, 1806, ...,1906' (Van de Walle, 1974, p. 58). He adds in his footnote that this assumption includes an approximation: certain censuses, notably those of 1876 and 1881, took place late in the year; the census of 1871 occurred during the following year in the month of May (but nevertheless he treats it as having occurred on 1 January 1871).

In my opinion, this assumption may be appropriate, however it is difficult to determine the amount of bias it may introduce. To avoid the same kind of bias, I shall endeavour to locate the birth cohorts through the censuses which will then enable me to reconstruct demographic rates.

4.1.2   Locating the Cohorts

Since births and deaths correspond to yearly intervals, I propose finding the quinquennial cohorts of 1 January 1901 to 31 December 1905, of 1 January 1896 to 31 December 1900, and so on for successive censuses, without yet worrying about biases linked to the declaration of age, such as age heaping. This process of correcting the censuses conducted in the months of March, April, or May, other than for the year of 1872 may be spurious refinement, especially since under-registration and false declarations of age must then be treated. This initial process of correcting therefore applies essentially to 1872, 1876, and 1881.

We can take as an example the census of May 1872. The population by *département* was first published by yearly intervals of age from 0 to 24 years, and then by quinquennial intervals of age. I collapse original intervals to form new groups of 0–17 months, 1 year and 6 months – 6 years and 5 months, 6 years and 6 months – 11 years and 5 months, etc, in order to identify the quinquennial cohorts present at the end of the month of May 1872, and which were respectively 0–4 years old, 5–9 years old, etc, on 1 January 1871.

In order to do this, for a given *département*, let p_x denote either the post-twenty-four year population of age between x and $x + 4$, or the pre-twenty-four year between x and $x+1$. The cumulated function starting from the older ages can then be formulated as: $F_x = \sum_{i=x}^{\omega} p_i$, where ω indicates the maximal age of life published in the *SGF* tables. I run a cubic spline interpolants exactly through the points $\{x, F_x\}$, so that $s(x) = F_x$.[1] Once the interpolant s is determined, it is easy to interpolate it in order to slice F according to the age groups which interest me.

A classification for the population present at the end of May 1872 is thus obtained according to the birth cohorts of 1 January 1871–May 1872, 1 January 1866–31 December 1870, 1 January 1861–31 December 1865, etc.

The same procedure was used for the other censuses, especially for those of 1876 and 1881, so that I can now follow each cohort during the course of the censuses of the century. The question of age heaping, however, still remains intact.

---

[1] There are various ways to achieve this function. Many of them have been described in Chapter 3, 'Interpolation and approximation', from the Library of Mathematical Programs *IMSL MATH/LIBRARY User's Manual*. The method developed by Akima (Akima, 1970) adequately preserves the general shape of the curve. It provides a $\mathcal{C}^1$ interpolant. See also Bartels, Beaty, and Barsky (1987) as a reference on splines.

4.2   First Treatment of the Poor Quality of the Censuses

4.2.1   Preliminary Examination

One of the important points of Van de Walle's book is the illustration of the poor quality of the nineteenth-century censuses. Among others, he cites Bourgeois-Pichat, who had already declared that it was well known that the size of the 20–24 year old age class was always ballooned, because adolescents tended to make themselves older and adults to make themselves younger. Van de Walle however posited that this was not verified for all censuses (p. 25). He also mentioned the 1886 census, where it had already been noticed that the 20–24 year old age group was abnormally inflated in that women made themselves younger, and also in that many foreigners were present in that age group. In this same report, the fact that infants were widely under-declared was also emphasized. Léon Tabah, cited in Van de Walle (1974), calculated that 12 per cent of children under 5 years old had been omitted in the 1851 census.

Van de Walle then conducted a few simple tests which demonstrated the necessity for reconstruction of the censuses. He started off with sound remarks such as: a cohort should not fluctuate in too violent a manner, but should progressively diminish in time (p. 27). After discussion, he dismissed the possibility of migrations as an explanation for the observed irregularities. The first test of the likelihood of the data consists, therefore, of following the cohorts from census to census.

He graphically represented the population aged from 15 to 49 years, and first compared it to the total population and to the total number of births by year of census, for certain representative *départements* (Charente, Creuse, Landes, and Finistère), and then for the population distributed according to year of birth for Hérault and Finistère. He concluded that *départements* where the series of censuses are coherent are rare, and he advised adjusting age distributions before using them.

Under the assumption that everyone had been recorded, Van de Walle only used global population sizes from the censuses in his reconstruction in order to fix net migratory flows.

I suggest a first method of correction which only more or less respects the global population size, but which supplies age pyramids coherent with the history of each cohort followed during the course of the century. This preliminary correction will enable me to tailor later estimates.

4.2.2   Preliminary Correction of the Censuses

I have already identified each of the cohorts through the successive censuses (e.g. the cohort of 1 January 1851–31 December 1855), whose size we know in May 1851, June 1856, ..., May 1872, December 1881, ... The age distribution of a cohort shows oscillations which I attribute, as did Van de

Walle, to age heaping and concerns all *départements*. For the moment, let us first focus only upon *départements* whose territory had remained intact from 1851 to 1906. They constitute a large majority.

4.2.3   Smoothing by Cohort of the Départements whose Territory had Remained Intact Between 1851 and 1906

By an adequate smoothing [2] of each cohort, I can both get rid of age heaping and estimate age pyramids on every 1 January of years ending in a 1 or in a 6.

This method demonstrates the advantage of preserving the importance, in terms of population size, of each cohort without interfering with the other cohorts present in the same censuses. It restores the pace of deterioration of the cohort, free of age heaping, without referring to some standard age distribution, as done in most correction methods (e.g. Manual No. X of the United Nations). Furthermore, as it is possible to weigh the observations using this smoothing method, I can attribute a more significant weight to the data belonging to the most reliable censuses. More specifically, the 1901 and 1906 censuses were attributed a heavy weight of 10^5, and the censuses of 1851 and 1896 were given a lighter weight (10 for 1861 and 1866, 1 for the others).

The censuses of 1901 and 1906, where the population is classified by year of birth, could display errors due to attraction to round years, such as '1850'. After examination of age pyramids for each *département*, this fear can be dismissed; this reinforces Van de Walle's findings.

An inconvenience could arise from the fact that the smoothing process may ignore patterns of in- and out-migration per quinquennial period. This issue had been addressed and demonstrated as dismissable by Van de Walle. Nevertheless, in order to improve the capacity of the smoothing to mould the rises and falls of the curve, I can adjust its flexibility by playing with the number of knots of the smoothers. Figures 4.1, 4.2, and 4.3 present examples of this. Another example is published in Appendix A.

---

[2] I have used the smoothing by variable knot *B-spline* least squares approximation (program 'bsvls' of the *IMSL* library). It consists of finding the best placement of knots which will minimize the least squares error to given data. In a formal manner, we look for the minimum of the functional:

$$F(a, \mathbf{t}) = \sum_{i=1}^{M} w_i (f_i - \sum_{j=1}^{N} a_j B_{j,k,\mathbf{t}}(x_j))^2$$

where x_j and f_i are respectively the abscissas and ordinates of the given points, in number M, weighted by w_i. $B_{j,k,\mathbf{t}}(.)$ a B-spline function, $\mathbf{t}$ is the N knot sequence $(t_1, \cdots, t_N)$ (cf. IMSL *User's Manual*, p. 537). The flexibility of this smoother comes not only from the fact that the knot sequence is variable and optimized, but that the given points can be weighed. This is useful with the *SGF* data, whose quality varies during the course of the censuses. The definitions and results on *B-splines* can be found in de Boor (1978).

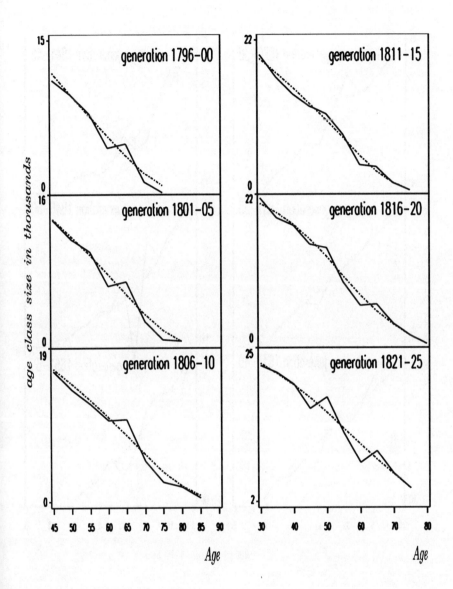

Figure 4.1 Example of age distributions for female generations 1796-1800 to 1821-25. In full line: *SGF* data. In dotted line: the smoothed values. *Département* of Finistère.

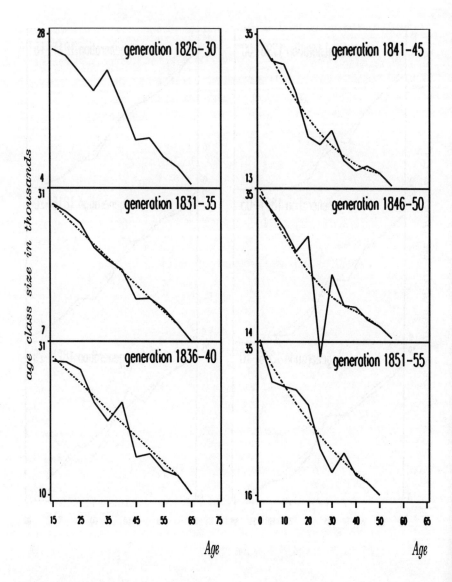

Figure 4.2 Example of age distributions for female generations 1826-30 to 1851-55. In full line: *SGF* data. In dotted line: the smoothed values. *Département* of Finistère.

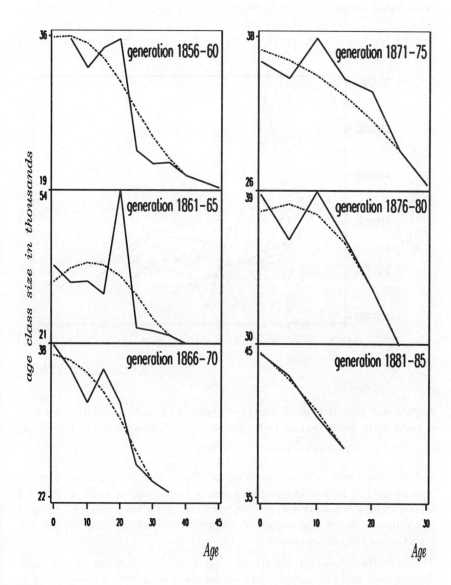

Figure 4.3 Example of age distributions for female generations 1856-60 to 1881-85. In full line: *SGF* data. In dotted line: the smoothed values. *Département* of Finistère.

Therefore, coherent pyramids are obtained in this reconstruction of censuses based on smoothed cohorts. Refer to Figure 2.6 of Van de Walle's book (1974, p. 36) reproduced from my own data (corrected on the bookkeeping level, see Chapter 3), in Figure 4.4. Between 1872 and 1896, I

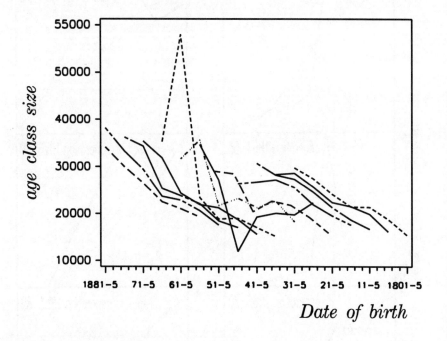

Figure 4.4 Distribution of the 15–49 year old female population by year of birth, *SGF* from 1851 to 1901, Finistère. Each line joins a same census.

find the same anomalies as did Van de Walle, and the same abnormally high number of women in the 20–24 year old age group in 1886. Figure 4.5 presents the same distribution, but corrected after smoothing by cohort. Not only do the censuses appear coherent, but we can find a plausible evolution of the cohort sizes.

This method, however, constitutes but a small step in the correction of the censuses, and functions only to render them as credible as possible so as to benefit from the information they conceal. These corrected censuses will mark out the method of reconstruction which will lead to new corrections for a final, coherent demographic picture.

I must first treat the *départements* created, suppressed, or modified between 1851 and 1906, to which this smoothing method is not necessarily appropriate.

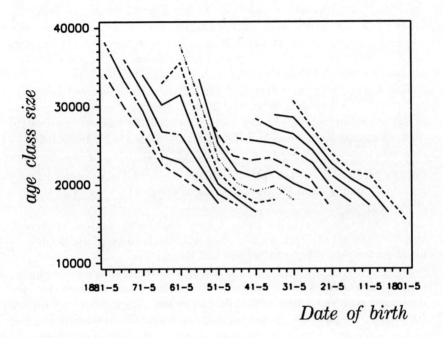

Figure 4.5 Distribution of the 15–49 year old female population by year of birth, from 1851 to 1901 after smoothing, Finistère. Each line joins a same census.

4.2.4   Period-Smoothing of Départements whose Territory was Altered between 1851 and 1906

Created Départements   The method of cohort smoothing still works for the period 1861–1906 for the following *départements* all created in 1861: Savoie, Haute-Savoie, Alpes-Maritimes.

Départements of the East   For the following *départements* of the East: Meurthe, Moselle, Meurthe-et-Moselle, Bas-Rhin, Haut-Rhin, Territoire-de-Belfort, and Vosges, modified or annexed by Germany in 1871, the follow-up is too short to smooth correctly, and I cannot rely on censuses of 1901 or 1906 for the lost *départements*. In order to smooth these *départements* from age heaping, I have resorted to the period-specific method recommended in Manual No. X of the United Nations.[3]

This method relies on a standard age distribution. I used the age distribution of a neighbouring *département*, corrected by the previous method of smoothing by cohort. In this case, I selected the age pyramids of the Meuse corresponding to each of the necessary dates (1856, 1861, 1866).

Slightly Modified Départements   From 1861 to 1906, the smoothing by cohort technique is valid for the following *départements*: Var, Landes, and Basses-Pyrénées.

For the years 1851 and 1856, I used the same method of period-smoothing based this time on corrected age distributions of the neighbouring *départements* of Lot-et-Garonne and Hautes-Pyrenées.

Further corrections must be made so that eventually the demographic series of these modified *départements* can be comparable in time: in 1861, the *département* of Var, whose population had risen to 300,365 at the time of the census, had lost the district (*arrondissement*) of Grasse which counted 68,054 individuals. Next to the original birth and death series, I also obtained these corrected series from 1851 to 1860, by multiplying the original numbers by $(1 - \frac{68,054}{300,365+68,054})$. This adjustment permits comparisons in time, and was repeated for each age group in the 1851 and 1856 censuses.

In 1857, the population of Landes, estimated at 309,832 by the census of 1856, relinquished 8,500 individuals to the population of the Basses-Pyrénées numbered at 436,442. Aside from the original series, I corrected births and deaths from 1851 to 1856 and age groups in 1851 and 1856 by respectively $(1 - \frac{8,500}{8,500+309,832})$ and $(1 + \frac{8,500}{8,500+436,442})$. These corrections

---

[3] See 'Smoothing of an Age Distribution', section entitled 'Comparison with a Standard Age Distribution' in Manual No X *Indirect Techniques for Demographic Estimation* (New York, United Nations, 1983, p. 244). There exist other methods, such as those based on the ratios of the enumerated population at a given age over the moving averages of the age group sizes centred on that age (Coale and Zelnick 1968; Shryock and Siegel, 1973), or based on the Demeny and Shorter technique (1975).

were made on the already smoothed pyramids, by the method mentioned
in Manual No. X of the United Nations.

4.3   First Correction of Vital Statistics

4.3.1   Births

Van de Walle basically put forward three points:

- Throughout the period of interest, the term 'stillborn' refers not only
  to children born dead, but also to children born alive who died before
  an official record of birth;
- in examining the sex ratio at birth by *département*, female births
  appear systematically under-registered. Nevertheless, the global registration for France improves progressively during the course of the
  century to reach a normal level after 1894;
- the quality of registration seems better in the north of France than
  in the south.

Like Van de Walle, my corrections of births are performed by the reconstruction method.

4.3.2   Deaths by Age

These series have not been considered by Van de Walle, who confined himself to series of total deaths, which he assumed to be correct. The data,
however, conceal a mass of information which I will attempt to exploit.

Descriptive Examination of the Series   As with the census series, they can
be biased through age heaping or even under-registration. Legoyt (cited
in Van de Walle, 1974), prior to becoming the head of the *Bureau de la
Statistique*, wrote in 1843 that the age of the deceased must have been
distorted, since the mayors had to accept more or less exact declarations
of witnesses in order to write down the age on the declaration. Yet my
systematic examination of all *départements* from 1856 on failed to identify
any obvious distortion of the numbers of deaths in terms of age. This was
also remarked by Van de Walle (pp. 71–3): he compared the distributions
of deaths by age published with those he reconstructed, on the basis of
Coale and Demeny's model life tables. For the 1900s, the adjustment is
excellent, for the 1890s, he suspected an attraction towards the 75 years
and older: there was a tendency to make the deceased still older; for the
years 1861 to 1865, he observed a slight excess of people under 30 years of
age, which he attributed to the excess mortality caused by tuberculosis.

My reconstruction method nevertheless incorporates a process of correction, based on the least squares smoothing of the probabilities of dying. It

would certainly be incorrect, for a given year, to smooth the age distribution directly, because it can be naturally deformed by passing cohorts of irregular size. It would be equally incorrect to smooth for a given cohort, since the distribution of deaths in this case could be naturally deformed by the irregularity of the mortality conditions of the moment.

I shall first treat the series of deaths by age in order to identify them by each successive cohort. I shall then have at my disposal annual death series for a given cohort (for instance the generation born between 1 January 1831 and 31 December 1835) by age.

Attribution of Deaths by Age to Each of the Cohorts The age intervals published in the *SGF* vary with years. They are presented in Table 4.1.

Table 4.1 Age intervals published in the *SGF*.

years	heading of the intervals
1855...1860	0–1 1–5 5–10 10–15 15–20 20–30 30–40, ..., 90–100 >100
1861...1865	0–1 1–5 5–10 10–15 15–20 20–5 25–30, ..., 95–100 >100
1866...1884	0–1 1–5 5–10 10–15 15–20 20–5 25–30, ..., 95–100 >100
1885, 1886	0–1 1–2 2–3 3–4 4–5 5–10 10–15 15–20 20–5, ..., 95–100 >100
1887	not published
1888...1891	0–1 1–2 3–4 4–5 5–10 10–15 15–18 18–20 20–5, ..., 95–100 >100
1892...1896	0–1 1–2 2–3 3–5 5–10 10–15 15–18 18–20 20–5, ..., 95–100 >100
1897...1902	0–4 5–9 10–14, ..., 80–85 >85
1903...1906	0–4 5–9 10–14, ..., 95–100 >100

The year 1861 serves as a good example. I have available total numbers of deaths $d_{[x_i, x_{i+1}]}$ classified by age intervals $[x_i, x_{i+1}]$: 0–1, 1–4, 5–9, 10–14, ..., 95–99, >100. In order to attribute these annual deaths to the proper months, I need the monthly distribution of deaths by *département*. It is only for the whole of France that the distribution of deaths $d^F_{[x_i, x_{i+1}]}(j)$ by month j and by age class $[x_i, x_{i+1}[$, where F denotes the whole of France is published (for example, Table XVII p. 14, *SGF* vol. 1904). I can then obtain the probability distribution $\delta_j([x_i, x_{i+1}[) = \frac{d^F_{[x_i, x_{i+1}]}(j)}{\sum_k d^F_{[x_i, x_{i+1}]}(j)}$.

I thus allocate the total number of deaths $d^h_{[x_i, x_{i+1}]}$ for the age class $[x_i, x_{i+1}[$, for each *département* h over the 12 months of the year, so that a total number of $d^h_{[x_i, x_{i+1}]}\delta_j([x_i, x_{i+1}[)$ is assigned to the month j in *département* h.

In this text, I proceed to omit the subscript h representing the *département* to simplify notation.

In summary, I have distributed deaths over an age × month grid, where post 5 year ages are quinquennial, and pre-5 year ages are annual.

The next step is to apply a bi-dimensional smoothing, in order to allocate deaths as accurately as possible to each triangle of the Lexis diagram 'cohort × $[a, a+1[$', where a is age, in integer number. Note that this reallocation within the Lexis diagram does not change the total number of deaths observed for a given age class (see Figure 4.8). If 477 deaths for example are observed in the $[1, 4]$ age class, the total number of deaths after reallocation is again 477.

Because the deaths are counted from the oldest age to birth, that is to say in reverse order of age, so as to begin with low numeric values, the bi-dimensional distribution for any month j is defined as follows:

$$\begin{cases} f(110-y,j) &=& d_{[y,y+4]}\delta_j(y,y+4) & y=5,10,\cdots,95,100 \\ f(109,j) &=& d_{[1,4]}\delta_j(1,4) \\ f(110,j) &=& d_{[0,1]}\delta_j(0,1) \end{cases}$$

which I complete by stating that $f(0,j)=0$, because there is no record of death exceeding 110 years old, and for all i $f(i,0)=0$ which signifies that, on 1 January, at 12.00 am, no death had been registered for the new year.

The corresponding cumulated distribution is (age i, month j) (see Figure 4.6):

$$F(i,j) = \sum_{i'\le i}\sum_{j'\le j} f(i',j')$$

I now simply smooth this grid by bi-dimensional *B-splines*[4] to obtain the value at any point, and then to partition it again as finely as possible. The interpolant can calculate any value on the two-dimensional grid of the cumulated distribution of deaths by ages and months without changing given values (which are themselves cumulated from the original *SGF* data). This property allows the total number of deaths for a given age class to remain untouched. Practically limited by computing time, I cut each square one year of age × one year of time into 24 × 24 cells. This seems large enough (since an attempt at 36 × 36 cells barely changes the results).

[4] I run the surface smoother, obtained as tensor product of univariate spline interpolants through the given points $\{(x_i, y_j, f_{ij})\}$, where $1 \le i \le N_x$ and $1 \le i \le N_y$. It has the form:

$$\sum_{m=1}^{N_y}\sum_{n=1}^{N_x} c_{nm} B_{n,k_x,\mathbf{t}_x}(x) B_{m,k_y,\mathbf{t}_y}(y)$$

where k_x and k_y are the orders of the interpolants, $\mathbf{t}_x$ and $\mathbf{t}_y$ are the corresponding knot sequences. It must then satisfy the constraint:

$$\sum_{m=1}^{N_y}\sum_{n=1}^{N_x} c_{nm} B_{n,k_x,\mathbf{t}_x}(x_i) B_{m,k_y,\mathbf{t}_y}(y_j) = f_{ij}$$

(cf. *IMSL Math/library*, routine 'bs2in').

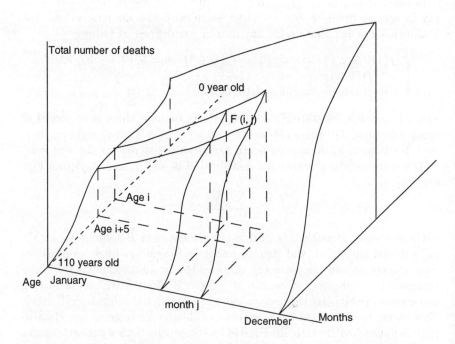

Figure 4.6 Cumulated distribution of deaths according to an age × month grid.

To attribute the deaths $d_t^g([a, a + 1[)$ of cohort g year t between ages a and $a + 1$, I add up the small squares of the inferior triangle and add up half of the diagonal squares (schema on Figure 4.7):

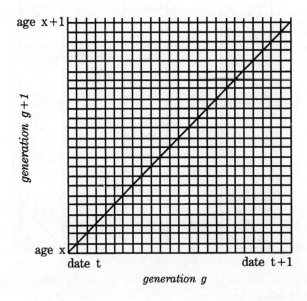

Figure 4.7 Partitioning of numbers of deaths in one year according to a 24×24 grid, adding up over the entire squares of the inferior triangle and over half the diagonal squares.

$$d_t^g([a, a + 1[) = \sum_{l_j < l_x} f(x + l_x, l_j) + \sum_l \frac{f(l + x, l)}{2}$$

An example is given in Table 4.8. The partitioning operation is carried out for each year. For the five consecutive years separating two censuses, for instance from those of 1861 and 1865, I reassemble the preceding portion by cohorts, by successively adding across the small superior triangles of the Lexis diagram and then across the inferior triangles (see Figure 4.9).

$$d_{1861 \rightarrow 1865}^g([a, a+4[) = \sum_{u=0}^{4} d_{1861+u}^g([a+u, a+u+1[) + \sum_{u=0}^{4} d_{1861+u}^g([a+u-1, a+u[)$$

The deaths of a quinquennial cohort can be obtained by simply adding up the deaths of five annual cohorts.

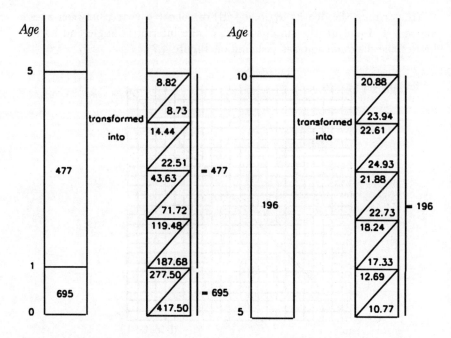

Figure 4.8 Example of partitioning of number of deaths by cohort and by age: *département* of Ain in 1855.

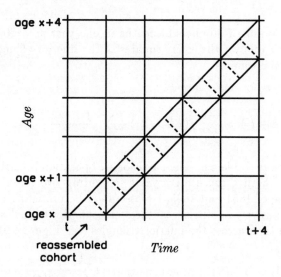

Figure 4.9 Reassembling deaths of a cohort between two successive censuses.

This was done for all series of death by age and by *département* available between 1856 and 1905 (statistics of deaths by age begin only from 1856).[5]

4.3.3   Ready for the Reconstruction

I finally begin the reconstruction between 1856 and 1906 on the following data by *département*:

- the censuses adjusted on the 1st of every January of the years ending with a '1' or with a '6' from 1851 to 1906, classified by quinquennial age, smoothed of age heaping and of obvious anomalies of declaration for groups at least 5 years of age. Beneath this age level, I expect to find under-registration. The definitive adjustment will be generated during the course of the reconstruction;
- the series of feminine deaths from 1856 to 1906, by quinquennial age and by quinquennial cohort;
- from 1836 to 1906, the annual series of feminine 'live' births (published as such), which we know may suffer from under-registration ; the annual stillborn 'series' (published as such) of feminine gender, the annual series of total numbers of deaths;
- from 1801 to 1835, the annual birth series classified by gender (excluding stillborns), the annual series of total numbers of deaths;
- the tables classifying the French population between *département* of census and *département* of origin in 1891, 1896, and 1901. In practice, I will only use the 1901 table, which is coherent on the book-keeping level;
- the distribution of foreign women by *département* in the 1901 census (entitled 'Population présente totale par nationalité', p. 422) and that published in the 1851 census (entitled 'Population selon la nationalité' p. 140).

Since the series of deaths by age begin only in 1856, I have imagined two successive methods linked one to the other: the first one uses deaths by age and goes back in time from 1906 to 1856; the other starts from 1801 and ends at the junction of 1856. The censuses from 1801 to 1846, which I judge hardly reliable, have been deliberately ignored.

In the following chapters, we will see how this method will permit us to depart from some of Van de Walle's hypotheses, such as the calculation of migrations or under-registration. However, as in his methodology, there is

---

[5] For the smoothing to accurately reflect the shape of the pyramid, it is important to 'guide' it as much as possible. Notably, to reflect the strong decrease at young ages, one must at least know the size of the 0–1 year age group when it is necessary to compensate for the lack of yearly classification of age for the 0–5 year age group. Therefore, from 1898 to 1906, one must consider this 0–1 year old age group by *département*. These statistics are published separately in Table XXXVI of the 1898 *SGF* volume, and in Table XXXIV in the 1899 to 1906 volumes). At the other end of the age pyramid, I interpolated to identify the pre-1806 generations and the 'undeclared ages'.

a recursive effect in that the data is part of the reconstruction only to the extent that this latter permits progressive correction of the data.

5

Reconstruction of the Population

5.1   Van de Walle's Method

There are several important differences between my data and those used by Van de Walle. Enumerated below are the main variants:

- he used only quinquennial total death series: 1856–1860, ..., 1901–1905 instead of deaths by age;
- he used only total female population size at the actual dates of the censuses, or its interpolated value in 1811, 1816, 1826, which he assumed valid on the 1 January in 1801, 1806, ..., 1871, ...1906;

Furthermore, his model is fully based on three assumptions which are only partial support for the foundation of my model:

- he assumes that, for each *département*, the age structure in 1801 is that of a stable population. The mortality is derived from west or north Coale and Demeny model life tables, the growth rate is the difference between crude birth and crude death rates estimated for the period of 1801–1805;
- these model life tables, either north or west according to the quality of the fit, are used to 'project forward' the feminine population by age;
- he uses an identical schedule of migration by age.

The underlying principle of the reconstruction is similar to that of Lee's (1974) 'inverse projection' method. The age pyramid constituted of the total number $p_t(a)$ of the age class $[a, a + 4]$ on date t (initial date $t_0 = 1801$) is modified according to the Coale and Demeny model life table of probabilities of dying $_5q_a(t)$, such that:

$$
\begin{cases}
D_{[t,t+4]} &= \sum_a p_t(a) {_5}q_a(t) \\
p_{t+5}(a+5) &= p_t(a)(1 - {_5}q_a(t)) +_5 w_a \left(P_{t+5} - \sum_a p_t(a)(1 - {_5}q_a(t))\right) \\
p_{t,t+5}(0) &= B_{[t,t+4]}
\end{cases}
$$

where $D_{[t,t+4]}$ is the total number of deaths from 1 January of year t to 31 December of year $t + 4$; $B_{[t,t+4]}$ is the total number of births for the same time period; $_5w_a$ is the invariable migration schedule by age; and P_{t+5} is the total population size for date $t + 5$.

The poor quality of the data led Van de Walle to make necessary adjustments to this method. An example of the difficulties involved in working with the data is that the declared population size at the 1801 census is less than the estimation obtained by subtracting births from, and adding deaths to, the population size recorded in 1846. If the declared population size is kept, the gap would be too wide between reconstructed numbers and those declared at the most reliable censuses (according to Van de Walle, prior to the 1901 census, those of 1851, 1856, 1861, and 1866 are the most reliable).

The information provided by deaths by age was neglected by Van de Walle. This led him to impose an artificial migration schedule, to keep away urban *départements* and to rely more or less on vital statistics. The consideration of the statistics of total numbers of deaths by age does not bring a superfluous detail: it makes us totally rethink the general reconstruction, bringing new foundations through the estimation of under-registration, producing *département-* and time-specific migration age distributions, and making possible the consideration of all *départements*, urban as well as rural.

5.2   A Dynamic Reconstruction of the French Population by Département, 1856–1906

5.2.1   Principle

My goal is to integrate spatial dynamics with temporal demography. This concern has been expressed in many works such as Chiang (1968) and Rogers (1975). The point is to incorporate the notion of interdependency between regions to the classical demographic process. Migratory flows—internal or external—to a given set of regions then appear dynamic as a demographic whole. This may have an effect upon the way the evolution of populations is described and on the analysis of demographic structures.

I shall thus construct a sequence of matrices, each one calculated per quinquennial period between two censuses, revealing mortality forces for each *département* and the structure of net migratory distributions for each *département*.

5.2.2   Equations

The Demographic Space-Time Process as a Non-Homogeneous Markov System   Following a given cohort, let us note:

N = total number of *départements* at moment t;

$p_j(x)$: continuous function of exact age x giving the population of age x at time t in *département* j, $p(x) = (\cdots, p_j(x), \cdots)'$;

$B^i(t)$: total number of births year t in *département* i

$\tilde{B}^i(t)$: corrected total number of births year t in *département* i

$\nu_j(x)$: (instantaneous) force of out-migration at age x, time t, *département* j;

$m_{ji}(x)$: instantaneous probability that an individual of age x goes to *département* i knowing that he emigrates from *département* j and remains in France, $(\sum_{i \neq j} m_{ji}(x) = 1)$;

$\mu_j(x)$: (instantaneous) force of mortality at age x in *département* j;

$_h q_x^j$: probability of dying between age x and age $x + h$:

$$_h q_x^j = 1 - e^{-\int_0^h \mu_j(x+u)\,du}$$

$D_j([x, x + h[)$: total number of deaths between age x and age $x + h$ in *département* j from the cohort which was of exact age x on 1 January of year t:

$$D_j([x, x + h[) = \int_0^h p_j(x + u)\mu_j(x + u)\,du$$

$_h r_x^j$: probability of out-migration between age x and $x + h$:

$$_h r_x^j = 1 - e^{-\int_0^h \nu_j(x+u)\,du}$$

$_h \rho_x^j$: net migration rate between age x and $x + h$:

$$_h \rho_x^j = \frac{p_j(x + h)}{p_j(x)(1 - {}_h q_x^j)} - 1$$

Between instants u and $u + du$, a given cohort evolves as indicated in Figure 5.1.

In a France totally closed to migrations to and from abroad, the evolution equation for *département* i reads into a forward Kolmogorov equation:

$$\frac{dp_i}{du}(x+u) = -p_i(x+u)(\nu_i(x+u)+\mu_i(x+u)) + \sum_{j \neq i} p_j(x+u)\nu_j(x+u)m_{ji}(x+u)$$

$$(5.1)$$

which accounts for a non-homogeneous Markov process.

The corresponding matrix equation is linear with non constant coefficients:

$$\frac{dp}{du}(x + u) = \Delta(x + u)p(x + u) \tag{5.2}$$

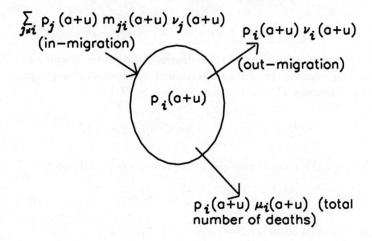

Figure 5.1 Evolution of the population of a given *département* i between instants u and $u + du$.

where Δ is the matrix (N, N):

$$
\Delta = \begin{pmatrix}
\cdot & -(\nu_i(x+u) + \mu_i(x+u)) & \cdot & \nu_j(x+u)m_{ji}(x+u) & \cdot \\
\cdot & & \cdot & & \cdot \\
\cdot & & \cdot & & \cdot \\
\cdot & & \cdot & & \cdot
\end{pmatrix}
$$

The deaths occurring between instants t and $t + h$ satisfy the equation:

$$
D_i([x, x + h[) = \int_0^h \mu_i(x+u)p_i(x+u)\, du \tag{5.3}
$$

Equations 5.1 and 5.3 highlight the two elementary forces of the demographic process: force of mortality and force of migration. The population numbers will be derived from this play of forces.

Kolmogorov's equation for Markov processes has given birth to an abundant literature in demography, focused on multi-state transition tables, or 'decrements-increments'. The reader can find sufficiently complete accounts of these theories in, for example, Rogers (1975, 1980).

Hypotheses of Calculation

Review of Currently used Hypotheses The presentation I give of the process can be compared to that in Schoen (1988). I note $\pi_{ij}(x, h) = \text{prob}(S(x + h) = j/S(x) = i)$ the transition probabilities of the Markov process S, where $\pi_{ij}(x, h)$ is the probability that an individual in state i at age x be in state j at age $x + h$ (states are at the number of $k + 1$, the $(k + 1)^{\text{st}}$ being death). If the existence and the continuity of all transition forces are assumed, the force of transfers from state i to state j at age x is:

$$
\eta_{i,j}(x) = \lim_{h\downarrow 0} \pi_{ij}(x, h)/h, \quad \text{for } i \neq j
$$

Here, we have simply:

$$
\begin{cases}
\eta_{i,j}(x) &= \nu_i(x)m_{ij}(x) \quad \text{for } i \neq j \text{ and } j \neq k+1 \\
\eta_{i,k+1}(x) &= \mu_i(x) \quad i = 1, \cdots k
\end{cases}
$$

To calculate this multi-state table, Schoen (1988) suggested the following methods:

- the linear approximation, consisting of assuming linearity over the interval $[x, x + h]$ of the functions $l_{ij}(x + u)$, the survival probability in state j at age $x + u$ knowing that one is alive in state i at age x;
- 'the mean transfer function', refining the preceding function by adding the quadratic approximation of μ_i to the linear approximation of $l_{ij}(x + u)$;

- the cubic method, consisting of taking $l_{ij}(x+u)$ as a cubic polynomial passing through $l_{ij}(x-h), l_{ij}(x), l_{ij}(x+h), l_{ij}(x+2h)$;
- the method of constant forces, consisting of assuming $\mu_i(x) = \mu_i$ and $\nu_i(x) = \nu_i$ in the age interval $[x, x+h]$.

The first three possibilities require knowing the number of transfers from state i to state j between ages x and $x+h$; they are unknown in this study. The last hypothesis of calculation, the constant infinitesimal forces over the intervals $[x, x+h]$ is the most currently used.

The Hypothesis of Relative Constancy of Intensities   Relative to these four calculation tricks, Greville (1948), and later Chiang (1968, p. 244) (see also Brouard, 1986), suggested a broader hypothesis, also mentioned in Schoen (1988, p. 29), which consists of assuming that *relative* forces are constant over each interval $[x, x+h]$:

$$\frac{\eta_{ij}(x+u)}{\sum_j \eta_{ij}(x+u)} = c_x^{ij} \quad \text{for } i \neq j \quad j = 1, \cdots k$$

where c_x^{ij} is independent of time u, but remains a function of the interval $[x, x+h]$ and of the transition risk $i \to j$. This hypothesis allows the intensity $\eta_{ij}(x+u)$ to vary in absolute value, but constrains it to remain a constant proportion of total intensity over the interval $[x, x+h]$ (Chiang, 1968). This hypothesis is much more flexible than the one more currently employed of constancy of absolute forces in the interval.

There are two risks in our study: out-migration $\nu_i(x)$, which is made up of $N-1$ risks $m_{ij}(x)\nu_i(x)$ and mortality $\mu_i(x)$. The hypothesis of relative constancy of intensities reads as:

$$m_{ij}(x+u)\nu_i(x+u) = c_x^{ij}\mu_i(x+u)$$

in the interval $[x, x+h]$, where c_x^{ij} is constant in the interval $[x, x+h]$. By adding over j, I also have:

$$\nu_i(x+u) = c_x^i \mu_i(x+u)$$

in putting $c_x^i = \sum_{j \neq i} c_x^{ij}$.

The hypothesis of relative constancy of intensities is well suited to analytically solve the system (5.2), although it requires meticulous calculation. I am aware that ν and μ have no reason to be proportional on $[x, x+h]$, but my purpose is simply to approximate $\int \nu_i$ as best as possible, which I do with $c_x^i \int \mu_i$.

Transformation of the Equation of Change of States   On the basis of this hypothesis, equation (5.1) becomes:

$$\begin{aligned}\frac{dp_i}{du}(x+u) = {} & p_i(x+u)\left(-(c_x^i+1)\mu_i(x+u)\right) \\ & + \sum_{j \neq i} \frac{p_j(x+u)}{p_i(x+u)} m_{ji}(x+u)c_x^j\mu_j(x+u)\right)\end{aligned}$$

Within the interval $[x, x+h]$, we know that forces of mortality from distinct *départements* will have approximately the same shape and will differ only by level; I can then approximate the term $\mu_j(x+u)$ by $\epsilon_x^{ji}\mu_i(x+u)$, where ϵ_x^{ji} does not depend on time u, but only on the interval $[x, x+h]$ and on *départements* i and j. This hypothesis is analogous to the hypothesis of relative constancy of intensities, apart from the fact that the two compared intensities do not come from the same *département*, and thereby not from the same population. This hypothesis can be written by relying on the fact that the functions μ_i and μ_j are mortality functions, and generally have more or less the same shape on a same quinquennial interval $[x, x+h]$, potentially differing only by level.

Moreover, as age group sizes $p_i(x+u)$ evolve relatively slowly in relation to the others, I can approximate on $[x, x+h]$, ($h = 5$ years in general):

$$\frac{p_j(x+u)}{p_i(x+u)} \approx \frac{p_j(x+h) + p_j(x)}{p_i(x+h) + p_i(x)} \quad 0 \le u \le h$$

The choice of destination of out-migrants from j to i, $m_{ji}(x+u)$, can be taken similarly as evolving slowly, so that it can be considered as not depending on u:

$$m_{ji}(x+u) \approx m_{jix} \quad 0 \le u \le h$$

Integration of the Instantaneous Demographic System Equation (5.1) now becomes:

$$\frac{dp_i}{du}(x+u) = p_i(x+u)(-(k_x^i + 1)\mu_i(x+u)) \tag{5.4}$$

in putting:

$$k_x^i = c_x^i - \sum_{j \ne i} \frac{p_j(x+h) + p_j(x)}{p_i(x+h) + p_i(x)} m_{jix} c_x^j \epsilon_x^{ji}$$

The integration of the system constituted by (5.3) and (5.4) is then classic (Chiang, 1968). Equation (5.4) is integrated in:

$$p_i(x+h) = p_i(x) \left(e^{-\int_0^h \mu_i(x+u)\,du} \right)^{k_x^i + 1}$$

and (5.3) becomes:

$$\begin{aligned}
D_i(x, x+h) &= p_i(x) \int_0^h \mu_i(x+u) e^{-(k_x^i+1)\int_0^u \mu_i(x+v)\,dv}\,du \\
&= \frac{p_i(x)}{k_x^i+1} \left(1 - (e^{-\int_0^h \mu_i(x+v)\,dv})^{k_x^i+1} \right)
\end{aligned}$$

hence:

$$k_x^i + 1 = \frac{p_i(x) - p_i(x+h)}{D_i(x, x+h)}$$

If $_hq_x^i$ designates the probability of dying between x and $x + h$ for *département i*,

$$_hq_x^i = 1 - e^{- \int_0^h \mu_i(x+v)\,dv}$$

I deduce that:

$$1 - _hq_x^i = \left(\frac{p_i(x + h)}{p_i(x)}\right)^{\frac{D_i(x,x+h)}{p_i(x) - p_i(x+h)}} \tag{5.5}$$

Matrix Equation of Integrated Migratory Intensities   I can now estimate the net migration rates ρ_x^i. Equation (5.1) now reads:

$$k_x^i \ln(1 - _hq_x^i) = - \int_0^h \nu_i(x+u)\,du + \sum_{j \neq i} \frac{p_j(x + h) + p_j(x)}{p_i(x + h) + p_i(x)} m_{jix} \int_0^h \nu_j(x+u)\,du \tag{5.6}$$

This system constituted of N equations for N *départements* is singular of rank $N - 1$, because of the constraint for all i, $\sum_{j \neq i} m_{jix} = 1$. This constraint implies that the total of out-migrants equals the total of in-migrants within France: $\sum_i \nu_i(x + u)p_i(x + u) = \sum_i \sum_{j \neq i} m_{jix}\nu_j(x + u)p_j(x + u)$. Even if I had the parameters m_{jix}, I would not be able to determine a unique solution of Equation 5.6, but only a line of possible solutions.

I must subsequently be content with calculating net migration rates, whose integral on $[x, x + h]$ is equal to $k_x^i \ln(1 - _hq_x^i)$ (see Equation 5.6). By taking the exponential of this term, I define the rates of net migration $_h\rho_x^i$ as:

$$\begin{aligned} 1 + _h\rho_x^i &= e^{- \int_0^h \nu_i(x+u)\,du + \sum_{j \neq i} \frac{p_j(x+h)+p_j(x)}{p_i(x+h)+p_i(x)} m_{jix} \int_0^h \nu_j(x+u)\,du} \\[2mm] &= \frac{1 - _hr_x^i}{\Pi_{j \neq i}(1 - _hr_x^j)^{\frac{p_j(x+h)+p_j(x)}{p_i(x+h)+p_i(x)} m_{jix}}} \end{aligned}$$

which is also:

$$1 + _h\rho_x^i = (1 - _hq_x^i)^{k_x^i} \tag{5.7}$$

The discrete evolution equation now reads:

$$p_{x+h}^i = p_x^i(1 - _hq_x^i)\frac{1 - _hr_x^i}{\Pi_{j \neq i}(1 - _hr_x^j)^{\frac{p_j(x+h)+p_j(x)}{p_i(x+h)+p_i(x)} m_{jix}}} \tag{5.8}$$

which is also:

$$p_{x+h}^i = p_x^i(1 - _hq_x^i)^{1 + k_x^i}$$

For the sake of clarity, I have presented my methodology under the assumption of no external migrations (immigration and emigration). We know that France can be considered as a more or less closed system throughout the nineteenth century. Foreign migration was not significant and the term representing net migration rates at the level of France as a whole $\sum_{i=0}^{\infty}\left(p_{x+h}^{i}(t+h)-p_{x}^{i}(t)+D_{i}(x,x+h)\right)$ is small and can be easily incorporated into System 5.6.

5.2.3 Putting It All into Practical Use

Estimation and Smoothing of Probabilities of Dying In Equation (5.5), $\frac{D_{i}(x,x+h)}{p_{i}(x)-p_{i}(x+h)}$ is estimated by

$$\frac{\int_{x_{l}}^{x_{l+h}}D_{i}(x,x+h)dx}{\int_{x_{l}}^{x_{l+h}}(p_{i}(x)-p_{i}(x+h))dx}$$

which is simply the ratio of observed deaths between t and $t+h$ of the cohort which was between x_{l} and x_{l+h} years old at t, $x_{l}=0,5,\ldots100$, divided by the difference of the corresponding population sizes.

The numerator of the preceding ratio is taken from my earlier portioning of deaths by cohort and by year. The denominator is simply drawn from corrected censuses. In the same fashion, the term $\frac{p_{i}(x+h)}{p_{i}(x)}$ of (5.5) is approximated by $\frac{\int_{x_{l}}^{x_{l+h}}p_{i}(x+h)dx}{\int_{x_{l}}^{x_{l+h}}p_{i}(x)dx}$. I thus obtain an estimate $_{h}\hat{q}_{x_{l}}^{i}$ of the quinquennial (for $h=5$ years) probability of dying within the calendar period $[t,t+h[$ over $[x_{l},x_{l+h}[$ at t.

The probabilities of dying obtained within a calendar period $(_{h}\hat{q}_{x}^{i})_{x=0,5\cdots}$ rest then on the values of p_{x}^{i}, which are smoothed from the published censuses, and of numbers of deaths, deduced from those published. To obtain the demographic coherence of the reconstruction of mortality, the idea is to work with these probabilities of dying in relating them to model life tables. Subsequently, I look for the entry e of a Ledermann single entry model life table, after changing them into probabilities within a calendar period (see the end of this chapter for details) to select the Ledermann model life table $(_{h}q_{x}^{L}(e))_{x}$ which minimizes the least square distance to the observed life table $(_{h}\hat{q}_{x}^{i})_{x}$:

$$\text{Min}_{e}d\left((_{h}q_{x}^{L}(e))_{x}-(_{h}\hat{q}_{x}^{i})_{x}\right)$$

where d is a distance between the two life tables $(_{h}q^{L}(e))_{x}$ and $(_{h}\hat{q}^{i})_{x}$. For the distance d, I tried, for ages ω_{a} and ω_{b} to be determined:

- sum of squares of the differences of logarithms:

$$\text{Min}_{e}\sum_{x=\omega_{a}}^{\omega_{b}}\left(\log(_{h}q_{x}^{L}(e))-\log(_{h}\hat{q}_{x}^{i})\right)^{2} \qquad (5.9)$$

- sum of squares of the simple differences:

$$\text{Min}_e \sum_{x=\omega_a}^{\omega_b} \left({}_h q_x^L(e) - {}_h \hat{q}_x^i \right)^2 \tag{5.10}$$

- sum of squares of relative differences of logarithms:

$$\text{Min}_e \sum_{x=\omega_a}^{\omega_b} \left(1 - \frac{\log({}_h q_x^L(e))}{\log({}_h \hat{q}_x^i)} \right)^2 \tag{5.11}$$

The ages ω_a and ω_b are chosen as far apart from each other as possible in order to improve the fit, but also to avoid biases at extreme ages, which most probably suffer from under-registration or bad declaration. Experimentation led me to take $\omega_a = 5$ years and $\omega_b = 60$ years.

Criterium 5.9 favours the fit to the youngest ages, while Criterium 5.10 favours the fit to the oldest ages. Criterium 5.11 lies in between. The choice depends on the reliability of the estimated probabilities of dying. From 1871 to 1906, over the whole set of *départements*, the average relative difference between the estimates of life expectancy through Criterium 5.9 and through Criterium 5.10 fluctuates in time around 3.5 per cent. The similar relative difference between the estimates of life expectancy through Criterium 5.11 and through Criterium 5.10 is also approximately constant over time, around 1.9 per cent. However, the solution yielded by Criterium 5.9 corresponds to higher life expectancies and thus to lower reconstructed population sizes than those produced by Criterium 5.10. When comparing with estimates coming from the *SGF* or from Van de Walle, I am led to choose Criterium 5.10, which implies that estimated probabilities of dying are more reliable at older ages.

This quest for the best model life table based on least squares is similar to a smoothing by a known function $({}_h q_x^L(e))_x$. It is at this point that I definitely correct the series of deaths by age, which could be biased by age heaping or by under-registration. The fit is generally rather good, which was a pleasant surprise (for me at least), indicating that data are not in the end so bad. The *département* of Finistère is an example where registration is likely to have been of lower quality, as illustrated at various periods in Figure 5.2. In Appendix A, the example of the département of Seine, the most urban one with the city of Paris, is presented, as well as that of Gironde, which was intermediate between rural and urban (with the city of Bordeaux), and that of Creuse, which was rural.

Reconstruction of the Censuses   It is also at this point that I can correct the censuses and establish a certain demographic coherence. In fact, once the net migration rates within a calendar quinquennial period ${}_h \rho_x^i$ are calculated in Equation (5.7), I can go back in time and infer from $p_{x+h}^i(t+h)$

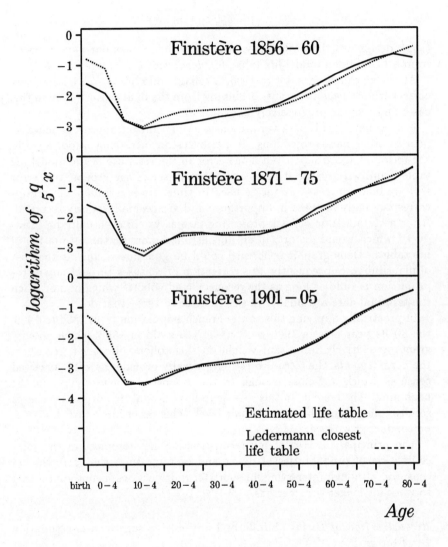

Figure 5.2 Examples of probabilities of dying within a calendar quinquennial period estimated directly. Examples of their fitted probabilities of dying taken from a Ledermann model life table.

a new estimate $\tilde{p}_x^i(t)$ of the total number $p_x^i(t)$ of survivors in the age group $[x - h, x]$ at time t through the equation deduced from (5.8):

$$\tilde{p}_x^i = \frac{\tilde{p}_{x+h}^i}{(1 - {}_h q_x^{i,L})(1 + {}_h \rho_x^i)}$$

(${}_h q_x^{i,L}$ designates the probability of dying within a calendar period drawn from a Ledermann model life table, for *département i*, at age $[x, x + 4]$).

At the terminal census $t = 1906$, a reliable one, $\tilde{p}_x^i = p_x^i$. I iteratively correct from census to census, beginning from the final census (1906 in this case) and moving progressively back in time.

Unfortunately, this backward reconstruction suffers from the same weakness as other back-projections: it attributes an increasing importance to the terminal age group. Even if the error in the estimate of the model life table is limited because it relies on the whole set of age groups, this error will gradually increase as we go back in time, since terminal age groups correspondingly increase in importance and are generally poorly recorded. After a certain time of back-projecting, a bias would eventually be introduced which would distort, in an uncontrolled manner, the estimation of life tables. Demographic coherence could be guaranteed, but at the cost of plausibility. Subsequently, this correction of censuses through my retro-projection is valid as long as the reconstructed cohorts which do not reach the terminal date are smaller in size relative to those that do.

In practically applying this to the French population from 1856 to 1906, the 80–84 year olds in 1906 were 30–34 years old in 1856, which already grants a relatively important weight to this cohort. However, for all of the *départements*, the retro-projection generally provides us with corrected censuses which are close enough to the smoothed censuses used in the beginning. The benefit, in this case, is to have now at my disposal censuses solidly coherent on the demographic level. This procedure must, however, be conducted with care.

The principal interest of my reconstruction lies foremost in the joint estimation of probabilities of dying and of migrating; the correction of censuses, although interesting for short-term projections, is not guaranteed to work for longer time periods.

Reconstruction of Births   Similarly, I am able to suggest a re-estimation $\tilde{B}^i$ of births B^i :

$$\tilde{B}^i = p_0^i \frac{\Pi_{j \neq i}(1 - {}_h r_B^j)^{\frac{p_j(0)+B^j}{p_i(0)+B^i} m_{jix}}}{(1 - {}_h q_B^{i,L})(1 - {}_h r_B^i)} = \frac{p_0^i}{(1 - {}_h q_B^{i,L})(1 - {}_h \rho_B^i)} \qquad (5.12)$$

where 'B' is the subscript related to births.

The ratio $\tilde{B}^i/B^i$ of reconstructed births divided by published births would give an indication of the under-registration of births. This evaluation of under-registration can be criticized in arguing that it relies heavily on the Ledermann model, especially at young ages. The possibility of estimating under-registration of births is reflected here by the gap between directly estimated, and Ledermann probabilities of dying. Some might argue that Ledermann life tables with double entries could be taken to reflect better mortality at young ages. However, this would prevent us from estimating under-registration, or, more specifically, the opportunity of giving an estimate of under-registration is given by the relative rigidity of single entry life tables.

I will nevertheless examine the spatial and temporal distribution of the ratio $\tilde{B}^i/B^i$, seen as an indicator of under-registration.

Reconstruction of the Coale Index I_f   Finally, for each *département* and each available date, I calculate, as did Van de Walle, the overall Coale index I_f:[1]

$$I_f = \frac{B}{\sum_{x=20}^{49} p_x h(x)} \quad \text{and} \quad \tilde{I}_f = \frac{\tilde{B}}{\sum_{x=20}^{49} \tilde{p}_x h(x)}$$

where $(h(x))_{x=20,\cdots 49}$ is the age-specific fertility distribution of the Hutterites, a small population living in North America, chosen as a reference because it has one of the highest fertility patterns. The latter is given in Table 5.1.

Table 5.1 Fertility of the Hutterites.

age	15–19	20–24	25–29	30–34	35–39	40–44	45–49
rate	0.300	0.550	0.502	0.447	0.406	0.222	0.061

source: Coale 1969.

If, on the odd chance, published births B are greater than reconstructed births $\tilde{B}$, I will consider as valid the greatest of the two estimates $\sup(I_f^i(t), \tilde{I}_f^i(t))$.

5.2.4   Sensitivity Analysis

Death Under-Registration and Age Heaping   I have simulated a closed population by age over 11 quinquennial periods (12 censuses). Starting from an initial age pyramid on 1 January in year 1, age pyramids at year 6, 11,

---

[1] For an introductory presentation of this index used in historical demography in absence of suitable data, see Van de Walle (1974, p.128), Woods (1986, p.26), or Weir (1982).

Table 5.2 Sensitivity to age heaping and under-registration of deaths (in per cent) (11 quinquennial periods).

under-registration of deaths (%)	age heaping in %	mean relative error in estimated life expectancy at the		mean relative error (std) in pop. size over the 11 periods
		6th period	1st period	
0	0	0.0	0.0	0.0 (0.0)
0	10	-0.1	-0.5	-0.1 (1.1)
0	20	-1.5	-2.2	0.1 (2.2)
0	30	-3.5	-5.7	0.8 (3.4)
0	40	-9.0	-13.0	2.7 (5.2)
5	0	0.5	0.5	3.0 (2.5)
5	10	0.0	0.0	3.2 (3.0)
5	20	-1.2	-1.7	3.7 (4.1)
5	30	-3.0	-5.0	4.9 (5.8)
5	40	-9.0	-12.0	7.8 (9.2)

..., 56 are successively obtained by applying a life expectancy at birth of 40 years for example and a renewal $B(t) = B(1)\exp(0.01t)$, where $B(t)$ is the total number of births during year t, for a growth rate of 0.01.

This age pyramid series is then distorted by imposing an age heaping ζ and a death under-registration ξ, except for the last two periods, where age pyramids are left untouched, so as to imitate the good quality of the 1901 and 1906 censuses. The simulated age heaping consists in declaring a proportion ζ of $(a-5)$ year old people and the same proportion ζ of $(a+5)$ year old people as aged a years old instead of their actual age, where a is a round number 0, 10, 20, ..., 90. The death under-registration rate ξ is taken as constant over the age distribution. The under-registration of births is not a parameter, because the total number of births intervenes neither in the estimation of life expectancy nor in the smoothing of the pyramids.

Cohorts issued from the age pyramid series are then smoothed to get rid of age heaping as in Figures 4.1, 4.2, and 4.3, deaths are allocated to cohorts, and the life table is estimated using 5.10. Table 5.2 presents the results of such simulations. This table shows a good correction of age heaping as well as the importance of death under-registration, responsible for a rapid growth of errors in population size. The error in life expectancy depends more on age heaping than on death under-registration. The level of errors in general is satisfactorily small (−12 per cent or −13 per cent in life expectancy after 11 periods of reconstruction with 40 per cent of age heaping).

Influence of Net Undercount in Censuses   In modern censuses, post enumeration surveys show that net undercounts by age group and area can
vary widely. Therefore, it is important to study how results are affected by
net undercounts varying by age and *département*. In the period 1871–1906,
during which the French territory was kept the same, the backward reconstruction was run for each *département* with censuses altered, respectively
−5 per cent, +5 per cent, and +10 per cent at each age with the actual
statistics on deaths by age and births. The positive values correspond to
the suspicion that actual censuses are themselves undercounts. Said differ-
ently, if the +10 per cent re-evaluation of the actual censuses is regarded as
the reference, the +5 per cent represents a net undercount of $1.05/1.1 \approx 4.5$
per cent to this reference, the actual censuses (0 per cent) a net undercount of $1.00/1.1 \approx 9.1$ per cent and the −5 per cent a net undercount of
$0.95/1.1 \approx 13.5$ per cent.

Figures 5.3, 5.4, 5.5, and 5.6 show the average errors affecting the estimates of life expectancy at birth, of the fertility index, of birth under-
registration and of population size respectively. Each point of the lines
represents the mean over 87 *départements* for a given quinquennial period,
and each figure must be read from right to left, because the reconstruction
runs backward from 1906 to 1871. Lines corresponding to the various undercounts considered are generally not parallel, showing that the accuracy
of estimates worsens when running farther back in time. As was expected,
with undercount increasing, fertility increases as well and life expectancy
decreases. Errors affecting fertility are high (7 per cent after 7 periods for
4.5 per cent undercount, 14.5 per cent for 9.1 per cent undercount, and
23.5 per cent for 13.5 per cent undercount), while errors on life expectancy
reach 3 per cent, 6 per cent, and 10 per cent in the three cases of undercount. This sensitivity of results adds another caution of the accuracy of
fertility indexes with imperfect data.

Errors on population sizes turn out to be very stable and close to the
undercount imposed on the initial data. This comes from the fact that
censuses which serve as a basis for the calculation of demographic forces
are modified only in the direction of greater coherence, not with the idea
of a dramatic revision. Errors affecting estimates of under-registration at
birth on the contrary vary greatly, because the probability of dying from
birth to [0, 4] years old vary more rapidly than the life expectancy to which
it is linked.

Finally, this sensitivity analysis shows that estimates on life expectancy
are more reliable than those on fertility, and that a systematic net undercount on censuses could not be corrected to find the final population size
estimates. In some sense, this is reassuring, because it shows how close to
data the reconstruction works. Indeed, I do not claim to have discovered

the truth concerning past populations, but my aim has been to respect the material at my disposal and to extract the best information as rigorously as I can. That is why I have insisted on the notion of coherence rather than on those of truth or reality.

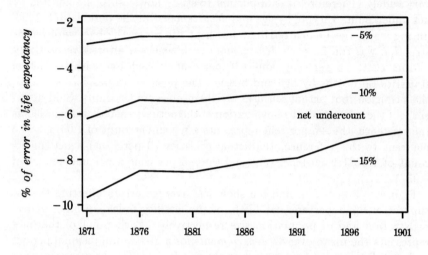

Figure 5.3 Sensitivity of mortality estimates to census net undercount.

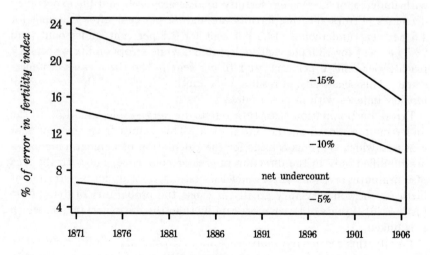

Figure 5.4 Sensitivity of fertility estimates to census net undercount.

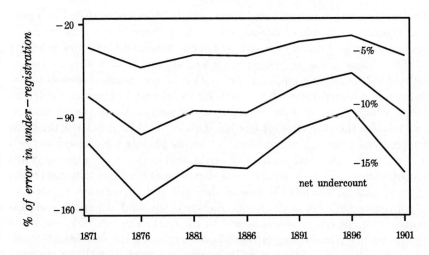

Figure 5.5 Sensitivity of under-registration rates at birth to census net undercount.

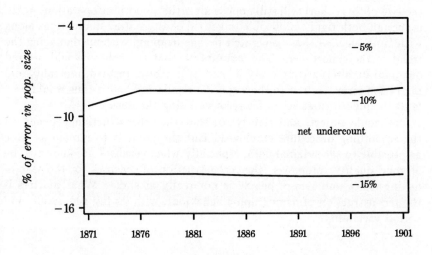

Figure 5.6 Sensitivity of population size estimates to census net undercount.

5.2.5   *Discussion*

The reconstruction method used from 1856 to 1906 has consisted in a general algorithm capable of dealing with extant flawed data: adjustment of census dates, preliminary smoothing (in the weighted least squares sense) of the cohorts across successive censuses, allocation of deaths to precise cells of the Lexis diagram, joint estimation of age-specific probabilities of dying and net migration rates, search for the closest Ledermann model life table, which gives internal demographic coherence to the reconstruction and enables the correction of deaths. This corrected life table is the basis for projecting the age pyramid of the census at date t backward to $t - 5$ and to correct the total number of births within $[t - 5, t]$. This backward reconstruction of age pyramids needs to rely on at least one terminal census of good quality, which is the case of the 1901 and 1906 French censuses.

An important asset of the reconstruction is the weak dependence of estimates from one quinquennial period to the next. The sole link consists in the preliminary smoothing of the cohorts, replacing the original SGF census data. One could argue as follows: why not work directly on the SGF data, estimate age-specific mortality and migration rates for each cohort, then smooth these series with ad hoc procedures, and then reconstruct? First, no correct work can be done directly on age pyramids showing obvious and significant anomalies. Secondly, only a cumulated distribution evolving regularly is appropriate for smoothing. If a cohort experiences a mortality crisis or a sudden in- or out-migration flow, the time-evolution of the size of this cohort will still appear after the smoothing operation, which is enough both rigid and flexible to get rid of alternating fluctuations along with time, such as those generated by age heaping, without damaging the trend of the cohort size. The assumption that the cohort would in- and out-migrate alternatively every 5 years is unlikely. Instead, mortality and migration series are not to show specific regularity, and it thus would be a fault to smooth these series for reconstructing the data.

One could object, and rightly so, that the reconstruction depends on the smoothing procedure employed. But the point is to remain as close as possible to the original data, especially when censuses are known to be of good quality. Moreover, the reconstruction of censuses for the sake of having exact numbers of people is not really at stake. What matters is the reconstruction of demographic behaviour, with its full age, space, and period variability.

5.3   Reconstruction of the Population from 1801 to 1856

The second part of the reconstruction runs from 1806 to 1856, and bears a greater resemblance to that of Van de Walle. The results obtained from 1856 to 1906, mainly the reconstructed pyramids by *département* in 1856, the matrices of migratory intensity by age and by *département*, and the shift between calculated and adjusted life tables are now once more ready for use.

According to Van de Walle, the 1806 census, in spite of contemporary criticism, is much more reliable (1974, p.19) than any other in the first half of the century and, moreover, it was conducted concisely (Biraben, 1970). The second reconstruction starts then from 1806 and runs to 1856.

5.3.1   Changes of Territory

Départements Altered from 1856 to 1861   For purposes of comparing the populations from 1856 to 1860, modifications were made to the populations of Landes, Basses Pyrénées, and Var altered in 1861 by law. In the reconstruction from 1806 to 1856, I respectively restore to these *départements* their territories prior to the alteration of 1861. (Consequently I must change the reconstructed populations of 1856: for instance, for Var, which had a population of both genders of 300 365 in 1861, and which in the same year had lost 68 054 people, the reconstructed population $p_x^{rec}(1856)$ of age x becomes $p_x^{rec} \times (1 + 68\ 054/300\ 365)$. This same procedure applies to all other altered *départements*).

Created or Modified Départements from 1806 to 1856

- The 1821 census, volume I, p. 32, states that:
  'By the senatus-consulte of the 2nd of November 1808, the *département* of Tarn-et-Garonne has been created at the expense of neighbouring *départements*; the surface and the population in 1801 of the territories thus detached are indicated hereafter: (Par le senatus-consulte du 2 novembre 1808, le département de Tarn-et-Garonne a été créé aux dépens des départements voisins; la superficie et la population en 1801 des territoires ainsi détachés sont indiquées ci-aprés) (Peuchet et Chanlaire, Statistique de la France, 1808-11).

Lot: arrondissement de Montauban, entier (12 cantons)	1,912	116,000
Haute Garonne:arrondissement de Castelsarrasin, entier (7 cantons)	1,220	66,000
Lot et Garonne: cantons d'Auvillar, Montaigu et Valence de l'arrondissement d'Agen	420	25,000 ,
Gers: canton de Lavit de l'arrondissement de Lectoure	210	13,000
Aveyron: canton de Saint Antonin de l'arrondissement de Villefranche	195	8,000
TARN-ET-GARONNE	3,957	228,000

This information can be used to correct the population numbers of each of the five *départements* listed above, in such a way that the territories from 1806 to 1808 are adjusted to those of 1809 and after. One can see that the same results are obtained by correcting in the following manner:

$$P^i(1806) = P(1806) \times P^i(1821)/P(1821)$$

where $P(1821)$ is the feminine population size of the six *départements* at the 1821 census, and $P(1806)$ that of the five *départements* (occupying the same territory) in 1806. $P^i(t)$ is the feminine population size of *département i* at year t. The same applies for births and deaths.

Since it matches up with the number published in 1821 (one finds 114,929 women in 1806 in the Tarn-et-Garonne, to compare to the 228,000 published in 1821) this second method seems better, since it allows one to estimate feminine births as well as deaths.

• Like Van de Walle, I compare the recorded population size in 1806, as well as the total numbers of births and deaths from 1806 to 1814 respectively to those from the *arrondissement* of Gex, which had been omitted in the publication of 1837, and then deduct them from the two *cantons* lost by the *département* of Ardennes in 1815 (see Van de Walle p. 56, and the 1821 census, volume I, p. 33).

5.3.2   Principle of the Reconstruction 1806–1856

In 1806, for each *département i*, a stable population of size P^i is constructed with a model life table $(q_x(e^i))_{x=0,\cdots,100}$ where e^i is a parameter (in this case I take a Ledermann model life table with single entry e^i, (the life expectancy at birth)), and a growth rate κ^i. In other words, for *département i* and age $[x, x+4]$:

$$p_x^i(1806) = p_x(e^i(1806), P^i(1806), \kappa^i(1806))$$

Starting from this initial population, the challenge is to reconstruct the series of age pyramids $(p_x^i(t))_{x=0,\cdots 90}$ for each *département i*, so as to minimize the distance between a given age pyramid $(\breve{p}_x^i(1856))_x$ and the age pyramid $(p_x^i(1856))_x$ reconstructed by this present method, in respect to the three starting parameters $e^i(1806), P^i(1806), \kappa^i(1806)$. In this case, it is advantageous to work with $(\breve{p}_x^i(1856))_x$ reconstructed by the prior method, the one which runs backward in time from 1906 to 1856.

Both reconstructions of 1806 to 1856, and of 1906 to 1856, are linked to each other only by a narrow junction, which is the correspondence of age pyramids by *département* in 1856 reconstructed by the two differing methods. In order to obtain the correspondence, I can vary the three parameters to modify the shape and the dimension of the initial age pyramids. These parameters have limited variance: we expect $e^i(1806)$ to be found only a few years from the reconstructed life expectancy in 1856–1860, which implies intervals going approximately from 25 to 40 years of age. The same restriction applies for the growth rate in that we expect it to be close to the difference between the growth rate of births and the growth rate of deaths around 1806. The population size $P^i(1806)$ should be equal or slightly greater to that published in the 1806 census.

The difficulties, however, are not negligible. We can trust neither the total numbers of births or deaths, which suffer no doubt from under-registration, nor the numbers published between 1806 and 1856, and least of all the published age pyramids.

This justifies my reliance on results obtained from the first reconstruction for the structure of migrations and under-registration of births and deaths. This second part of the reconstruction, although appearing more like that of Van de Walle by the choice of initial stable populations which are projected forward, extends the method I have developed in the first reconstruction from 1906 to 1856, and tests its consistency. It is the coherence found between these two distinct methods which justifies the entire reconstruction on a demographic level.

5.3.3 Multi-state 'Forward' Projection

Beginning from age pyramids in $t_0 = 1806$, $p_x^i(t_0) = p_x(e^i(t_0), P^i(t_0), \kappa^i(t_0))$ assimilated to stable populations of parameters $e^i(t_0), P^i(t_0), \kappa^i(t_0)$, I can draw the sequence of age pyramids through the aging process formalized by Equation 5.8, which I recall here:

$$p_{x+h}^i = p_x^i(1 - {}_hq_x^i)(1 - {}_h\rho_x^i)$$

and by the birth process:

$$p_0^i = B^i(1 - {}_hq_B^i)(1 - {}_h\rho_B^i) \tag{5.13}$$

In order to restore the data damaged by hidden under-registration, I must incorporate a pattern of errors on life tables, capable of overcoming the under-registration of deaths, and I must consider that the recorded *SGF* total number of births can be re-estimated. The fixed element in this second part of the reconstruction is the reconstructed age pyramids of 1856. All the other data are uncertain and must be treated with caution.

Modelling Net Migration Rates $({}_h\rho_x^i)$ Van de Walle used a schedule of age-specific migratory rates fixed for all *départements*. I can render the reconstruction more flexible by imposing *département*- and age-specific net migratory rates, instead of a schedule which does not account for growth differentials between *départements*.

The sequence of matrices $({}_h\rho_x^i)_{x,i}$ estimated from 1856 to 1906 are extrapolated to the period 1806–1856. We may think that migration was taking off after the middle of the century in France. A simple experiment

76 *Reconstruction*

corroborates this assertion: by imposing the age-specific migration rates estimated for 1861–1865 on the whole period 1806–1855, the computation shows unrealistic reconstructions for most *départements*. Age pyramids are distorted from 1806 to 1856 in a very unlikely manner. A solution yield-ing sensible results consists in forcing migration rates rapidly to zero while running back from 1851–1855 to 1806–1810. The rate of decrease is simply extrapolated from those of 1856–1860 and 1861–1865, or artificially when the data are fluctuating too much in those periods. This assumption of near zero migration rates in the first half of the century has the advan-tage of producing sensible results, showing consistency with the results of 1856–1860 and after. This is true for almost all *départements*, except Seine, Rhône, Bouches-du-Rhône, Gironde, and Hérault. It is no accident that these *départements* are the most urbanized ones. For them, putting migra-tion to zero before the middle of the century produces hugely distorted age pyramids. On the contrary, imposing the rates calculated for the period 1856–1860 or 1861–1865 to these exceptional *départements* yields very con-sistent results, as regards all the reconstructed variables (fertility, mortality, etc.) and smoothly evolving age pyramids.

In summary, net migration rates have been taken as rapidly decreasing to zero while running back from 1851–1855 to 1806–1810, except for the 5 *départements* mentioned above, for which rates are maintained at their 1856–1865 level.

Modelling Life Tables   The probabilities of dying $(_hq_x^i)_{x=B,0,\cdots,\omega}$ are taken from the Ledermann model life table satisfying the approximated death equation:

$$D_i(t) = p_x^i\,_hq_x^i(1 + \frac{_h\rho_x^i}{2}) \qquad (5.14)$$

where $D_i(t)$ represents the total number of deaths recorded in the *département* i during the quinquennial period $[t, t+h[$ [2,3].

We know in general that total numbers of deaths suffer from under-registration. In adjusting the probabilities of dying $(_hq_x^i)_x$ to the closest Ledermann model life table with respect to least squares for the sequence

---

[2] I noted that tables N^{os} *83 to 91* of vital statistics by gender of the *SGF* volume, *Territoire et Population*, 1837, conceal an important error: from 1817 to 1825, the line entitled 'SEINE-ET-MARNE' corresponds in fact to *Seine-Inférieure*, that entitled 'SEINE-INFERIEURE' to *Seine-et-Oise*, that entitled 'SEINE-ET-OISE' to *Seine-et-Marne*, and similarly for the years 1831 and 1832 (Tables 97 and 98). These errors are not repeated in the large recapitulative tables of births and deaths with no distinction of gender (N°s 102 et 105).

[3] Deaths by age of SEINE in 1870 and 1871 have not been published, except for total numbers: 37,886 women in 1870 and 40,610 in 1871 (pp. 107 and 165, Tables 11 of *SGF*, 1870). I applied then the structures of deaths from SEINE-ET-OISE to missing SEINE for the same years. Similarly, births from SEINE are not published in detail, (legitimate, illegitimate); we only have access to total numbers by gender (same table references).

of reconstructions of 1906 to 1856, I have ascertained that the differences generally appear mainly at young ages, and more specifically for $_5q_B$ which goes from birth to the age class $[0, 4$ years old$]$, and for $_5q_0$, which goes from the $[0, 4$ years old$]$ to the $[5, 9$ years old$]$. Moreover, we know that total numbers of births are also questionable. One is prompted, therefore, to reconstitute a deliberately biased model life table $(_hq_x^i)_x$ on the basis of an actual Ledermann table $(_hq_x^{i,L}(e))_x$ of entry e. This biased table should take into account these two types of under-registration, through a correction term denoted $\mathcal{C}\mathrm{orr}(x, i)$:

$$\text{for all } x = B, 0, \cdots \omega, \quad _hq_x^i = \mathcal{C}\mathrm{orr}(x, i)_hq_x^{i,L}$$

The reconstruction from 1906 to 1856 makes it possible to estimate the correction factors $\mathcal{C}\mathrm{orr}(x, i)$ by extrapolation starting from the sequence $_hq_x^i(t)/_hq_x^{i,L}(e_{[t,t+4]}^i)$ $(t = 1856, 1861, \cdots, 1901)$. Practically, I have taken the mean over the two periods 1856–1860 and 1861–1865:

$$\mathcal{C}\mathrm{orr}(x, i) = \left(_hq_x^i(1856)/_hq_x^{i,L}(e_{1856}^i) + _hq_x^i(1861)/_hq_x^{i,L}(e_{1861}^i)\right)/2 \quad (5.15)$$

Thus, without touching the suspect total number of births, I can match the declared total number of deaths (through death Equation 5.14) and generate valid age pyramids starting from these births (Equations 5.8 and 5.13). Practically, as under-registration of deaths is present mostly for young ages, I consider only two correcting factors, one for $x = B$ and the other for $x = [0, 4$ years$]$ (the probabilities of dying are within a calendar period). The other $\mathcal{C}\mathrm{orr}(x, i)$, $x = 5, \cdots, \omega$ can be taken equal to 1, because of the empirical closeness of the adjusted Ledermann table to the life table directly calculated in the reconstructions 1906–1856.

It is worth noting that the reconstruction turns out to be sensitive to these correction factors. If for all i, $\mathcal{C}\mathrm{orr}(0, i) = 1$ are taken, then trends of the sequences of life expectancies $e_{[t,t+4]}^i$ or of fertility indexes $I_f^i(t)$ appear broken around 1856, which is not justified by the compared evolution of death and birth series, especially if no correction factor (that is $\mathcal{C}\mathrm{orr}(B, i) = 1$, $\mathcal{C}\mathrm{orr}(0, i) = 1$) is introduced.

Correcting Total Numbers of Births and the 1806 Census   On the first run of the 1806–1856 algorithm, the best 1806 age pyramid is selected as the one which, projected forward, gives the 1856 age pyramid as close as possible to the 1856 target age pyramid. From 1806 to 1856, the corresponding population was submitted to the mortality modelled by modified life tables which produced exactly the *SGF* total number of deaths, was renewed by *SGF* total number of births and altered by age-specific net migration rates.

The 1856 age pyramid obtained in this manner can be distinct from the target. The gap between the two pyramids is transferred to the total numbers of births in this way:

$$\frac{B^{(n+1),i}_{[1851-x,1855-x]}}{B^{(n),i}_{[1851-x,1855-x]}} = \frac{\breve{p}^i_x(1856)}{p^{(n),i}_x(1856)} \qquad x = 0, 5, 10, \cdots, 45 \qquad (5.16)$$

where superscript (n) denotes n^{th} run estimates. Thus $B^{(n),i}_{[1851-x,1855-x]}$ represents the total number of births in *département i* at the quinquennial period $[1851 - x, 1855 - x]$, estimated at the beginning of the nth run, $p^{(n),i}_x(1856)$ is the estimate of the total number of women aged $[x, x + 4]$ on 1 January 1856 in *département i* estimated at the end of the nth run, $\breve{p}^i_x(1856)$ is again the (unchanged) target constituted by the total number of women aged $[x, x + 4]$ on 1 January 1856 in *département i*. At the first run, $B^{(1),i}_{[1851-x,1855-x]}$ is of course equal to the *SGF* total number of births.

As the reconstruction starts from 1806, Equation 5.16 applies only for the correction of cohorts, which were aged under 50 years old at the 1856 census. The good fit after the 45–49 age class is obtained by extending the correction iteration 5.16 to the 1806 census itself, that is to say by superseding the total number of births $B^{(n),i}_{[1851-x,1855-x]}$ by the total number $p^{(n),i}_x(1806)$ of women aged $[x - 50, x - 46]$ on 1 January 1806:

$$\frac{p^{(n+1),i}_x(1806)}{p^{(n),i}_x(1806)} = \frac{\breve{p}^i_{x+50}(1856)}{p^{(n),i}_{x+50}(1856)} \qquad x = 0, \cdots, \omega \qquad (5.17)$$

The age ω is the age limit to which the correction is applied. Its value is obtained by trial and error: taking the 1806 *SGF* census untouched imposes a heavy constraint on the reconstruction. It is like bending too rigid a bow between 1806 and 1856: the reconstruction produces clearly artificial discontinuities at the 1856 junction. Moreover, all that we know about the censuses of the nineteenth century prevent us from taking the 1806 *SGF* census for granted. On the other hand, applying correcting iterations of Equation 5.17 for too high ω gives too much reliance to the estimates of the age class sizes at the 1806 reconstructed census. Indeed, trying ω to its maximum, 35 years (that is 85–89 years old in 1856), produces inconsistent results. Therefore, I tried every value of ω from 0 to 30, and checked the results for consistency. The solution $\omega = 10$ turned out to be the most satisfactory for the whole set of *départements*. Thus the three first age classes of the 1806 census are corrected according to Equation 5.17: the age classes 0–4, 5–9, and 10–14 years old. The other age classes remain uncorrected, implying occasional disparities at the junction of 1856 for ages over 65 years. Fortunately, these disparities remain negligible compared to the rest of the 1856 age pyramid. This enables one to obtain a very close agreement between 1856 age pyramids calculated by the 1806–1856 reconstruction and the 1856 'target' age pyramid.

The migration pattern must also be fine-tuned: if net migration rates are fixed too low or too high, new cohorts born after 1806 induce impossibly distorted age pyramids from 1811 to 1856 by generating a drop or a rise in levels of population numbers. The re-estimation of births from 1806 to 1856 and the three first age classes of the 1806 census should normally not disturb some rule-of-thumb 'smoothness' in the age pyramid series. Successive trials indicate that this constraint is best satisfied by putting net migration rates as rapidly decreasing to zero from 1855 to 1806, except for some specific *départements*, which afterwards turned out to be the most urbanized ones, and for which it is better to keep migration rates by age equal to those of the 1856–1860 period.

Correction algorithm (5.16) converges numerically for all the *départements* considered. The speed of convergence varies from one *département* to the other, but in general 6 or 7 iterations are enough to obtain a perfect fit between the projected age pyramid in 1856 and target. Figure 5.7 shows an example of convergence.

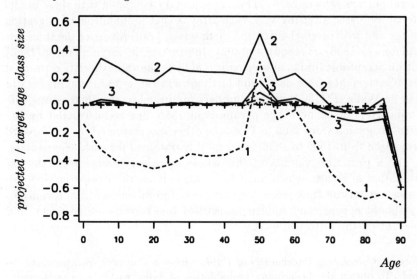

Figure 5.7 Example of convergence of the projected age pyramid in 1856 to the target (here, *département* of Seine). The digits on the curves indicate the number of iteration.

Equation 5.16, while permitting the production of consistent age pyramids from 1806 to 1856, yields estimates for under-registration of births as:

$$\frac{B^{(0),i}_{[1851-x,1855-x]}}{B^{(\infty),i}_{[1851-x,1855-x]}}$$

One a posteriori test for the goodness of this estimate is to check whether its time series 1806–1855 is smoothly connected to the time series of the estimates from 1856–1906. In this latter period, each estimate is calculated independently for each *département* and each quinquennial period. The credibility of both reconstructions will be increased if the whole series 1806–1906 looks smooth and makes sense. Fortunately, this is the case (a pleasant surprise!).

The overall Coale index, which is a measure and does not enter directly in the reconstruction, is corrected the same way for year t:

$$\tilde{I}_f^i(t) = I_f^i(t)\frac{B_t^{(\infty),i}}{B_t^{(0),i}}$$

which defines the corrected overall Coale index.

Running from 1806 to 1856   Thus, in summary, equipped with these model life tables biased at young ages, with arrays of net probabilities of migration by age and with original death and birth series, I optimize over the three parameters $e^i(1806)$, $P^i(1806)$, $\kappa^i(1806)$. In practice, in varying only $e^i(1806)$ within acceptable limits, in keeping $\kappa^i(1806)$ as the value directly estimated for *département i* from death and birth growth rates, and in taking, as did Van de Walle, $P^i(1806)$ as the numbers published in the 1806 census, the similarity between both age pyramids in 1856, one reconstructed by the retro-projection from 1906 to 1856, the other reconstructed by the forward projection from 1806 to 1856, is acceptably obtained for each *département*.

The a posteriori validity of this whole machinery comes from the examination of results which must look coherent on the demographic level, consistent on the time series level (some temporal rule-of-thumb continuity should appear, and sudden unjustified breakdowns are suspect), and relevant on the historical level.

Note on Calculating Probabilities of Dying within a Calendar Quinquennial Period   To obtain the Ledermann probabilities of dying within a calendar quinquennial period, I proceed as follows: a single entry e makes it possible to compile the list of quinquennial probabilities of dying, through the formula:

$$\log_{10}(_5\bar{q}_x) = a_x + b_x \log_{10}(100 - e)$$

The coefficients a_x and b_x are published in Ledermann's book *Nouvelles tables types de mortalité* (PUF, 1969). A parabolic smoothing yields the probabilities of dying in annual $_1\bar{q}_x$. These latter are then transformed into probabilities within a calendar year $_1q_x$ through the formulas established in Wattelar (1980) and in Pressat (1983):

- for $x = $ birth, $_1q_B = 0.89 _1\bar{q}_0$

- for $x = 0$,

$$_1q_0 = 1 - \frac{(1 - {}_1\bar{q}_0)(2 - {}_1\bar{q}_1)}{2.(1 - {}_1\bar{q}_B)}$$

- for $x = 1$ to 88 years old,

$$_1q_x = 1 - \frac{(1 - {}_1\bar{q}_x)(2 - {}_1\bar{q}_{x-1})}{(2 - {}_1\bar{q}_x)}$$

- at 89 years old and 90 and above, approximations lead to the following equations:

$$x = 89 \text{ years} \qquad _1q_{89} \quad = \quad 1 - \frac{(1 - {}_1\bar{q}_{89})(1 - m_{90+})}{(2 - {}_1\bar{q}_{89})(2 - m_{90+})}$$

$$x = 90 \text{ years} \qquad _1q_{90+} \quad = \quad m_{90+} . \frac{1 - {}_1\bar{q}_{89}}{2}$$

Instead of these simple formulas, one could also pass from probabilities of dying to probabilities of dying within a calendar year by an appropriate smoothing.

We then return easily to the calendar quinquennial period in considering a fictitious stationary population. We count the total number of survivors either by adding up the total number of survivors from annual cohorts aged $[x, x+4]$ at time t, or by following the total number of survivors from annual cohorts aged $[x-1, x+3]$ during 5 additional years:

$$(1 - {}_1q_B)\Pi_0^{x+4}(1 - {}_1q_i)\left(1 + \sum_{j=5}^{8}(\Pi_5^j(1 - {}_1q_{x+i}))\right)$$

$$= (1 - {}_1q_B)\Pi_0^{x-1}(1 - {}_1q_i) \times \left(1 + \sum_{j=0}^{3}(\Pi_0^j(1 - {}_1q_{x+i}))\right)(1 - {}_5q_x)$$

Hence the probability of dying within a calendar quinquennial period ${}_5q_x$.

Part II

Results and Dynamics

Part II

6

Perspectives on France as a Whole

6.1 Population Size

6.1.1 Summing up over all Départements

Van de Walle applied his general method of reconstruction to the whole of France. It was difficult for him to link this reconstruction on a national level to the sum of the *départemental* reconstructions, because he was missing the urban *départements* and those created, modified, or lost during the course of the century (Van de Walle, 1974, p. 123) (namely, Alpes-Maritimes, Bouches-du-Rhône, Meurthe-et-Moselle, Moselle, Bas-Rhin, Haut-Rhin, Rhône, Savoie, Haute-Savoie, Seine, Seine-et-Oise, Territoire de Belfort). He therefore had to settle for comparing only the age distributions (pp. 132-36).

As I have included all the *départements*, it is interesting to compare my results added over all *départements* to those presented on France as a whole by various authors. In fact, from 1806 to 1861, I have considered *all départements*, including Tarn-et-Garonne for which I have prolonged demographic data for the years 1807 and 1806 (as this *département* was non-existent until 1808). The territories of the *départements* which formed Tarn-et-Garonne were returned to their respective territories after 1808.

In the reconstruction from 1856 to 1861, the *départements* correspond to their respective territories of 1861, in particular Var, Landes, and Basses-Pyrénées. Subsequently, in the estimation of the national population of 1856, I have added the population of 68,054 people from the district of Grasse (united to Alpes-Maritimes in 1860 by a law decreed 23 June 1860) divided by two to obtain the number of women. In 1861, the following three newly created *départements* are entered into the analysis: Alpes-Maritimes, Savoie, Haute-Savoie.

From 1866 to 1870, although they were still French, I have dismissed the following *départements* annexed by Germany in 1871: Meurthe, Moselle, Bas-Rhin, and Haut-Rhin for that quinquennial period. Moreover, the *SGF* data ends in 1868 for these *départements*, because the volume of vital statistics (*SGF nouvelle série, Tome I, 1871*) was drafted only after the war.[1] In the calculation of the French population from 1866 to 1870, for the sake of comparison with other authors, I add the feminine population of these four *départements* taken directly from the *SGF*, to the sum of the *départements* in 1866.

From 1871 (initially from the 1872 census) to 1906, all of the *départements* enter into the analysis (including Meurthe-et-Moselle and Territoire-de-Belfort).

As a result of these changes of territory, I have preferred not to use my method to reconstruct directly the national population. In fact, to undertake the smoothing by cohort, I must either extrapolate the *départements* that are missing during certain periods, or reduce the territory under investigation. Like Van de Walle, I would have to be satisfied with comparing only the age distributions, instead of the age pyramids. To reconstruct *département* by *département* and then sum across them is therefore more satisfactory.

6.1.2   The Population Reconstruction of Bourgeois-Pichat

Van de Walle also compared his results to the earliest reconstruction made by Bourgeois-Pichat (1951, 1952, and 1965). This latter reconstruction at the national level begins in 1776 and includes both genders. Van de Walle noted that Bourgeois-Pichat considered the registrations of deaths as complete, the ages at death as exact, and foreign migrations as negligible (Van de Walle, 1974, p. 136).

Annually from 1806 to 1901, Bourgeois-Pichat classified deaths according to their dates of birth, which permitted him to calculate the survivors of each generation on 1 January of each year by subtracting, from the initial cohort size, the deaths that had occurred from the time of the birth of the generation. By adding other hypotheses, he repeated this process prior to 1806. Van de Walle rightly criticized this method and argued that it left many unanswered questions. An excellent critical review of Bourgeois-Pichat's reconstruction is made in Weir (1994).

---

[1]'Avant de donner un aperçu du mouvement de la population de France pendant les années 1869, 1870 et 1871, nous devons avertir le lecteur qu'à raison des perturbations causées par la dernière guerre dans les services publics, les administrations préfectorales des deux anciens *départements* du Haut-Rhin et du Bas-Rhin n'ont pu fournir aucun document relativement à l'état civil. Les démarches faites, depuis, auprès des autorités allemandes, n'ont pas donné de résultats au moyen desquels on pût combler cette regrettable lacune' (*SGF* nouvelle série, Tome I, 1871). (Before having any idea on vital statistics on the population of France in 1869, 1870, and 1871, we must caution the reader that the administrations of the *Prefectures* of the two former *départements*, Bas-Rhin and Haut-Rhin, have been unable to provide us with any information on civil status. This is due to the troubles in the public service caused by the last war. None of the steps taken with the German authorities was effective enough to fill this regrettable deficiency).

6.1.3 Comparison

Comparison of my results with Bourgeois-Pichat, Van de Walle, and the *SGF* is represented in Figure 6.1.

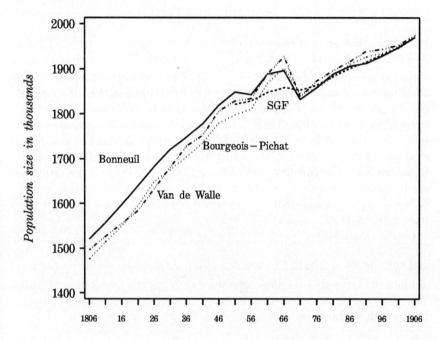

Figure 6.1 Female population of France, 1806–1906.

My reconstruction before 1856 has produced larger total numbers of young women from 0 to 15 years old, thus resulting in a higher estimate for the population size. It is symptomatic that Van de Walle's estimate and mine converge gradually from 1806 to 1851. By the way, it is worth noting that the growth rate is smaller and more regular in mine than in Van de Walle's.

After 1861, my estimation gives a smaller population size than that of Van de Walle. Both of them show a very pronounced dip at the time of the war of 1871, contrary to that of the *SGF*. It is interesting to note that the *SGF* number in 1871, corresponding to the 1872 census which was conducted in difficult conditions, is higher than the other estimates. This suggests that the impact of the war could have been underestimated.

Note that from the census of 1856 to that of 1861, the rapid growth of population size is due to the integration of three *départements* and not to any steep natural growth. In fact, the stagnation from the 1851 census to that of 1856 indicates a slowing down of intrinsic population growth. In the same manner, the trough after 1871 is due to the loss of *départements* annexed by Germany.

6.2   Mortality and Fertility

With the same precautions exercised for the changes of territory, I calculate the life expectancy at birth $e^F_{[t,t+4]}$ for France for each quinquennial period [t, t+4] ($t = 1806, 1811, \cdots, 1901$). The technique is similar to the one I have used at the *département* level (after replacing the subscript and the superscript 'i' by 'F' in the equations to indicate France as a whole): from 1856–1860 to 1901–1905, I have used Equation 5.5 and minimization 5.10; from 1806–1810 to 1851–1855, correction factors for $x = B$ and $x = [0, 4 \text{ years}]$ were used according to Formula 5.15 and inserted into Equation 5.14. For this first half of the century, I have used the estimated age pyramid for France by simply adding up over all *départements*, instead of searching to fit the 1856 age pyramid obtained by the reconstruction from 1906 to 1856.

I have also calculated the overall Coale index $I^F_f(t) = \dfrac{\sum_i B^i([t,t+4])}{\sum_{x=20}^{49} \sum_i \tilde{P}^t_x h(x)}$ and the corrected overall Coale index $\tilde{I}^F_f(t)$ obtained by replacing the total number of births B^i with the corrected one $\tilde{B}^i$ in the previous expression. The superscript i covers the entire range of *départements* under consideration, which again varies with changes in French territory.

6.2.1   *The Reconstruction of National Mortality by Meslé and Vallin (1989)*

Meslé and Vallin (1989) relied on two specific periods of the nineteenth century for their reconstruction: 1851–1856 and 1896–1901. Detailed annual data for deaths by age of the national population were published during these periods. They extrapolated them from the whole of the century, and related them to the populations in the middle of the year obtained by linear interpolation of Bourgeois-Pichat's reconstitutions. Of those, they deduce mortality tables by annual age. There as well, the registration of deaths is assumed to be complete. The series of life expectancies which they obtain are very close to that of Van de Walle (Figure 6.2).

6.2.2   *Comparison of Mortality*

The comparison of the reconstituted or reconstructed mortality series is represented on Figure 6.2. Although my estimations $e^F_{[t,t+4]}$ are almost independent from one another from 1856–1860 onward, a certain coherence of the temporal series emerges.

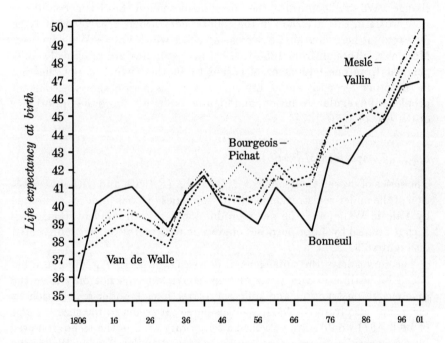

Figure 6.2 Life expectancy at birth, France as a whole, 1806–1906.

Trends and fluctuations are generally similar to those of Van de Walle and to those of Meslé-Vallin. The difference comes from the beginning of the century, where my curve supports a more pessimistic view of life expectancy during the First Empire. A rapid recovery from 1806–1810 to 1811 and after puts the estimate of life expectancy over the others until 1826–1830. After 1841–1845, my estimate is clearly below the others. We must also remember that there is no homogeneity in the territory considered: in my reconstruction, I try to allow as much as possible for the changes of territory, including all *départements*, whereas Van de Walle excluded urban *départements* and those which have had 'intractable problems of border change'. We shall confirm in the following discussion that living conditions were worse in the city than in the countryside: urban *départements* taken into account here thus have a decreasing effect which Van de Walle ignored. Moreover, although from 1856 to 1906 my estimates are practically independent from one quinquennial period to another, which is not the case in the other reconstitutions, my curve over this period shows a coherent profile and a regular evolution, and highlights slightly more the importance of the war of 1870–1871.

6.2.3 Comparison of Fertility

The series of overall Coale indexes $\tilde{I}_f(t)$ and $I_f(t)$ (with and without correction of the under-registration at birth), the series of Coale indexes estimated by Van de Walle, and the net reproduction rate estimated by Bourgeois-Pichat divided by 3, for purposes of graphic representation, are represented on Figure 6.3.

The curves have the same general decreasing aspect. The difference between my estimates and those of Van de Walle stems not only from the different reconstruction and different correction of under-registration at birth, but also from the territory considered. It seems to me that the war of 1870–1871 would have provoked a temporary drop in the trend, followed by a recovery, a feature that can be seen neither by Van de Walle who avoided urbanized *départements* nor by Bourgeois-Pichat who considered registration as complete. An intriguing result suggested by Figure 6.3 is the regular decline of the $\tilde{I}_f$ curve, apart from the depression due to the Franco-Prussian war, whereas Van de Walle's estimate and non-corrected I_f clearly exhibit evidence for a baby-boom, what Van de Walle (1974, p. 179) nicknamed 'the ski-jump'. In the $\tilde{I}_f$ curve, there is only a temporary ten-year stagnation, from 1856 to 1865, before the drastic drop at the time of the 1870–1871 war. Moreover, the $\tilde{I}_f$ curve looks more fluctuating in the short term, such as the mini baby-boom of 1846–1850 or the short drop of 1821–1825. At the *départemental* level, Van de Walle (1974) presented the time series of I_g, the indicator of marital fertility, for 'selected *départements*' on his Figure 7.3 (p.180 of his book). He commented upon

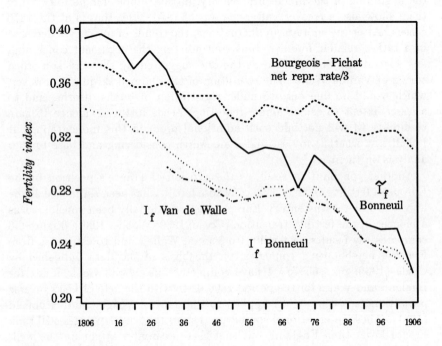

Figure 6.3 Fertility indexes for France as a whole, 1806–1906.

this figure, noting that the baby-booms occurred 'at different levels and at different dates, and had different intensities', and that this phenomenon 'may be analogous to the "baby-boom" of the 1940s and 1950s in much of the Western world—a temporary reversal of long-term trends'. On Figures 6.4 and 6.5 are plotted the I_f estimated by Van de Walle for the same *départements* which he had selected in his Figure 7.3 (p. 180). This I_f series show very similar evolutions to the I_g ones originally chosen by Van de Walle. In juxtaposition, I have plotted my own $\tilde{I}_f$ series on Figures 6.4 and 6.5. These $\tilde{I}_f$ series look more irregular in the short term, especially at the beginning of the nineteenth century, in the Napoleonic period. All of them show also a recovery after the war of 1870–1871, that is at the 1876 census. After the short-term fluctuations, the trends of my curves decrease in a rather regular manner, thus contradicting the argument concerning any special baby-boom such as the one suggested by the very smoothed curves of Van de Walle. The refutation of the claimed ski-jump, however, which would be due only to under-registration of births, deaths, and to a lesser extent to census under-reporting, needs further evidence to gain credibility. I will not add such additional proof in this monograph, but I shall test whether my estimates are worth considering and base further analysis on them.

Another concomitant result is the revision of France's position in the European fertility decline. France, whose fertility has been estimated as the lowest in nineteenth-century Europe, has traditionally been considered as a pioneer in the fertility transition (Coale, 1969, Woods, 1986). Figure 6.6 compares my results on fertility to Van de Walle's and to estimates from France's neighbouring countries, on the basis of the data published by Coale (1969, pp. 55–7). I have completed the overall Coale index for England and Wales for the period 1806–1846 with the help of Lee's inverse projection (see Chapter 2) applied to the data of Wrigley and Schofield (1981). These international comparisons show that my estimates still rank France lower than England, but that these estimates attenuate the well-known considerable gap. With this in mind, although I still fear that my correction by Ledermann model life tables are too strong and could tend to overestimate $\tilde{I}_f$, the international comparison raises serious questions about the claimed advance of France in the European demographic transition. Spatial differentiation in France was more extreme than was possible in England, for example, so that the quality of estimates for regions with bad registration can play a crucial role in the aggregate calculation at the national level. My estimates compared to those of the Princeton project pull France back into the group of other European countries, while still maintaining it at the advanced front of the decline. Under-registration is once again the key factor responsible for this revision. However, other pieces of evidence are needed for this suggestion to gain credibility, because my findings rely heavily on model life tables. I shall, however, carry on

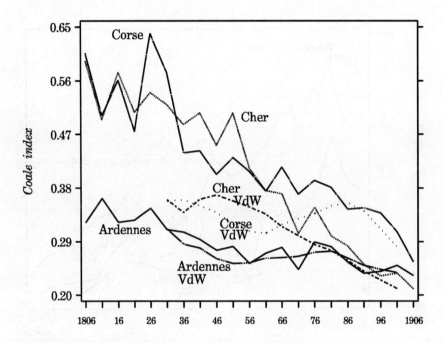

Figure 6.4 $\tilde{I}_f$ series compared to Van de Walle I_f, for the *départements* selected by Van de Walle as representative of the so-called 'ski-jump' (continued on the next figure).

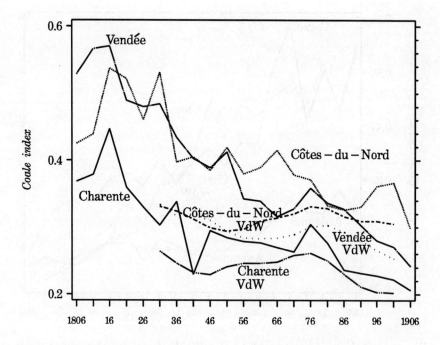

Figure 6.5 $\tilde{I}_f$ series compared to Van de Walle I_f, for the *départements* selected by Van de Walle as representative of the so-called 'ski-jump'.

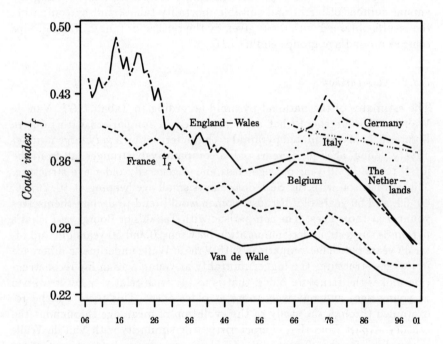

Figure 6.6 Overall Coale indexes in some neighbouring countries of France compared to France $\tilde{I}_f$ estimates. *Source* Coale 1969.

exploiting their consequences by further considering $\tilde{I}_f$ as the best estimate.

6.3   Age Pyramids

6.3.1   The 1851 Age Pyramid According to Tabah

Tabah (1947), prior to Bourgeois-Pichat, had proceeded to a reconstitution of the French pyramid in 1851. In summary, his method consists of evaluating the surviving population of successive generations by using the annual number of births and suitable mortality tables, and by comparing the results obtained with those given by the census for ranges of age groups centred around age groups ending in 0.

6.3.2   Comparison

The estimates of the national pyramid according to Tabah, *SGF*, Van de Walle, and Bourgeois-Pichat are represented in comparison with mine in Figures 6.7. My estimated pyramid is characterized by a very large number of very young, aged [0, 4] years old, a comparatively stronger fall from the [0, 4] to the [5, 9] year old age class and a generally older age structure. The comparison with the *SGF* data shows small age heaping at 10, 20, 30, 40, 50, and 60 years old, because women would tend to declare themselves younger at those ages. The comparison with Tabah's or Bourgeois-Pichat's pyramids suggests under-enumeration between 20 and 50 years old and after 65 years old. The comparison with Van de Walle underlines a difference in the age structure: the higher mortality at young ages in my reconstruction makes the structure older, that is to say with relatively fewer women at young ages and relatively more at older ones. This point will be re-examined through the study of the evolution of mean age throughout the century. Apart from that characteristic, the similarity with Van de Walle is very high for the 20 year olds and above, the dissimilarity is evident for the under 20 year olds. The difference comes from my re-estimations of mortality and total number of births.

6.4   Correcting Under-Registration Alters our View of the Transition

In summary, the comparison with other authors (who either ignored urban *départements* or considered registration as complete) shows that my estimates portray a national population more numerous at younger ages, submitted to higher mortality and endowed with higher fertility. This tendency will emerge again in the regional analysis to follow and will colour my rereading of the French demographic transition.

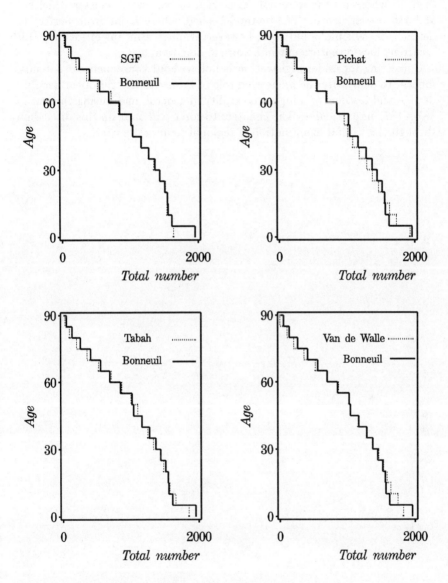

Figure 6.7 Feminine pyramid in 1851, France as a whole.

Put simply, the reconstruction leads me to count an 'invisible' population, made up of the infants whose births were not registered before they died, or whose deaths were not registered, or who were registered neither at birth nor at death. The method I suggest here is far from perfect to detect this invisible population; however, it offers a means of tackling this recurrent flaw often present in historical demography.

Correcting for under-registration is not without consequences: it tends, indeed, to demystify the pioneering role of France in the European fertility decline and testifies to a higher mortality in general, and during the war of 1870–1871 in particular. The chapters to come will back up this discussion through the careful examination of regional temporal patterns.

7

The French Transition of Fertility

Fertility transitions have been much debated in the demographic literature. The subject deserves much attention and this chapter will be devoted to the description of the stratified evolution of fertility and to the search for possible space-temporal linkages. In Chapter 8, other factors characterizing the transition will be reviewed. In Chapter 9, the debate will return to fertility, and its space-time dynamics in connection with other demographic variables: mortality and migration, but also urbanization.

7.1 Diffusion Effects in the Fertility Transition

7.1.1 The Diffusionist Approach

In the analysis of demographic changes during the nineteenth century, two temporal scales are usually distinguished: the long run, represented by contrasted evolutions throughout space, and the short run, reflected by short-term fluctuations from one year to the next. The theory of spatial diffusion of innovations in geography is one possible model to enlighten the historical processes at work and to help us understand the change of variables varying at different points of the geographical field.

The pioneering work of Hägerstrand (1952, 1953) has made the theory of diffusion a common theme in geography (Brown 1968, Cliff and Hagett 1988, Saint Julien 1990). In this theory, two main schemes are suggested to explain the process of diffusion of an innovation:

1. re-localizing diffusion: innovative centres migrate like a wave throughout space, while former locations are gradually weakened or even abandoned;

2. expanding diffusion: phenomena spread throughout space from the initial kernel, similar to an oil stain. The innovation diffuses first to the nearby neighbourhood, but the expansion also takes the route of the hierarchical structure of places, when potential adopters are

heterogeneously distributed along space: the diffusion is called 'hierarchical'. In this case, innovation propagates by invading 'down' the steps of the hierarchy (see J. B. Racine and C. Raffestin, 1984).

Hägerstrand distinguished four phases of the process:

1. At the beginning, innovative centres contrast strongly with far away regions;
2. new centres then emerge with rapid growth in far away regions, while the regional contrast regularly decreases;
3. the innovation is generalized to the whole space;
4. with the growth rate of the innovation slowing down, all locations converge to saturation of the phenomenon.

In addition, Hägerstrand pointed out the importance of barrier effects, such as physical obstacles or cultural conservatism and resistance.

Such a theory must be kept in mind when looking at the transition of mortality, fertility, or migration over time and space. In the case of mortality, innovation can reflect any change in living conditions, either negatively, such as an epidemic, a war, or a famine, or positively, such as improving hygiene.

Fertility change through time and space is more difficult to explain, although diffusionist explanations are now common in the literature. For example, Rosero-Bixby and Casterline (1993) seem to take for granted that 'substantial historical and contemporary evidence points to the existence of diffusion effects on the timing and space of fertility transition'. They present a model of diffusion coming from the epidemiological 'Susceptible-Latent-Infectious-Removal' model. Unfortunately, their analysis is related neither to historical data, nor sufficiently to the spatial question. The much debated question is, however, whether an individual adjusts his or her fertility to socio-economic conditions, or if he or she adopts an innovation propagated through diffusion.

Cleland and Wilson (1987) favoured the diffusion of ideas and information flows, what they called 'ideational change', over other explanations centred on material change, and Freedman (1987) supported the notion of quasi-independent forces spreading through national networks of communication and transportation. The two influences, adaptation to local circumstances or diffusion of an innovation such as contraceptive knowledge or technology, are important to distinguish as the mechanism responsible for the transition. However, while Carlsson (1966) supported the adjustment hypothesis on Swedish data, Knodel (1977) and Watkins (1987) emphasized the 'natural' aspect of pre-transition fertility and the irreversibility of fertility transition as evidence in favour of the innovation hypothesis. Coale and Watkins (1986), summarizing the Princeton European Fertility Project, contested that the geographic distribution of socio-economic pressures toward fertility adaptation can explain pre- or post-transition regional differences in Europe. Knodel (1974) and Lesthaeghe (1977, 1983, 1992) came to similar conclusions.

Bean, Mineau, and Anderton (1990) tackled the spatial problem directly in a study of an American Mormon population. They were restricted to only three time periods: 1871–1890, 1891–1910, and 1911–1930, which is very few to conduct a time series analysis, although they wrote that they had 'a considerable period of time' (p. 212). Their temporal follow-up is even reduced to two time units, when they decided to study the change from one period to the next. By taking averages over periods as long as 20 years, these authors are hindered in their search for causal dynamic relationships. However, they had access to more precise data than this present study, such as interval to first birth, average birth interval, length of final birth interval, and age at last birth. They used cluster analysis 'to identify regional or community similarities in the patterns of fertility change over time and the underlying forms of fertility-limiting behaviour'. Unfortunately, they acknowledged the difficulty 'of addressing the debate of adaptation and innovation in full', although they finally claimed to be convinced by the adaptive argument.

Here, despite the advantage of encompassing a whole century divided up into twenty quinquennial periods, I do not dispose of many demographic variables which could help me address the 'stopping' versus 'spacing' behaviour which is debated at length in Bean et al. (1990). Moreover, my doubts regarding the nineteenth-century data (elaborated earlier, in Chapter 1, section 1.3) provide justification for not calculating a legitimate fertility Coale index. It is true that the overall Coale index I use here is confused by the fluctuations of illegitimate fertility, which is more related to social and clerical controls than to family limitation. Van de Walle's calculation of I_g (1974), the legitimate fertility index, shows the difficulty of obtaining a good unquestionable estimate, as I have explained in the introduction of this book. Considering that only the overall Coale index is limiting, but its estimation is better, I will try to show that valuable results on the dynamics of the transition can be obtained.

I wish to take advantage of 100 years of observation less in order to enter the modern, but common, debate about the determinants of fertility or the individual motivations 'underlying the transition', than to depict the French transition in terms of spatial organization and changing evolution, and to search for any space-time synergy between the three basic demographic behaviours involved in the transition. After the following global description of the evolutions of the main demographic variables, the richness of the time series available will permit the econometric investigation of their space-time dynamics. The absence of data at the individual level is counterbalanced by the abundance of temporal spatial data at the macro level, a perspective which deserves attention, as I will try to show.

7.1.2   The Transition of Fertility

Classification of Départemental Trajectories to Gain in Readability   In order to facilitate reading, the evolutions of the *départements* are regrouped
with the help of a multivariate data analysis, of hierarchical ascending
classification.

This method consists in producing a set of partitions, each partition
corresponding to a certain degree of similarity shared by *départements*
regrouped within each subset of the partition, or to a certain degree of
dissimilarity between members belonging to different subsets of the partition. The notion of dissimilarity must be employed with care. Here, for
the purpose of clustering, *départements* are considered as belonging to $I\!R^T$,
where T is the time dimension, specifically $T = 20$ quinquennial periods.
They constitute a cloud of points in $I\!R^T$, and are grouped whenever the
inter-class inertia is maximum and the intra-class inertia is minimum. This
is the so-called Ward method for Euclidean distances (see Saporta 1990).
Here, the partition chosen is the one yielding both sufficient details on the
mortality differentials and a readable map. *Départements* belonging to the
same class can indeed be represented with the same colour on a map of
France. Here, this map is a 'temporal' map, synthesizing 20 maps, one for
each of the 20 census dates. Information condensed in this way is more
readable than a film showing the succession of 20 maps, because space-
time is considered as a single object of study. Moreover, the regrouping
has the advantage of polishing fluctuations specific to one *département* and
to reflect directly space-time correlations. Moreover, the *département* as a
geographical elementary unit is dictated by the nature of the data. The
knowledge of the evolution of each single *département* has little interest,
if this evolution cannot be connected with the ensemble of the remnant
territory. In other words, the *départemental* specificity is less important
in my mind than its contribution to some possible collective arrangement.
Thus, the classification helps delineate homogeneous subsets to the French
space, naturally shaping geographical types with homogeneous behaviour.

Fertility over Time and Space   In the case of fertility evolutions, six large
classes emerge from the hierarchical ascending classification, apart from
three *départements* (Finistère, Haute-Vienne, and Lozère) which appear
marginal. No inter-*départemental* connection has been postulated a priori
for the classification, so that the regrouping of neighbouring *départements*
on Figure 7.1 brings a piece of news and sheds light on the evolving structure of the French space.

The time series of the means over each class is represented on Figure 7.2.

The fertility decline seems to be driven from three leading poles, forming
a triangle inscribed in the French hexagon: Normandy-Pays de Loire at

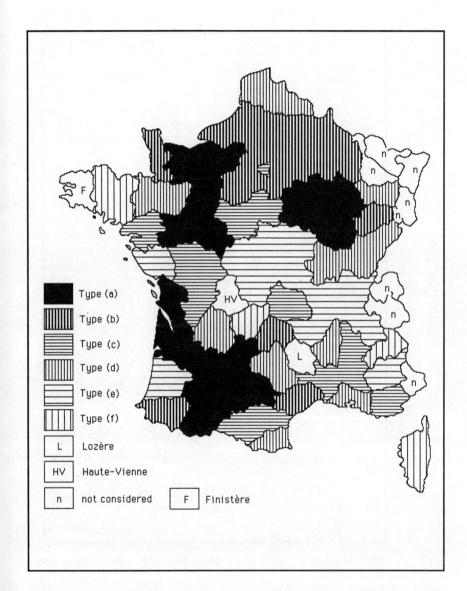

Figure 7.1 Temporal map showing the decline of the overall Coale Index $\tilde{I}_f$.

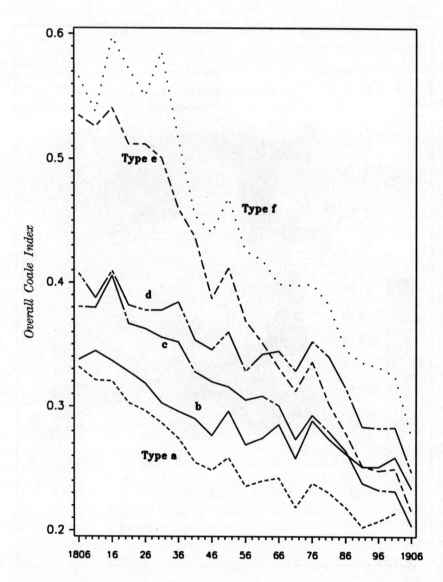

Figure 7.2 The decline of the overall Coale index $\tilde{I}_f$, by geographical Types.

the western corner, Champagne (in fact, Champagne and the north of Burgundy) at the eastern corner, and the Garonne Valley (plus Charentes) at the south-western corner. Figure 7.3 shows how intricate are the declines of fertility. Each one after the other, Champagne and the Garonne Valley, take the leadership on the fertility decrease front, while Normandy-Pays de Loire maintains its rank in-between. The three curves remain constantly near to each other, in level and tempo of decrease. The study of French

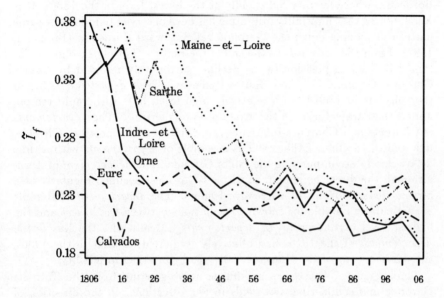

Figure 7.3 Overall Coale Index $\tilde{I}_f$ of the three leading regions (the Garonne Valley is restricted to its less fertile *départements*: Haute-Garonne, Gers, Lot-et-Garonne, and Tarn-et-Garonne).

rural fertility from the '39 villages survey' (Henry, 1972, 1978; Henry and Houdaille, 1973; Houdaille 1976) had shown a relative regional homogeneity before the decline which started after the mid-eighteenth century. In this survey, four regions only were distinguished (north-eastern, north-western, south-eastern, and south-western quarters), which mix up each leading pole with more fertile *départements*. It was thus impossible to make out a differentiated evolution and to point out any leader in the transition. H. Le Bras (1988) already noticed that the division of France into four parts was unable to reveal the actual complexity of the country and that the 'quarters' are far from homogeneous. In a more precise study, Blum, Houdaille, and Tugault (1987) have shown that the fertility decline in the Garonne Valley (one of our leading poles) started just before the French Revolution, and accelerated after 1795. The diffusion of fertility limitation, if diffusion was actually the phenomenon at work, should have had three distinct sources. A detailed inspection of the *départements* by each of these three poles reveals that this process is gradual.

In the Garonne Valley, Figure 7.4 shows that the *département* of Tarn-et-Garonne was the most advanced in the fertility decline at the beginning of the century. In the 1820s, it was caught up by the *département* of Lot-et-Garonne and Gers, thus in the direction of the regional metropolis of Bordeaux, whose fertility fell rapidly at the lowest level in the 1830s. It is worth noting that nuptiality migration has been observed to follow the same pattern of moving down the Garonne valley toward Bordeaux (Bonneuil, 1992). From 1836 onwards to the end of the century, Lot-et-Garonne maintained its leading position in the decline, successively rejoined by Haute-Garonne, Gironde, Lot, and Hautes-Pyrénées. These *départements* began their decline in 1806 from a relatively high level, but, with rapid tempo, united their trajectories to the group of lowest fertility. The *départements* of Charente and Charente-Inférieure immediately to the north of Gironde, followed the decline of the previous ensemble of *départements* with a time delay, closely accompanying the fall of Gironde. The *département* of Tarn, although the direct neighbour of Tarn-et-Garonne, declined regularly at a certain distance from the successive leaders. The *département* of Hérault is particularly notable for showing oscillations between the lowest and the highest level of this group of *départements*. Meanwhile, the less fertile *départements* of the 1810s had relatively stagnated, so that in the 1900s, the *départements* of the Garonne Valley had converged in fertility.

Thus, Figure 7.4 suggests a diffusive wave starting from the Tarn-et-Garonne and conquering new fields in two directions: in the direction of Bordeaux (Lot and Lot-et-Garonne then Gironde), which extended afterwards to the north (Charentes), and simultaneously to the south, which was also gradually attained (Gers then Hautes-Pyrénées and Haute-Garonne). The eastern side of the Garonne Valley, with the *département* of Tarn and to some extent that of Hérault, were caught up in the wave with a certain delay.

Such a progression can be seen in the other two poles. In Normandy, Figure 7.5 shows that the two contiguous *départements*, Calvados and Eure, were far below the others in 1806. They were rapidly joined by the contiguous *département* of Orne. These three *départements* constituted a very cohesive subgroup, which then stagnated during the whole century at its low level. A second subgroup had Indre-et-Loire (which does not directly border the first subgroup) as leader and two followers: Sarthe and Maine-et-Loire. They declined regularly and cohesively so as to rejoin the first subgroup. In Champagne, the third pole, the diffusion seems to have run from the east (Haute-Marne and Côte-d'Or) to the west (Yonne and Aube), as Figure 7.6 shows. The time delays observed within each of these three poles are summed up on Figure 7.7.

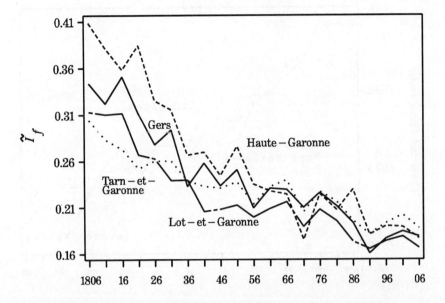

Figure 7.4 The decline of fertility in *départements* of the Garonne Valley (selection of the less fertile ones).

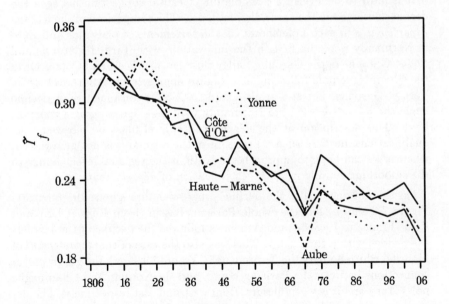

Figure 7.5 Fertility decline in Normandy-Pays-de-Loire.

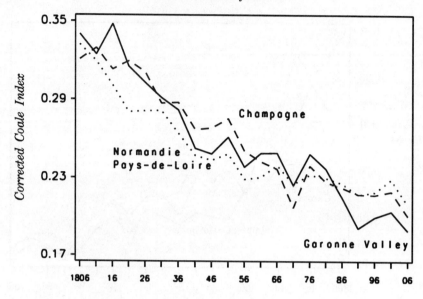

Figure 7.6 Fertility decline in Champagne.

It is hard to believe in a possible direct causal connection between the declines observed in the three distinct poles. The comparison of the leading *départements* in each pole shows that *départements* of Calvados and Eure in Normandy were the first in the innovation, with Tarn-et-Garonne and Lot-et-Garonne in the Garonne Valley close on their heels and Côte-d'Or in the Champagne pole following at a slightly higher level. After 1871–1875, Tarn-et-Garonne, Lot-et-Garonne, and Côte-d'Or continued their decline while the *départements* from Normandy went on stagnating at a constant level. This description at the *départemental* level must be received with qualifications, because such a precision in the estimates is not guaranteed, whereas we can hope to approach the truth at the regional level, thanks to the smoothing coming from the classification of *départements*.

On the national scale, the decline progressed throughout the territory. Figure 7.2 shows that the whole Parisian Bassin, from Eure-et-Loir and Ile-de-France to Picardie and Ardennes followed the decline of the less fertile regions with a time delay. This was also the case of the *département* of Manche, which borders the Norman pole. Figure 7.1 shows the geographical connections between the Parisian Bassin and the Norman and Champagne poles: they are direct neighbours, from west and east respectively. The decline spread to the borders of the poles: Seine-Inférieure (now called Seine-Maritime), Loire-Inférieure (now called Loire-Atlantique), Centre, Poitou, Pyrénées, Provence, Auvergne, and Paris itself. Then it reached the pe-

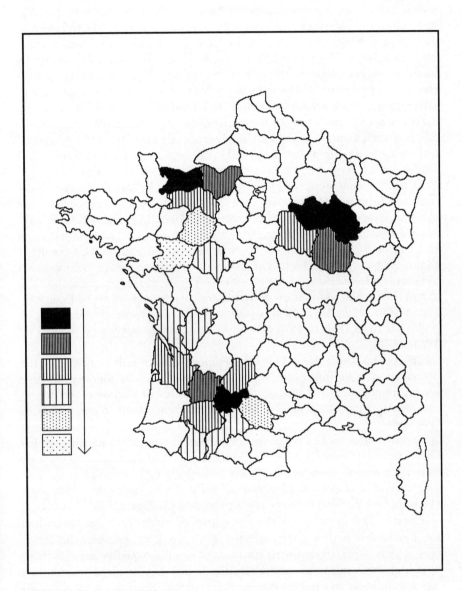

Figure 7.7 Geographical representation of the differential declines in the three poles. The earlier the decline, the darker the representation of the *département*.

riphery of France: Nord, the Rennes Bassin, Vosges, Jura, and the Rhône valley, before the 'rural enclaves' of France, the most backward regions: first, Limousin, Brittany, Hautes-Alpes, and Corsica; and, finally Finistère and Lozère. Meanwhile, Centre-Loire, contiguous to Rhône-Alpes, started very high, at the level of backward regions, but declined very rapidly to join the northern level at the end of the century. It is interesting to note the quasi-parallelism of the various declines on Figure 7.2, except for the latter group which accelerated abruptly its fall of fertility. This made the 'fertile heart of France' at the beginning of the nineteenth century (Centre, Rhône-Alpes, Limousin, and Brittany), gradually move from the geographical centre to the periphery at the end of the century: Brittany, Nord, Jura, Rhône Valley, Aveyron, Pyrénées-Orientales, and the Dordogne.

At this regional level, the baby-boom mentioned by Van de Walle to have occurred from mid-century until the 1880s is hardly existent, apart from the temporary recovery after the war of 1870–1871. Thus, the regional analysis confirms the surprising result already seen at the national scale in Chapter 6 of the erasing of the well-known 'ski-jump'. This result, if confirmed by other studies to come, is relatively important, in so far as some authors (Le Bras, 1988) have put some emphasis on this phenomenon. For example, the new estimation of overall fertility for the whole of France by David Weir (1994, p. 316), using data from family reconstitutions, shows a plateau from 1850 to 1875 instead of the upsurge advocated by Van de Walle (1974).

The general description of spatio-temporal trends tells in favour of the propagation of an innovation wave: leading poles whose followers in time are rigorously arranged in space, and respond to the decline of fertility in compliance with the degree of isolation we know about *départements* at that time.

Another clue to the diffusion hypothesis is the homogenizing of behaviours or, in other words, the reduction of the dispersion of fertility indicators among *départements*. This homogenizing is reflected in the regular decline of the standard deviation computed at each census date over the whole set of *départements* and represented on Figure 7.8.

The standard deviation of the non-corrected index, I_f, is far lower than the standard deviation of the corrected index, $\tilde{I}_f$. One reason for this difference is that *départements* with statistics of mediocre quality are also those with high birth rates. Under-registration would then artificially lower high fertility indexes, and reduce standard deviations. However, both standard deviations are decreasing globally with time, if not at the same rate.

Figure 7.8 also shows that the time of the war of 1870–1871 corresponded with a temporary upsurge of the dispersion. After 1886, the decline was resumed. Together with the decrease of the standard deviation over the country, the contrast between the least and most fertile *départements* at the beginning of the century faded away, so that at the beginning of the twen-

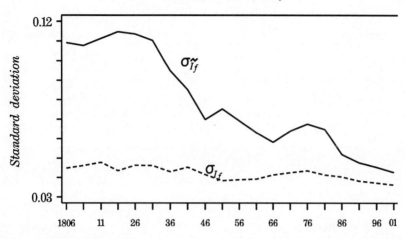

Figure 7.8 Evolution of the standard deviation '$\hat{\sigma}$' in Overall Coale Indexes $\tilde{I}_f$ and I_f.

tieth century, French behaviour appeared more alike in all *départements* than it had throughout the nineteenth century.

The inter-relationship between geographical types in terms of fertility has been presented so far in a descriptive manner. Levels and trends have been examined, and the spatio-temporal contrast indicates for a possible diffusion phenomenon on the mean and long-run scale. An econometric analysis will be conducted in Chapter 9 to clear up the space-time pattern of the transition. Before dealing with the global dynamics of demographic behaviours, where fertility plays a major role, in connection with mortality, migration, and urbanization, Chapter 8 presents the results obtained on these other variables, in the form of a general description similar to that of this Chapter. Resulting demographic factors such as age structure or population growth also deserve to be presented in a space-time panorama.

8

Changing Mortality, Migration, and Populations

This chapter presents the changes in other demographic components, aside from fertility. The technical apparatus (descriptive analysis of temporal trends, visualization of space-time aggregates) is the same. The reader unfamiliar with the classification technique should, therefore, read the preceding chapter.

8.1 Mortality

Figure 8.1 shows the improvement of life expectancy at birth by *département* from 1806–1810 to 1901–1905. The evolutions of the *départements* have been regrouped again with the help of a hierarchical ascending classification (same aggregation Criterium and distance as in the preceding chapter). The time series of means over each class is represented on Figure 8.2. The space-time transformation in terms of living conditions largely resembles that of fertility. At the beginning of the century, France is divided into three large sections: a large diagonal strip with relatively low mortality, going from the northern border to the Pyrénées passing by Ile-de-France, Normandy, and the lower Loire Valley, Poitou-Charentes, and Aquitaine. This north-east to south-west diagonal is surrounded by higher mortality regions: Brittany on the western side and Centre-Loire, Jura, Rhône-Alpes, and the Mediterranean coast on the eastern side. As the century progressed, this arrangement was altered, as life expectancy in the region of Centre took off to become the highest in 1901–1905, while the Norman façade, Ile-de-France, and Provence stagnated and shifted downward from experiencing the highest to the lowest life expectancy, relative to the rest of France. The turning point seemed to be 1866–1870, partially coinciding with the war of 1870–1871. It looks as if the drop during this period was never recovered, entailing stagnation till 1886–1890 at least. At the end of the century, relatively low life expectancy in Brittany and the

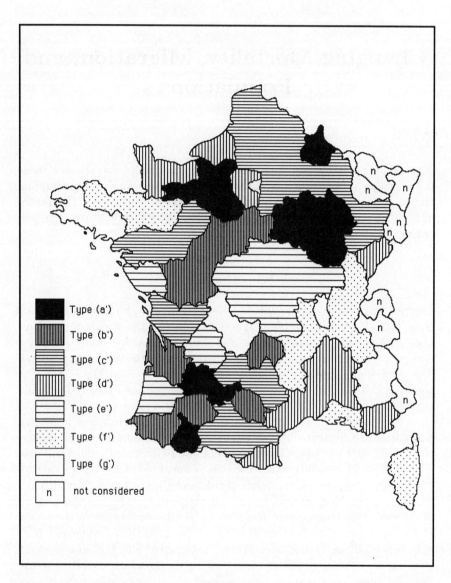

Figure 8.1 Temporal map of life expectancy at birth, from 1806–1810 to
1901–1905.

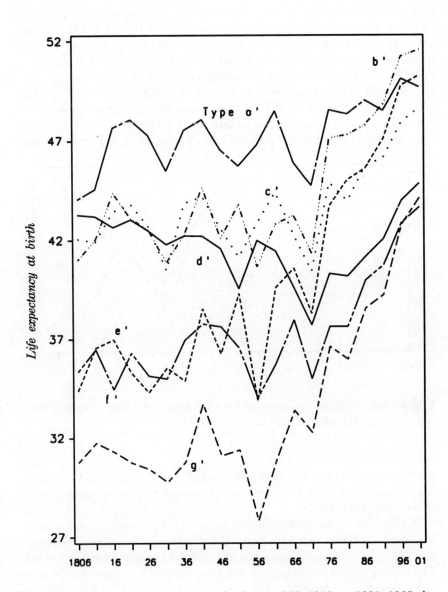

Figure 8.2 Life expectancy at birth, from 1806–1810 to 1901–1905, by homogeneous ensembles (the abscissa t designates the beginning of the quinquennial period $[t, t+4]$).

Norman façade on the north-west, Rhône-Alps and Provence in the South-East, and Limousin in the centre contrasted with higher life expectancy in the large strip going from the Belgian-German border to the Spanish one. Throughout the century, Champagne and part of Burgundy, non-maritime Normandy, Poitou, and part of the Garonne Valley managed to keep their leading position, just marking a momentary stagnation after the war of 1870–1871. These regions overlap importantly the three leading poles mentioned in the fertility analysis, establishing a precise connection between trends of mortality and of fertility. Chapter 9 will be devoted to this question. From a global point of view, Figure 8.3 shows that mortality

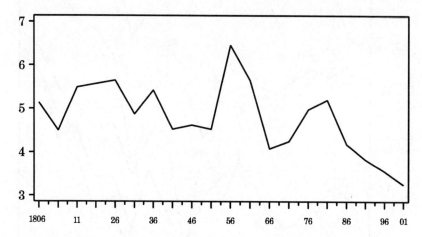

Figure 8.3 Standard deviation of life expectancy at birth over the French *départements* throughout the nineteenth century.

conditions were converging throughout the century. A notable exception to this homogenizing was the 1851–1865 period, which was marked by numerous epidemics, and the 1871–1880 one, corresponding to the consequences of the 1870–1871 war.

Mid-century, 1856–1865, seems to have been the turning point separating relative general stagnation from take-off, whereas the war of 1870–1871, although marked by temporary troughs, did not change the general trends. The leading geographical type at the beginning of the century (the three poles) managed to maintain their position, while second leaders were relatively regressing (maritime Normandy and Mediterranean coast), and new leaders appeared (Centre Loire). It is interesting to note that this new leader is precisely a region surrounded by the three poles, which could reveal a driving impetus on the part of neighbouring *départements*. This incitement effect is characteristic of a diffusive phenomenon. The innovative centre kept the leadership, though with a new comer hard at its heels, while the others (Brittany, Rhône-Alps) followed at a distance. Globally however, the dispersion decreased and situations converged.

8.2 Net Migration

8.2.1 Changing Age Distributions

Figure 8.4 represents the typology of the evolutions of distributions of age-specific net migration rates (age varies from birth to [60–64]) obtained through a hierarchical ascending classification. As before, the aggregation Criterium is the maximization of central second momentums and the distance is the usual Euclidean distance. At each period, each *département* is characterized by 14 age-specific net migration rates (one at each age class). Thus, from 1856–1860 to 1901–1905 (10 quinquennial periods), each *département* entering into the classification is determined by 14 × 10 variables.

Figures 8.5, 8.6, and 8.7 represent the distributions of net migration rates by age in 1856–1860, 1886–1890, and 1901–1905.

They show how differentials in migration intensity by age closely reflect the urban hierarchy. Paris was far above the rest with high in-migration before 25 years of age, followed by the most urbanized regions: Ile-de-France, Bouches-du-Rhône (city of Marseilles), Alpes-Maritimes (city of Nice), then Gironde (city of Bordeaux), Hérault (city of Montpelier), and Rhône (city of Lyon) in 1901–1905; in 1856–1860, Gironde, Hérault, and Rhône received more net in-migration than Ile-de-France, Bouches-du-Rhône, and Alpes-Maritimes; in 1886–1890, these two groups were comparable. The reversal of the order of the most net in-migrating regions is then clearly visible. Correspondingly to this net in-migration in these urban regions, net out-migration was at its maximum between 5–9 and 20–24 year old classes, especially in the Alps and Normandy, or in the most rural areas, such as Brittany, Massif Central, Pyrénées, and Isère, but also, to a lesser degree, in Aquitaine, north of Massif Central, Norman façade, Poitou-Charentes, Jura, and Vosges. It is important to note that no constraint was imposed in the reconstruction method that could force net-migration to be globally balanced, harmoniously distributed between positive and negative migration so as to make the total near to zero. It is therefore all the more fruitful to obtain consistent inter-regional patterns for distributions of net migration rates by age.

The distributions represented on Figures 8.5, 8.6, and 8.7 support an interpretation in terms of life cycle (seen from a transversal perspective). Net-migration from birth to 0–4 years old is estimated negative for urbanized regions and relatively highly positive in rural regions. This result is coherent with what we know about migrations of the very young: children born in urban regions were rapidly placed under the care of a wet-nurse

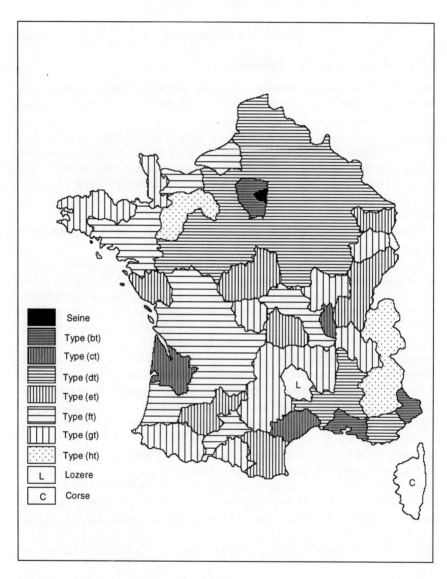

Figure 8.4 Temporal map of age-specific distributions of net migration rates.

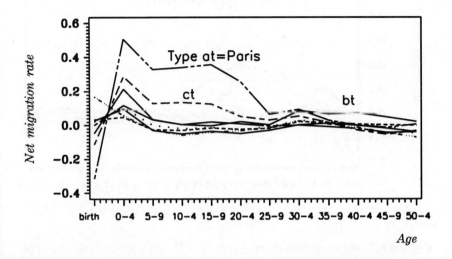

Figure 8.5 Net migration rates by age in 1856–1860 by geographical types.

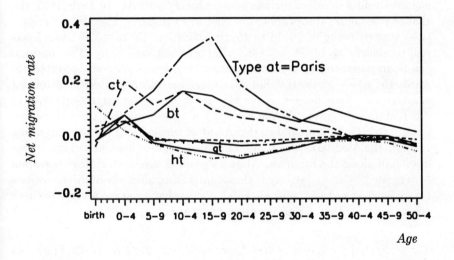

Figure 8.6 Net migration rates by age in 1886–1890 by geographical types.

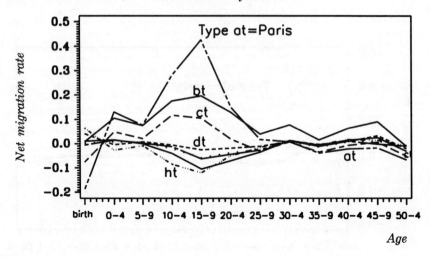

Figure 8.7 Net migration rates by age in 1901–1905 by geographical types.

in the rural *départements* surrounding urban centres. From 0–4 to 5–9 and 5–9 to 10–14 years old, children returned to maternal homes, which is reflected by the change in sign of net migration rates in 1901–1905: in rural regions, the positive value at birth turned into a negative one, while negative values in urban regions became highly positive. In 1856–1860, the change was not so abrupt, but the trend was the same. The wave of migrations started rising at 10–14 to 15–19, peaked at 15–19 to 20–24 and was still significant at 20–24 to 25–29, after which it died away. This upsurge can be imputed to pre-nuptial migration, which was generally directed towards the cities, and migration after marriage which was directed toward employment opportunities. After 30 years of age, net in-migration varied in different urban centres. While Paris, Lyon, Bordeaux lost their attractive power after 25–29 years old to the extent of turning into net out-migrating centres, the Mediterranean coast and Ile-de-France kept absorbing immigrants all along the life span. After 45 years of age, a returning migration is suggested by the relatively high out-migrating intensity of urban regions (with Bordeaux, Lyon, and above all Paris), balanced by weakly positive (though not in 1886–1890) in-migration of rural regions.

8.2.2 *Spatial Evolution of Net Migration from 20–24 to 25–29 Years Old*

The migration of 20–24 to 25–29 year old women is of particular interest because women were then at their most fertile age. Moreover, this moment in the life cycle is also an important age for migration, although not as much as 15–19 to 20–24. Figure 8.8 was based on the now commonplace hierarchical ascending classification with the same specification as before. Figure 8.9 represents the (non-weighted) means over each class of Figure 8.8. Paris once again had a positive in-migration rate, which was more or less constant, except for the trough of the war of 1870–1871, which affected the 1866–1870 period. The next period, 1871–1875, showed a little recovery after the war. While the most urban regions after Paris maintained a high and constant level of attractiveness all along the second half of the century, the recently annexed *département* of Alpes-Maritimes, with its city of Nice, took off so as to become the first in-migration French pole, relative to its population. The direct neighbours of Paris and Marseilles, Ile-de-France and Var, also kept regularly increasing net in-migration rates. Poitou-Charentes, the lower Loire Valley, the Parisian Bassin, the Garonne Valley, and Nord-Pas-de-Calais lost their weak, but attractive power to become out-migrating regions. The rest of France was out-migrating, and Figure 8.9 shows a remarkable regular fall into negative values. It is important to remember that each estimation is independent from one date to the next. It is thus a pleasant surprise to find such smooth time series, which speak in favour of a regular process of growing migration, some becoming more and more in-migrating with others increasing their out-migration flow. The period of 1871–1875 appears to be a breaking point, after which Alpes-Maritimes took off and already out-migrating regions accelerated their flow. Figure 8.8 shows that France was divided into two ensembles arranged around urban centres. The first one regroups slightly out-migrating regions: northern France centred around Paris, the Garonne Valley and Poitou Charentes, and a part of the Rhône Valley. The second ensemble regroups growing out-migrating regions, which were the most rural ones: Brittany, Massif Central, Landes and Pyrénées, the Alps. Discovering that towns attracted people and that people left rural regions may be no surprise; however Figures 8.8 and 8.9 give a precise and in my opinion an acute glimpse at the arrangement of the territory in terms of migration, and a fresh view of the rhythm and change of the spatial process at work.

8.2.3 *Migration in Space, Age, and Time*

Age distributions from birth to 60–64 years old show very similar evolutions during the second half of the century as does that of the sole migration rate from 20–24 to 25–29. Age distributions have been represented here at only three points in time (on Figures 8.5, 8.6, and 8.7) for fear of burdening the reader with too much detailed information. All the information obtained from 1856 to 1906 is synthesized on Figure 8.4, by regrouping time series of the age distributions. The vast region around Paris, the Parisian Bassin from the River Loire to the German and Belgian borders formed a first ensemble of weak out-migration. At the edge of this ensemble, rural regions drew a sort of circle, where out-migration apparently increased with rural-

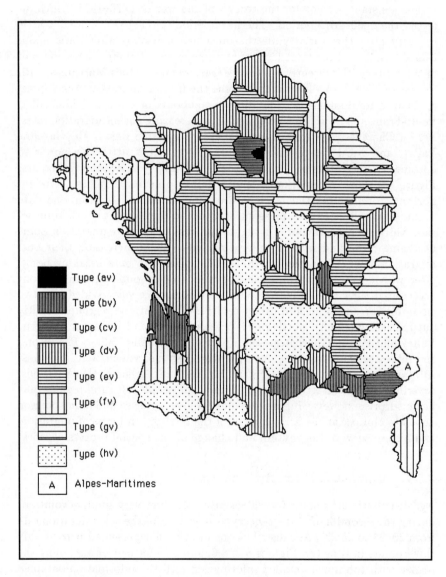

Figure 8.8 Temporal map of net migration rates from 20–24 to 25–29 years old.

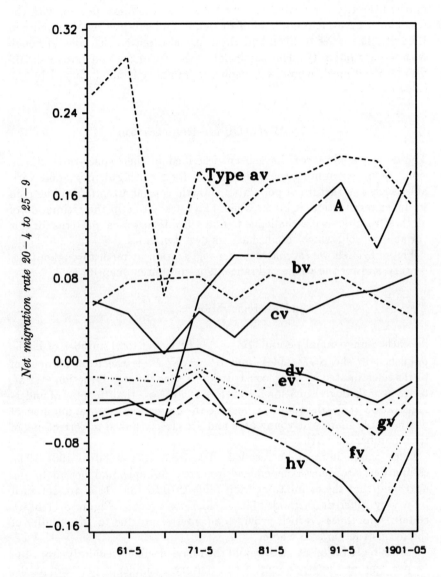

Figure 8.9 Net migration rates from 20–24 to 25–29 years old in the geographical types of the preceding figure.

ity (but this assertion requires further evidence). Close to Paris, a small circle gained an important attractive power. The same pattern found in northern France is repeated around Marseilles to a lesser degree, with the small out-migrating hinterland of Provence, and sub-pole as Montpelier in Hérault. The cities of Lyon and Bordeaux also played this role, although with weaker intensity. The particular cases of Corsica and Lozére should also be mentioned, whose well-known marginality is not betrayed by the calculus.

8.3   Birth Under-Registration

The demographic forces have been described in their space-time dimension. Before examining the consequences for resulting demographic variables such as structure or population growth, special attention will be paid to under-registration of birth, which plays a key role in the estimation of all these results. It is a challenge to find sensible historical patterns for this variable as well, which should have its own dynamics.

Figure 8.11 shows estimated under-registration at birth throughout the century and for the whole of France. The computed quantity is:

$$\text{under} - \text{registration} = 1 - \frac{B^F}{\tilde{B}^F}$$

for each quinquennial period. $B^F = \sum_i B^i$ is the total number of births published in the SGF tables, and $\tilde{B}^F = \sum_i \tilde{B}^i$ is the total number of births re-estimated by the reconstruction, either through Equation 5.12 after 1856 or through Equation 5.16 before 1856. Note that the map of under-registration at death is similar, because the corrections of total numbers of deaths apply mainly at young ages and are closely linked to corrections of total numbers of births.

Once again, it must be recalled that, from 1856–1860 to 1901–1905, estimations are quasi-independent from one quinquennial period to the next, and that the estimations from 1806–1810 to 1851–1855 are obtained by a very different method. The decline observed on Figure 8.11 has a certain smoothness, which provides an interesting clue to the validity of the reconstruction as a whole.

Under-registration at birth would then have declined regularly, from 14–15 per cent at the beginning of the century to under 6 per cent at the end. The regular trend did not exclude temporary ups and downs, notably in 1846–1850, a period of political trouble (the Revolution of 1848), and 1871–1875, a period covering war and its aftermath. The Revolution of 1830 could also be invoked for the upsurge of 1826–1830 and 1831–1835, but proving any link between deterioration of statistics and political ups and downs is beyond the scope of this book. Other factors may have played a role, like the personalities of the directors of the *SGF* and the handing over of office. This point has received attention in Chapter 3 on the more detailed data of errors of transcription. However, the imperfections of the reconstructions which permit estimating under-registration at birth from the *SGF* data must not be forgotten and the validity of Figure 8.11 must not be overrated. The comparison with Van de Walle who found only 5.1 per cent at the beginning of the century and a rapid decline of under-registration to zero remains troubling.

Figure 8.10 and corresponding Figure 8.11 show under-registration in time and space. Figure 8.12 presents the estimated rate for the whole of France (with changing territory). *Départements* which we know to have been backward in terms of statistical reliability showed the highest rates: Hautes-Alpes, Corrèze, Landes, and, to a lesser degree, Brittany, Haute-Vienne, Vendée, and Jura, but also Paris and the Rhône region with the big city of Lyon. This first ensemble of poor registration contrasts with two regions of very good statistics: the Parisian Bassin and a line going from the lower Rhône valley to the Garonne valley in the south. Both of these regions are surrounded by *départements* of still good, but a little worse quality in the data registration: Nord-Pas-de-Calais, Lower Normandy and Pays-de-Loire-Poitou-Charentes, Vosges and Haute-Saône; or the Pyrénées, the south of the Massif Central, the Rhône Valley and the Mediterranean Coast, shading gradually into the area of low quality data. Under-registration is thus arranged according to a precise pattern, with the Parisian Bassin as the perfect model (excluding Paris itself) surrounded by gradually worse quality regions when approaching the Massif Central or the far-eastern or far-western borders. Figure 8.12 may be striking, because under-registration is so high; however, these high values are concentrated in a few *départements* and Types (as) and (bs) with registration of good quality regroup most of the French territory.

8.4   Mean Age of Women

Ageing France is represented on Figure 8.13 and corresponding Figure 8.14. Mean age results from the demographic forces at work: falling fertility and mortality, and negligible foreign migration should generate an ageing population. Figure 8.14 illustrates this phenomenon clearly for nineteenth-century France, and it is no wonder that Figure 8.13 is a mixture of Figures 8.1 and 7.1: the three poles of low fertility and of low mortality are inhabited by the oldest women, whereas the youngest women live in the regions with highest mortality and fertility: Brittany, Limousin, Corsica, and Hautes-Alpes. Regions where fertility was waning rapidly while life expectancy was taking off were automatically those which were rapidly ageing: Centre-Loire, Rhône-Isère, Vendée, and Landes. The regularity

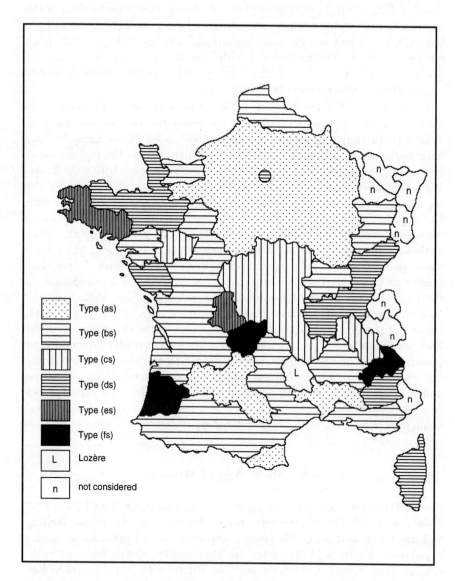

Figure 8.10 Temporal map of under-registration of births from 1806 to 1906.

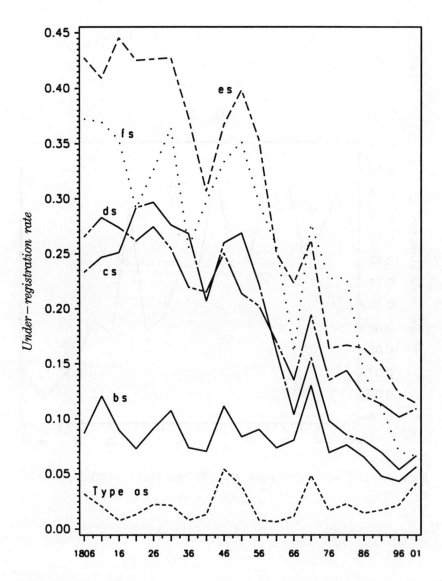

Figure 8.11 Under-registration of births from 1806 to 1906, by geographical types.

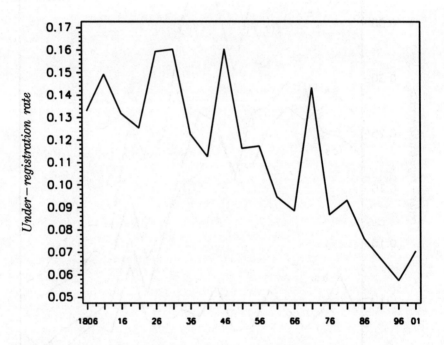

Figure 8.12 Under-registration of births from 1806 to 1906, for the whole of France.

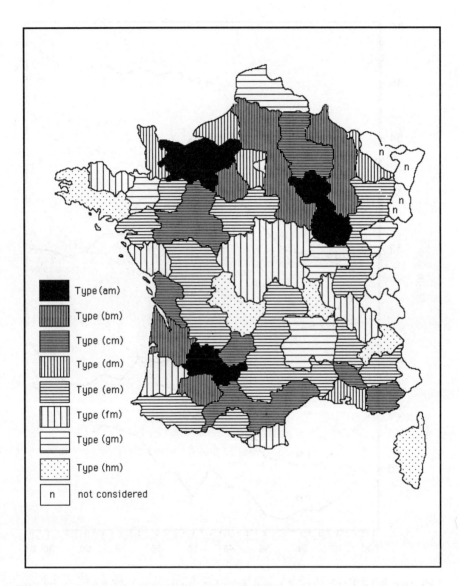

Figure 8.13 Mean age of women from 1806 to 1906.

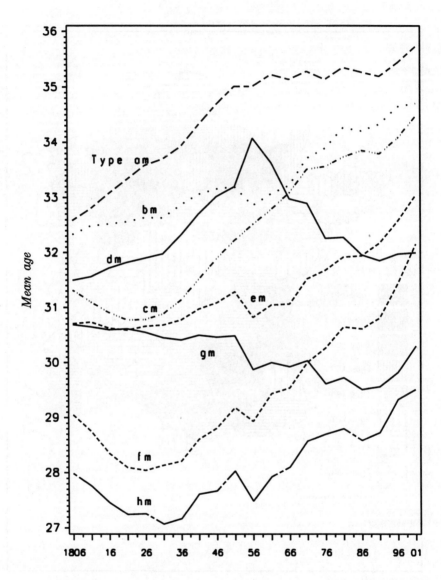

Figure 8.14 Evolution of mean age of women from 1806 to 1906, by geographical types.

of the ageing process shown on Figure 8.13, to which only Ile-de-France, Seine-Inférieure, Manche, and Bouches-du-Rhône were exceptions, provides a striking picture.

8.5   Population Growth Rates

Population growth rate is another noticeable result of the demographic forces. Figure 8.15 and corresponding Figure 8.16 reflect the changing structure of the French population: Paris, apart from a temporary sub-sidence in the 1850s, accelerated its population size far ahead of the rest; following behind, Lyon and Marseilles, the two next biggest cities, regularly slowing down their pace in contrast to Paris; Gironde, Ile-de-France, Nord-Pas-de-Calais, and also Meurthe replaced by Meurthe-et-Moselle from 1871 onwards, showed sustained growth. The rest of France started the century with population growth, but ended with population decline. The most dra-matic case was Normandy, Champagne, and the Garonne Valley (the three poles of fertility and mortality decline), as well as the Massif Central and southern Alps. Remarkably, the south-western region of population de-crease, the Garonne Valley contiguous to the Massif Central, forms a line going from Bordeaux to Lyon, while the Champagne-Burgundy depressed zone joins Lyon to Paris.

Thus, Figure 8.15 shows dramatically how the rural population was drawn from their home country to the cities. The temporal follow up and geographical regrouping of evolutions permits us to view the phenomenon more precisely.

8.6   The French Demographic Landscape: from Description to Systemic Analysis

This panoramic view of the French transition has shown regular evolutions and consistent patterns. After this description, we may wonder to what extent the declines in both mortality and fertility were linked to each other, and what role other variables such as migration, urbanization, or education may have played. To explore this question in greater depth, I shall exploit the efficiency of time series analysis and build an econometric model capable of bringing evidence to causal relationships.

The spatial context of the transition is a source of confusion, because simple methods such as visually comparing maps representing different variables, calculating simple correlations or χ^2 tests with *départements* considered as individuals are misleading. Spatial auto-correlations need special treatment, as many authors have pointed out (see Cressie, 1991 for references). For example, religion could have been an interesting variable to consider. Unfortunately, I do not dispose of time series showing the preva-

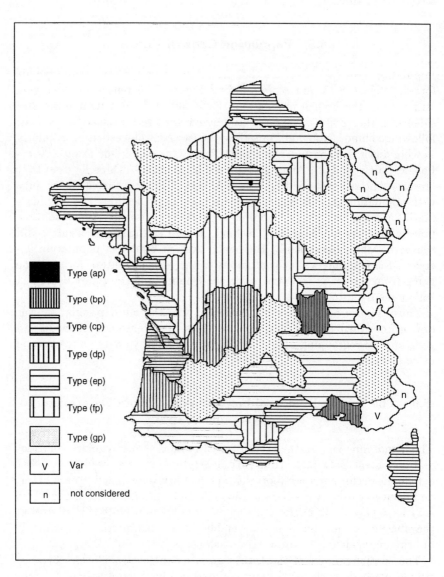

Figure 8.15 Female population growth rates from 1806 to 1906.

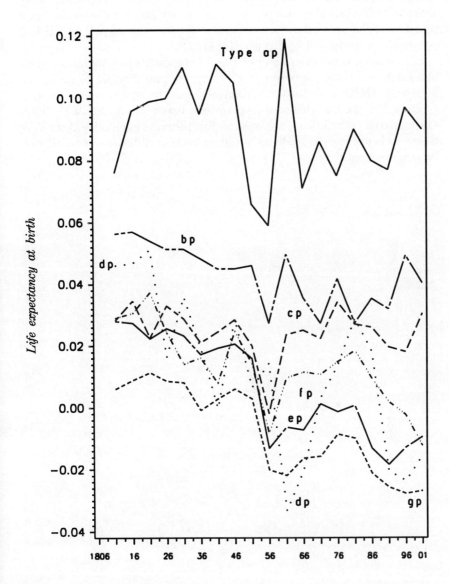

Figure 8.16 Female population growth rates from 1806 to 1906, by geographical types.

lence of Catholicism by *département* throughout the nineteenth century. A simple comparison of the map of non-juring priests in 1791 (Le Bras, 1988), apart from the fact that it does not look particularly similar to the maps that have been presented here, is insufficient for proving any causal link (see criticism addressed by Brunet, 1987).

Econometric time series analysis has its own limits and we must not be blinded by its power; however, the notions of causality are precisely defined and validated: in brief, a variable X would be said to 'cause' another variable Y if the knowledge of X permits a better prediction of Y. Time series analysis can prove a rigorous tool in testing explanatory theories of measurable phenomena, such as in the innovation/diffusion versus adaptation/adjustment debate.

9

Scope of the Transition

The previous chapter was devoted to the general description of demographic variables, with special emphasis on the spatial diffusion process of behaviours. However, the diffusion of a demographic behaviour can hide either adaptation to local circumstances or diffusion of an innovation. No mechanism underlying the processes observed in the preceding chapter has been suggested so far, although clues to understanding have gradually emerged, such as the presence of leading poles or the strong urban/rural contrast. This chapter begins with a panoramic view of the transition of demographic forces during the second half of the century. The three forces are combined to unveil the division of France into relatively homogeneous ensembles and its structuring around poles and cities. This still descriptive analysis helps introduce a dynamic model capable of explaining the decline of fertility in relation to 'meaning' variables: death, mobility, education, urbanization and, indirectly, subsistence capacity.

Before beginning the exposition, I present a traditional technique in data analysis, Principal Component Analysis, so that non-statisticians can also understand how this representation can reveal salient patterns of multivariate time series.

9.1 Principal Component Analysis for the Description of Multi-Dimensional Numerical Data

In the previous maps, only one variable (life expectancy or fertility index) was attached to *départements* through time. The classes obtained were relatively easy to interpret, since each category corresponded to an average temporal trajectory of the variable considered. In other words, *départements* which were considered in $I\!R^T$ for the purpose of clustering could also be viewed as evolving along a one-dimensional state space, constituted, for example, of life expectancy as in Figure 8.2. In a state space of more than one dimension, things do not appear so clearly. For example, distributions of net migration rates by age consist of 14 variables, one for each quinquennial age class, from birth to 60–64 year old women. For the sake of interpretative clarity, I have presented age distributions separately at different points in time (Figures 8.5 to 8.7) or only one age-specific rate through time (Figure 8.9). If attention is paid to the 20–24 age class, the most fertile one, the number of interesting forces can be restricted to three: fertility and mortality intensities and migration rate from 20–24 to 25–29 years old. *Départements* are thus to be viewed in a three-dimensional state space. Clustering temporal trajectories into three or more dimensions raises no more difficulty than in the one-dimensional case: a *département* at a given period is represented by a point in the space $I\!R^{3T}$, where T is the time dimension (=10 quinquennial periods, from 1856–1860 to 1901–1905). In the same manner as before, once classes have been built, average values of the variables at each date over *départements* belonging to a given class can be computed.

Fortunately, there exists a simpler and more concise procedure for exploring multi-dimensional data, which is Principal Component Analysis. In demography, it was notably used by Ledermann in 1959 to characterize mortality age distributions. I refer the reader to Saporta (1990) for a full presentation of this technique. Other references are Taylor (1977) for geographical data.

Assume that seven classes have been retained by the classification procedure, so that only seven geographical types are studied in their evolution through time (but the discussion would be the same if 87 *départements* were considered). Each type experiences average fertility, mortality, and net migration over the *départements* constituting this type. Time is represented by 10 quinquennial periods (1856–1860 to 1901–1905). Thus each 'period-geographical type' can be represented in a three-dimensional state space, the three axes of which are life expectancy, fertility, and migration. In other words, a point in this space determines a complete state of demographic behaviour. The 7×10 'period-geographical types' constitute then a cloud of points shaped like a rugby ball in this three-dimensional state space, reflecting a certain relationship between the three variables. The metric chosen is the usual diagonal metric of inverses of variances, $M = diag(\frac{1}{s_1^2} \cdots \frac{1}{s_3^2})$, where s_i is the standard deviation of the ith variable. This metric permits assigning the same importance to each variable, whatever its dispersion.

The axis of the rugby ball with maximum inertia can be computed and is called the first principal axis. Its centre of gravity corresponds to the average period-geographical type. The period-geographical types with lowest mortality and fertility are located at one end of the ball, while those having highest mortality and fertility are located at the other end. The second principal axis is orthogonal to the first one, so that the principal plane constituted by both these axes yields the best two-dimensional view. The more inertia cumulated by the two first axes, the more representative is the perspective given by the plane. The interpretation is made easier than directly in three dimensions, and the salient features of the data appear more easily. The greater the number of axes, the higher the loss of information, because p axes have been summarized into only two axes. But the gain in readability is helpful. Each location in the principal plane represents a demographic state, all the better when the two first axes involve a large fraction of the total inertia.

When dealing with such temporal data, joining the points belonging to the same geographical type successively with time permits drawing the trajectory of a given geographical type, for example type n°1-(1856–1860) to type n°1-(1861–1865), ..., and so on until type n°1-(1901–1905). Each type is then represented by a trajectory in the principal plane, thus tracing the best bi-dimensional picture of the temporal evolution of this geographical type in terms of demographic behaviours. We have thus compressed an important amount of information for over 50 years into a single readable picture.

9.2   The Structured French Space

In the present case of France in the second half of the nineteenth century, net migration indicated by the rate $_5\rho^i_{[20-24],[t,t+4]}$ of 20–24 to 25–29 year old women of the *département i* on time interval $[t, t+4]$, mortality indicated by life expectancy at birth $e^i_{[t,t+4]}$, and fertility at year t indicated by corrected overall Coale index $\tilde{I}^i_f(t)$, are the three variables included in the analysis (the data for these three variables is published in Appendix C). The 'observations' considered are the *départements* × quinquennial periods from 1856–1860 to 1901–1905, or 86 (for 1856) +89 (for 1861) +85 (for 1866) +7 × 87 (for each period from 1871 to 1906) = 869 observations. A hierarchical ascending classification (aggregation Criterium: maximization of central second moments, and Euclidean distance) is conducted. This classification permits regrouping the trajectories of *départements* through time and portraying the space-time behaviour in fertility, mortality, and net migration of young women. This classification is necessary to gain in readability. The number of classes has to be chosen with caution, so as to be both readable and keep enough variability. Seven classes have finally been retained. For each of them, I have calculated the (non-weighted) mean values of life expectancy, Coale index, and net migration rate from 20–24 to 25–29 year olds at each date.

A principal component analysis permits visualizing the active variables and following the 'trajectories' of the *départements* over the course of time on Figure 9.1. The first eigenvector is $-0.74\times$ life expectancy $+0.63\times$ Coale index $+0.25\times$ net migration rate. Mortality and fertility are then the dominant variables of Axis 1 and their contributions are nearly equal.

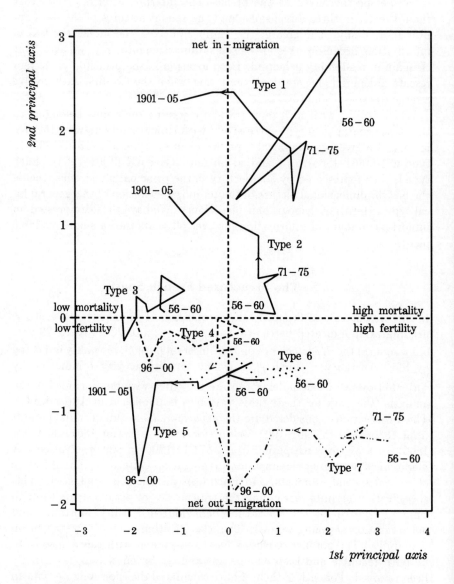

Figure 9.1 Principal component analysis, trajectories of the geographical types determined by the hierarchical ascending classification. The direction of time is indicated by the arrows, from 1856–1860 to 1901–1905. The point $(0, 0)$ is the mean point.

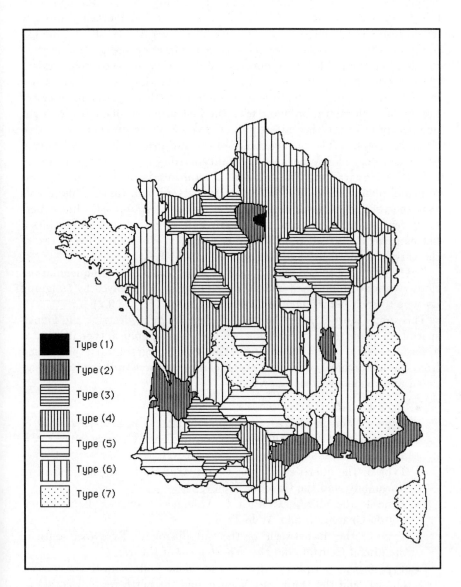

Figure 9.2 Temporal map of the hierarchical ascending classification (from 1856–1860 to 1901–1905).

Therefore, the first principal axis (59 per cent of total inertia) shows the simultaneous decrease in mortality and in fertility. It opposes high mortality and high fertility on the right-hand side to low mortality and low fertility on the left-hand side. The second eigenvector is $-0.12\times$ life expectancy $-0.49\times$ Coale index $+0.87\times$ net migration. Migration is then the dominant variable while mortality and fertility are negligible. Axis 2 (39 per cent of total inertia) is thus a net migration axis, opposing net in-migration Types 1 and 2 to net out-migration other Types (the intersection of the null migration plane with the first principal plane is a straight line nearly touching the trajectories of Type 3 and 4 on their respective '1871-75' points). The orthogonality of the two principal axes indicates a very weak dependency between mortality-fertility (which are very closely linked) and migration. The fraction of total inertia involved by the first principal plane is thus 59+39=98 per cent, a very high value. This reveals that the original three-dimensional state space is simplified, almost perfectly represented by a plane: the 'rugby ball' of visited states resembles a flat pancake. This trait results from the tight co-evolution between two of the variables, mortality and fertility.

The typology obtained on the basis of *départements* × quinquennial periods (without judging any spatial relation) can be displayed by assigning its type to each *département* on a map of France (Figure 9.2).

This map Figure 9.2 together with Figure 9.1 helps describe the French space-time demographic transition, while each geographical type illustrates a specific demographic behaviour. The seven geographical types issued from the hierarchical ascending classification can be numbered and designated approximatively as follows:

- Type 1: Seine (Paris);
- Type 2: the urbanized *départements* after Paris: *département* of Rhône (city of Lyon), the Mediterranean Coast, Gironde (city of Bordeaux), and Ile-de-France;
- Type 3: the infertile triangle: Champagne-Burgundy, non-maritime Normandy, and the Garonne Valley;
- Type 4: the 'diagonal': Picardy-Ardennes, Calvados, Loire Valley, Poitou-Charentes, and Aude-Tarn;
- Type 5: the 'in-between' or the 'sub-diagonal': Pyrénées, south of the Massif Central, and the *département* of Nièvre;
- Type 6: the 'periphery': Rhône and Saône Valleys up to the Vosges, Landes, and the Dordogne, Vendée, and the north-western coast;
- Type 7: the 'rural enclaves': Limousin, Ardèche-Lozère, Brittany, the Alps, and Corsica.

The numerical order corresponds a posteriori to an urban-geographical hierarchy, but its choice was made to facilitate the interpretation of the correlation matrix on Table 9.4, which will be presented later.

As the regrouped *départements* are more or less contiguous, a spatial pattern emerges, showing a strong resemblance to that of the economic gradients in 1830 obtained from 33 variables by Lepetit (1986). Specifically, the main features appearing now are urban hierarchy, differentials in life expectancy, and rural exodus.

Rural exodus is suggested on Figure 9.1 by the take-off of urbanized types (numbered 1 and 2) along the second axis, the axis of migration, together with the maintenance of rural Types 5, 6, and 7 in negative values along that axis. Differentials in living conditions can be read from the relative positions of the trajectories on Figure 9.1. The right-hand side of the first axis corresponds to higher mortality, the left-hand side to lower mortality. We can see that cities, or rather urban *départements*, were bad places for dwelling in terms of mortality—their trajectories stand behind, although they kept attracting people: their trajectories are highly positive on the second axis. The war of 1870–1871 can be detected from the momentary withdrawal of almost all urban trajectories (1 and 2) back to the right-hand side of Axis 1, reflecting the upsurge in mortality, with the simultaneous rising of all the other trajectories in 1866–1870 along Axis 2, reflecting the temporary fall of migration toward urban regions. At the next period, directions are inverted, indicating the recovery of former migratory movements.

The urban hierarchy is reflected by the order of the trajectories along Axis 2. Paris (*département* of Seine) had the leading position, followed by the regional metropoles of that time. Downward we find the infertile triangle studied in the previous chapter: the three poles, which are far ahead in terms of fertility and mortality decline. They occupy, therefore, the extreme left-hand side position on Axis 1. Their low position on Axis 2 visualizes the fact that these regions maintained very weak net migration. This can be interpreted as a great sedentarity (instead of a miraculous balance between high flows of in- and out-migrants), which could have a direct relationship with the low levels of fertility and mortality. The next section will be devoted to this question. Type 4, which I nickname the 'diagonal', passes just in the middle of the three poles, forming a diagonal strip over French territory. Demographic forces mimic those of the poles with a certain delay. The 'sub-diagonal', overlapping mountainous *départements*, from the Pyrénées as well as from the Massif Central, follows behind with an important delay and non-negligible out-migration. The 'diagonal' reappears to the south, in a less mountainous part of the south-west, just beside the pole of the Garonne Valley. The periphery was characterized above all by important out-migration, which increased with time. Finally, the rear-guard consisted of *départements* where fertility and mortality fell slowly, and where out-migration reached relatively significant proportions. This type corresponds exactly to the most isolated and rural *départements* of that time and, for this reason, can be nicknamed the 'rural enclaves'.

9.3 A Model of Transition

9.3.1 Available Co-Variates

The panoramic view taken on the system formed by the three demographic forces hints at a possible dynamical relationship between demography, urbanization, education, and isolation. Data on urban population exists from 1831 to today, they have been analyzed in Guérin-Pace (1993) [1]. At a given census at date t, the proportion of women living in cities provides a marker for urbanization at the *départemental* level. This proportion is obtained from the *SGF* statistics, by dividing half of the *SGF* total number of people recorded as urban in *département* i, say p_u^i, by the *SGF* total number of women, say $p^{f,i}$:

$$u(t) \equiv \frac{p_u^i(t)}{2p^{f,i}(t)}$$

Data on education come from the '3000 TRA families' survey undertaken by Dupâquier and Kessler (1992).[2] This survey gathers a representative sample of around 45,000 marriage certificates throughout the nineteenth century. One of its variables indicates whether each spouse could sign his or her certificate. It is thus possible to calculate the female proportion of signatures, call it $s([t, t+4])$, at every quinquennial period $[t, t+4]$ during the nineteenth century.

9.3.2 Synergy of Demographic Behaviours and the Role of Urbanization

A simple model is considered here to clarify what kind of synergy, detectable with the data exploited in this book, could govern demographic behaviours. Within each *département* i, the population p^i is divided more or less between rural population p_r^i and urban population p_u^i ($p^i = p_u^i + p_r^i$). In order to avoid the splitting up of land, children who do not inherit land are led to migrate to urban centres. The rural population is then more or less stagnant, at given technology: $\frac{dp_r^i}{dt} \approx 0$. The population growth rate for the *département* is thus finally concentrated in cities. Rural migrants in a city can be integrated only if the local economy has a sufficient growth rate. I thus assume that there is a limit $\theta^i(t)$ to the growth of the economic potential, which depends on resources, technology, and also people, so that:

$$B^i(t) - D^i(t) \leq \theta^i(t)p_u^i$$

where $B^i(t)$ and $D^i(t)$ denote births and deaths in *département* i at time t.

People who cannot find satisfactory jobs are inclined to search for employment elsewhere, in cities with a higher development rate. Thus,

---

[1] who generously allowed me to work on her dataset.
[2] to whom I am also grateful for offering me access to their dataset.

départements with out-migration can be considered to have already reached
their limit of development velocity $\theta^i(t)$, so that dissatisfied people out-
migrate (with variable t implicit for time and i for the *département*):

$$\frac{dp_u}{dt} = B - D + M = \theta(t)p_u \qquad \text{if, } M \leq 0$$

where $M(t)$ is the net total number of migrants at time t ($M > 0$ is net
in-migration, $M < 0$ is net out-migration). For *départements* with in-
migration, the limit of development may not be reached:

$$\frac{dp_u}{dt} = B - D + M \leq \theta(t)p_u \qquad \text{if, } M > 0$$

In this model, the economic perspectives in *département i* are experienced
by couples through a constraint imposed upon present and future jobs for
themselves as well as for their descendants. They thus react to the present
situation by tending to leave the country to search for a better life, and
by restricting the size of their families. However, the total number of
births cannot be planned directly. The control works at the individual
level, through the magnitude of change in the intensity to reproduce, or in
other words, in the will to limit family size. The relevant variable at the
individual level is thus $\frac{\partial f(a,t)}{\partial t}$, where $f(a,t)$ is the fertility rate at age a and
time t. Assuming cohort effect on fertility change is negligible compared
to period effect, changes on age-specific fertility is captured by a change
in total fertility rate, or, here, with historical data, in Coale indexes. The
change in overall Coale index is $\Delta \tilde{I}_f = \tilde{I}_f(t) - \tilde{I}_f(t-5)$, where t denotes
year t.

On what kind of changing information might people base their reaction? Among other things, they might perceive the growth of urbanization in their environment, they may hear about people leaving
the *département*, or they might experience worsening or improving living conditions, especially via the total number of surviving children at
a given moment. They could also be influenced by information coming
from people dwelling in other *départements*. The more mobility between
départements, the more behaviours can be expected to be mimetic. Finally, the more educated they are, the better informed they might be.
In summary, fertility change in *département i* is governed in this model
by the control $\Delta \tilde{I}_f^i$ which could depend on changing life expectancy at
birth $\Delta e^i(t) = e^i_{[t-5,t-1]} - e^i_{[t-10,t-6]}$, on changing migration intensity,
$\Delta \rho^i(t) = {}_5\rho^i_{[20-24],[t-5,t-1]} - {}_5\rho^i_{[20-24],[t-10,t-6]}$, where ${}_5\rho^i_{[20-24],[t-5,t-1]}$ denotes the migration rate from $[20, 24]$ to $[25, 29]$ years old on time interval
$[t-5, t-1]$, on changing urbanization $\Delta u(t) = u(t) - u(t-5)$, on changing
education $\Delta s^i(t) = s^i_{[t-5,t-1]} - s^i_{[t-10,t-6]}$, and on the influence of changes
in fertility behaviour in other types $\Delta \tilde{I}_f^{ij}$, $j \neq i$.

In Appendix C, the data are presented in full for the variables considered in the seven types of Figure 9.2.

The simple model of interactions leads, then, to a possible linear econometric system:

$$\Delta \tilde{I}_f^i(t) = (\Delta e_0^i(t), \Delta u^i(t), \Delta \rho^i(t), \Delta s^i(t))\beta^i + \epsilon_i(t) \qquad i = 1, \cdots, 7,$$
$$t = 1856, \cdots, 1906 \text{ by } 5$$
$$(9.1)$$

where β^i is a four-dimensional vector of coefficients, and where the variance-covariance matrix is assumed to be constant in time:

$$\text{cov}(\epsilon_i(t), \epsilon_i(t+5)) = 0, \quad \text{cov}(\epsilon_i(t), \epsilon_j(t)) = \omega_{ij}$$

The correlation $\frac{\omega_{ij}}{\sqrt{\omega_{ii}}\sqrt{\omega_{jj}}}$ reflects the importance of the link between geographical Types i and j, after the effects of mortality, migration, and urbanization. To obtain this correlation matrix, System 9.1 is estimated by a method suggested by Zellner (1962).

Including migration in the analysis reduces the series of observations to the period stretching from 1856 to 1906, which gives 10 periods, thus 9 values for the first differences representing the changes from one period to the next. Studying the system constituted by mortality and urbanization alone offers fewer, but longer time series, from 1831 to 1901, that is to say 16 dates or 15 values of first differences. Therefore, System 9.2 will also be studied:

$$\Delta \tilde{I}_f^i(t) = (\Delta e_0^i(t), \Delta u^i(t), \Delta s^i(t))\beta^i + \epsilon_i(t) \qquad i = 1, \cdots, 7,$$
$$t = 1831, \cdots, 1906 \text{ by } 5$$
$$(9.2)$$

where β^i is a three-dimensional vector of coefficients, and where the variance-covariance matrix is assumed to be constant in time:

$$\text{cov}(\epsilon_i(t), \epsilon_i(t+5)) = 0, \quad \text{cov}(\epsilon_i(t), \epsilon_j(t)) = \omega_{ij}$$

Systems 9.1 and 9.2 represent dynamic econometric models, where the structure of relationships between variables is given and where temporal delays are imposed a priori. Another version of Systems 9.1 and 9.2 which includes lagged $\tilde{I}_f^i$ into the set of covariates has been attempted, but no significant effect of this variable was found. I will thus focus attention on Systems 9.1 and 9.2 with no lagged effect on fertility. As for the covariates, the brevity of the time series considered does not allow the inclusion of other lagged effect of the covariates on the response, apart from the fact that all covariates except urbanization reflect the quinquennial period preceding the date t at which fertility is estimated. This is not a great loss, since the time unit here is the quinquennial period: a lagged effect implies an effect over more than five years, which is possible, but should not be essential.

Before analyzing the results, it may be useful to explain how I proceeded to avoid the technical difficulties specific to spatio-temporal data, especially questions of stationarity and multicollinearity.

9.3.3 Implementing the Econometric Model

Stationarity Systems 9.1 and 9.2 will be better treated if the time series to be dealt with are stationary. Stationarity is a mathematical and statistical property of time series data, upon which most probabilistic models are based. If the mean and variance of a time series are constant over time, then the time series is said to be *stationary*. In other cases, if either the mean or the variance is not constant over time, the time series is said to be non-stationary.[3] Formal statistical tests for the existence of stationarity were developed by Dickey and Fuller (1979) and Phillips and Perron (1988). Tables 9.1 and 9.2 show Dickey-Fuller and Phillips-Perron tests performed on each time series considered in the present study and their first differences.[4]

The statistics τ_τ and τ_μ of Dickey and Fuller must be compared to tables provided in Fuller (1976). Critical values are respectively -3.60 and -3.00 for a one-sided 5 per cent level for 25 observations. The statistics Z_t, single mean and zero mean, are given in Hamilton (1994). Critical values are again respectively -3.60 and -3.00 for a one-sided 5 per cent level for 25 observations. For both tests, the null hypothesis is 'non-stationarity'. Thus, Tables 9.1 and 9.2 show that every differenced variable can be taken as stationary, except urbanization in Type 2 and migration in Types 3 and 5. For these latter geographical types, differentiating migration twice also fails to produce stationary series. These series can thus be taken away from the econometric models where stationarity or first-order integration is required.

Multicollinearity Another difficulty stems from the collinearity of variables. 'The validity of inferences resulting from a regression analysis assumes the use of a model with a specified set of independent variables'.[5] Therefore, instead of working directly with the variables mentioned above, it is better to combine them to build orthogonal covariates, that is to say variables with null correlation between them. A preliminary principal component analysis (whose principle has already been presented in this chapter) has been run for each type i, with Δe_0, $\Delta\rho$, Δu, and Δs as active variables varying in time from 1856 to 1906, or, for the study with no

[3] For further references, see Judge et al. (1985).
[4] The Augmented Dickey-Fuller (ADF) accounts for serial correlation in the error term. Said and Dickey (see Hamilton, 1994) showed that the ADF test is valid asymptotically if the number of lags increases with sample size T at a controlled rate $T^{1/3}$. Here, $T \leq 21$ would indicate 2 lags, but I simply used DF because T is low.
[5] Freund and Littel (1991), *SAS System for Regression*, SAS Institute.

Table 9.1 Tests of stationarity Dickey-Fuller (DF) and Phillips-Perron (PP) for fertility index $\tilde{I}_f$ (21 observations), life expectancy e_0 (20 observations), and net migration rate ρ from 20-24 to 25-29 years old (10 observations).

Variable	Type	DF τ_τ	PP single mean Z_t	differenced variable	DF τ_μ	PP zero mean Z_t
	1	-0.41	-1.40		-4.97	-3.65
	2	-0.43	0.37		-5.38	-3.75
	3	-2.39	-1.26		-6.66	-5.90
$\tilde{I}_f$	4	-0.32	-0.72	$\Delta\tilde{I}_f$	-7.07	-4.57
	5	0.07	-1.08		-6.56	-4.29
	6	0.30	-0.13		-5.65	-2.99
	7	0.20	-0.74		-4.16	-2.75
	1	0.38	-0.74		-5.77	-4.76
	2	-1.11	1.12		-4.56	-3.61
	3	-1.95	0.95		-4.80	-4.34
e_0	4	-0.41	-0.86	Δe_0	-5.16	-4.15
	5	0.36	-0.34		-6.72	-5.33
	6	0.98	0.07		-5.62	-4.24
	7	0.70	0.06		-5.31	-4.01
	1	-5.81	-1.13		-5.43	-5.05
	2	-1.14	0.81		-7.01	-5.74
	3	-1.57	-1.40		-2.36	-2.29
ρ	4	-0.59	-1.19	$\Delta\rho$	-3.14	-2.96
	5	-0.70	-1.19		-2.66	-2.47
	6	-0.74	-1.38		-3.46	-3.22
	7	-0.64	-1.41		-3.09	-2.84

(continued...)

Table 9.2 Tests of stationarity Dickey-Fuller (DF) and Phillips-Perron (PP) for urbanization u (16 observations) and education s (21 observations).

Variable	Type	DF τ_τ	PP single mean Z_t	differenced variable	DF τ_μ	PP zero mean Z_t
	1	-3.17	1.51		-7.35	-2.01
	2	-1.58	-2.08		-2.20	-1.21
	3	-0.44	-0.07		-4.27	-0.51
u	4	-0.32	1.04	Δu	-6.48	-0.21
	5	-0.19	1.81		-7.50	-0.21
	6	-0.40	0.19		-5.53	-0.26
	7	-1.24	-1.42		-5.03	-0.90
	1	-2.52	-0.80		-5.46	-3.99
	2	0.08	-0.14		-4.53	-1.38
	3	-0.65	-0.91		-7.26	-3.12
s	4	0.87	1.53	Δs	-3.07	-0.31
	5	-0.35	0.15		-6.46	-3.55
	6	0.38	0.55		-4.31	-1.48
	7	1.20	1.13		-4.17	-2.31

migration, only with Δe_0, Δu, and Δs from 1831 to 1906. Principal component analysis uses linear transformations to create a new set of variables, called principal components. These new variables are jointly uncorrelated. Moreover, 'the first principal component has the largest variance of any linear function of the original variables (subject to a scale constraint). The second component has the second largest variance, and so on'.[6] The principal components can then be used as independent variables in a regression analysis (such an analysis is called principal component regression).

9.3.4 *Mortality, Urbanization, Education, and Diffusion in the Fertility Transition*

System 9.2 is thus changed into System 9.3

$$\Delta \tilde{I}_j^i(t) = (C_1^i(t), C_2^i(t), C_3^i(t))\beta^i + \epsilon_i(t) \qquad \begin{array}{l} i = 1, \cdots, 7, \\ t = 1831, \cdots, 1906 \text{ by } 5 \end{array}$$

(9.3)

where the variance-covariance matrix is assumed to be constant in time:

$$\text{cov}(\epsilon_i(t), \epsilon_i(t+5)) = 0, \quad \text{cov}(\epsilon_i(t), \epsilon_j(t)) = \omega_{ij}$$

Tables 9.1 and 9.2 show that first differences in life expectancy, education, and in urbanization are stationary. This does not imply that any linear combination of these variables should be stationary. Therefore, for each type, Dickey-Fuller and Phillips-Perron tests have also been performed on the principal components issued from Δe_0, Δu, and Δs. Although these tests are not reproduced here, they show that non-stationarity can be rejected in almost every case, or in other words, that, for each type, explanatory variables are both stationary and jointly independent (because principal components are orthogonal).

Running for 15 points in time, from 1831 to 1906, System 9.3 yields the results presented in Table 9.3.

The part of France where significant coefficients appear encompasses the most rural part of France (Type 5: south of the Massif Central and Pyrénées, and Type 7: the 'rural enclaves'), which corresponds also to the less advanced regions in the general decline (see Figure 9.1).

In these geographical types, the decline of mortality is associated with that of fertility in the short term. This result supports the idea of a mechanistic relationship between mortality and fertility when the fertility decline is still in its early stages. The same effect indeed seems to vanish with the advancement of the transition (such as in the ensemble of Types 1, 2, 3, 4, and 6). More surprising is the positive effect of urbanization on fertility in Type 7 as well as the negligible effect of education. In Type 5, urbanization

[6]ibid.

Table 9.3 Principal component regression on covariates: mortality, urbanization, and education (1831 to 1906, 15 observations).

Type	Variable	coefficient estimate	std error
1	$C_1 = -0.57\Delta e_0^* + 0.58\Delta u + 0.58\Delta s^*$	-	ns
	$C_2 = 0.82\Delta e_0^* + 0.34\Delta u + 0.46\Delta s^*$	-	ns
	$C_3 = 0.07\Delta e_0^* + 0.74\Delta u - 0.67\Delta s^*$	-	ns
2	$C_1 = 0.02\Delta e_0^* - 0.707\Delta u + 0.71\Delta s^*$	-	ns
	$C_2 = 1.00\Delta e_0^* - 0.03\Delta u + 0.71\Delta s^*$	-	ns
	$C_3 = 0.06\Delta e_0^* + 0.71\Delta u + 0.71\Delta s^*$	non statio.	
3	$C_1 = 0.64\Delta e_0^* + 0.47\Delta u - 0.61\Delta s^*$	-	ns
	$C_2 = -0.21\Delta e_0^* + 0.86\Delta u + 0.45\Delta s^*$	-	ns
	$C_3 = 0.74\Delta e_0^* - 0.16\Delta u + 0.65\Delta s^*$	-	ns
4	$C_1 = 0.60\Delta e_0^* + 0.73\Delta u + 0.33\Delta s^*$	-	ns
	$C_2 = -0.54\Delta e_0^* + 0.06\Delta u + 0.84\Delta s^*$	-	ns
	$C_3 = 0.59\Delta e_0^* - 0.68\Delta u + 0.43\Delta s^*$	-	ns
5	$C_1 = 0.72\Delta e_0^* + 0.67\Delta u - 0.19\Delta s^*$	-0.006	0.002
	$C_2 = -0.09\Delta e_0^* + 0.36\Delta u + 0.93\Delta s^*$	-	ns
	$C_3 = 0.69\Delta e_0^* - 0.65\Delta u + 0.32\Delta s^*$	-	ns
6	$C_1 = 0.49\Delta e_0^* + 0.66\Delta u - 0.57\Delta s^*$	-	ns
	$C_2 = 0.79\Delta e_0^* - 0.06\Delta u + 0.61\Delta s^*$	-	ns
	$C_3 = -0.37\Delta e_0^* + 0.74\Delta u + 0.56\Delta s^*$	non statio.	
7	$C_1 = 0.57\Delta e_0^* + 0.53\Delta u + 0.62\Delta s^*$	-	ns
	$C_2 = -0.61\Delta e_0^* + 0.78\Delta u - 0.11\Delta s^*$	+0.008	0.003
	$C_3 = 0.55\Delta e_0^* + 0.32\Delta u - 0.77\Delta s^*$	-	ns

System weighted $R^2 = 0.26$

The asterisk * indicates that variables are normalized; 'ns' means non-significant; C_i is the ith principal component; e_0, u, and s are abbreviated notations for $e_{0[t-5,t-1]}$, the life expectancy at birth from year $t-5$ to year $t-1$, $u(t)$, the urbanization rate at date t, and $s_{[t-5,t-1]}$, the mean fraction of signatures on marriage certificates from year $t-5$ to year $t-1$.
'non st.' means 'non stationary'.

has a negative effect on fertility. A simple way to evaluate the importance of urbanization among these latter two geographical types consists in multiplying the coefficient of urbanization in the principal component by the significant coefficient affected to this principal component. For example, in Type 7, the importance of urbanization would be $0.008 \times 0.78 = 0.006$. By proceeding in this way, it turns out that the influence of urbanization growth on fertility decreases according to the degree of advancement in the fertility decline: 0.006 for Type 7, -0.004 for Type 5, and non-significant for the other Types. For mortality, the same calculation supports again a decreasing effect along the order of advancement in the fertility decline (Figure 9.1): non-significant for the most advanced Types 1, 2, 3, and 4, but also for Type 6, -0.004 for Type 5, and 0.005 for Type 7.

Tugault (1975) has already examined some data on urbanization and fertility: he briefly compared crude birth rates in 1861 (from *SGF* data) in some rural and urban *départements* and noted that fertility seemed to increase with the degree of urbanization, except for Seine (city of Paris) where fertility was low. Results of System 9.2 based on the present follow-up over a century permit us to revise his arguments for the short term, by confirming the positive effect of urbanization on fertility for Type 7, but a negative effect in more advanced Type 5, and no further effect either in Type 6 or in the most advanced regions in the fertility decline. The temporal study thus adds an interesting nuance which cannot be seen from a static comparison between urbanized and rural *départements* at a given date: the advent of urbanization stimulated fertility in regions with relatively high fertility, but this effect must fall off in a later phase of the decline when relatively low levels of fertility were attained. Furthermore, and importantly, education appears to play no role in the short-term for the whole of France.

The finding that urbanization stimulates fertility at the beginning of the decline stands in concordance with Dyson and Murphy's thesis, according to which 'a fertility rise has to be viewed as an integral part of the opening phase of the transition' (1985, p. 432). These latter authors based their comments on a world-wide review of fertility transitions. The French baby-boom claimed by Van de Walle (1974) (which does not appear according to my reconstruction) is part of their argument, although the period from mid-century to the 1870s is not located at all at the 'opening phase of the transition'. However, the present short-term analysis confirms that the less advanced countries in the transition experienced the depressive effects of the improvement of mortality counterbalanced by the temporary favouring effects of the take-off of urbanization. I do not have here the resources to investigate the reasons underlying this phenomenon. Dyson and Murphy (1985) invoke the decline in the mean duration of breastfeeding as 'a prime candidate for the explanation', for developing countries as well as for 'historical Europe'.

Another mechanism capable of altering fertility must be searched for, such as the transfer of information and the diffusion of behaviours. The pattern of spatial interactions may not be as simplistic as the usual closest neighbour influence in use in spatial epidemiology (Cressie, 1991). A general structure of spatial interactions is revealed by the correlation matrix (ω_{ij}) issued from System 9.2 (estimated by Zellner's method of Seemingly Unrelated Regressions). This matrix is presented in Table 9.4. If the

Table 9.4 Correlation matrix $\text{cov}(\epsilon_i(t), \epsilon_i(t+5))$ in Equation 9.3, when fertility is explained by mortality, urbanization, and education (1831 to 1906).

geographical Type	1	2	3	4	5	6	7
1	1						
2	0.533	1					
3	0.339	0.721	1				
4	0.252	0.747	0.959	1			
5	-0.021	0.410	0.574	0.705	1		
6	0.247	0.680	0.800	0.865	0.638	1	
7	-0.092	0.225	0.546	0.618	0.730	0.670	1

perturbations are considered as multivariate normal, the hypothesis that a correlation r between two of them is non-significant is rejected when $| r | > 0.444$ for 20 observations (Fisher and Van Belle, 1993, p. 381).

Correlations in Table 9.4 turn out to be ordered along a four-fold pattern:

- the specificity of Paris, which is positively correlated with the second largest cities (Type 2). The correlation falls to zero for distant and rural regions (Types 3, 4, 5, 6, and 7);
- the urban hierarchy: Type 2, the most urbanized country after Paris, is linked to its neighbours, Types 3, 4, and 6, more weakly or non-significantly to rural far away regions (Types 5 and 7);
- the influence of the three poles (Type 3), which are positively related to all the other geographical types, especially to the periphery;
- the closest neighbour relationship and the interdependency of the French geographical types outside Paris (Type 1), which is reflected by the positive and significant correlations between one type and another, except the most isolated country, Type 7, which is not connected to the most urbanized regions Types 1 and 2. Correlations of this Type 7 seem to decrease gradually with increasing distance. The interdependency is strong between neighbours: as geographical types have been ordered on the map Figure 9.2 and Figure 9.1 to render Table 9.4 easier to read, it is symptomatic to see correlations decrease gradually either following the rows or following the columns

when starting from the diagonal of Table 9.4: the proximity to the diagonal indicates neighbouring geographical types, while geographical distance increases while going from the diagonal of Table 9.4 to the first column. Thus, the numbering of the geographical types reflects an urban-geographical hierarchy.

Although reduced to 10 values instead of 16, the study including migration can bring additional light to the understanding of the dynamics of fertility in time and space.

9.3.5 The Role of Migration in the Fertility Transition

The same procedure is used to handle System 9.1 as for System 9.2: principal component analysis with first differenced life expectancy, urbanization, and migration as active variables is performed to produce principal components for each geographical type. Thus, System 9.1 now becomes:

$$\Delta \tilde{I}_f^i(t) = (C_1^i(t), C_2^i(t), C_3^i(t), C_4(t))\beta^i + \epsilon_i(t) \quad i = 1, \cdots, 7,$$
$$t = 1856, \cdots, 1906 \text{ by } 5$$
$$(9.4)$$

where the variance-covariance matrix is assumed to be constant in time:

$$\text{cov}(\epsilon_i(t), \epsilon_i(t+5)) = 0, \quad \text{cov}(\epsilon_i(t), \epsilon_j(t)) = \omega_{ij}$$

These components are orthogonal, so that there is no more multicollinearity to fear between explanatory variables. As principal components are evolving in time (9 first differences from 1856–1860 to 1901–1905), Dickey-Fuller and Phillips-Perron tests help decide about stationarity, which is necessary to validate inference. Here, as could be expected from Tables 9.1 and 9.2, some components fail to be stationary and are removed from the model. The model is thus incomplete, but inference on estimated coefficients is valid.

Running for 9 points in time, from 1856–1860 to 1901–1905, System 9.4 yields significant coefficients for Types 1, 2, 4, and 5. The results are presented on Tables 9.5 and 9.6.

Urbanized regions Type 2, the three poles Type 3, and intermediary Type 4 (Loire Valley, Poitou-Charentes, Picardy-Ardennes) appear again with no significant coefficient. The relationship between mortality, urbanization, and fertility, which we observed for the whole century in Type 5 (south of the Massif Central and Pyrénées) is no longer valid for this second half of the century.

This time, Type 1, *département* of Seine (Paris), shows a negative influence of the third principal component, which combines migration and education in the same proportions: improving education depresses fertility, while growing in-migration favours it. The positive effect of urbanization

Table 9.5 Principal component regression on covariates: mortality, urbanization, education, and migration (1856 to 1906, 9 observations).

Type	Variable	coeff. estim.	std error
1	$C_1 = -0.59\Delta e_0^* + 0.56\Delta \rho^* - 0.36\Delta u^* + 0.45\Delta s$	-	ns
	$C_2 = -0.06\Delta e_0^* - 0.04\Delta \rho^* + 0.79\Delta u^* + 0.60\Delta s$	-	ns
	$C_3 = -0.17\Delta e_0^* + 0.61\Delta \rho^* + 0.48\Delta u^* - 0.61\Delta s$	0.034	0.010
	$C_4 = 0.79\Delta e_0^* + 0.55\Delta \rho^* - 0.10\Delta u^* + 0.26\Delta s$	non st.	
2	$C_1 = -0.65\Delta e_0^* + 0.34\Delta \rho^* + 0.09\Delta u^* + 0.67\Delta s$	non st.	
	$C_2 = -0.03\Delta e_0^* - 0.63\Delta \rho^* + 0.75\Delta u^* + 0.18\Delta s$	-	ns
	$C_3 = 0.61\Delta e_0^* + 0.60\Delta \rho^* + 0.47\Delta u^* + 0.21\Delta s$	-	ns
	$C_4 = 0.46\Delta e_0^* - 0.35\Delta \rho^* - 0.44\Delta u^* + 0.69\Delta s$	non st.	
3	$C_1 = 0.51\Delta e_0^* - 0.50\Delta \rho^* + 0.52\Delta u^* - 0.46\Delta s$	-	ns
	$C_2 = -0.19\Delta e_0^* - 0.53\Delta \rho^* + 0.34\Delta u^* + 0.75\Delta s$	non st.	
	$C_3 = 0.77\Delta e_0^* + 0.43\Delta \rho^* + 0.07\Delta u^* + 0.46\Delta s$	-	ns
	$C_4 = -0.33\Delta e_0^* + 0.55\Delta \rho^* + 0.77\Delta u^* - 0.06\Delta s$	non st.	
4	$C_1 = 0.38\Delta e_0^* - 0.60\Delta \rho^* + 0.61\Delta u^* + 0.35\Delta s$	-	ns
	$C_2 = -0.69\Delta e_0^* + 0.02\Delta \rho^* + 0.03\Delta u^* + 0.72\Delta s$	-	ns
	$C_3 = 0.61\Delta e_0^* + 0.51\Delta \rho^* - 0.21\Delta u^* + 0.57\Delta s$	non st.	
	$C_4 = -0.11\Delta e_0^* + 0.61\Delta \rho^* + 0.76\Delta u^* - 0.16\Delta s$	-	ns

(continued...)

Table 9.6 Principal component regression (mortality, urbanization, education, and migration as covariates) (1856 to 1906, 9 observations).

Type	Variable	coeff. estim.	std. error
5	$C_1 = \quad 0.62\Delta e_0^* - 0.29\Delta\rho^* + 0.65\Delta u^* - 0.32\Delta s$	-	ns
	$C_2 = \quad 0.08\Delta e_0^* + 0.72\Delta\rho^* - 0.09\Delta u^* - 0.68\Delta s$	non st.	
	$C_3 = \quad 0.53\Delta e_0^* + 0.55\Delta\rho^* + 0.06\Delta u^* + 0.64\Delta s$	-	ns
	$C_4 = -0.57\Delta e_0^* + 0.30\Delta\rho^* + 0.75\Delta u^* + 0.15\Delta s$	non st.	
6	$C_1 = \quad 0.57\Delta e_0^* - 0.62\Delta\rho^* + 0.53\Delta u^* - 0.06\Delta s$	-	ns
	$C_2 = -0.33\Delta e_0^* - 0.02\Delta\rho^* + 0.43\Delta u^* + 0.84\Delta s$	+0.008	0.002
	$C_3 = -0.36\Delta e_0^* + 0.32\Delta\rho^* + 0.71\Delta u^* + 0.50\Delta s$	+0.011	0.003
	$C_4 = \quad 0.65\Delta e_0^* + 0.71\Delta\rho^* + 0.15\Delta u^* + 0.19\Delta s$	-0.017	0.003
7	$C_1 = \quad 0.60\Delta e_0^* - 0.45\Delta\rho^* + 0.54\Delta u^* - 0.36\Delta s$	-	ns
	$C_2 = -0.12\Delta e_0^* - 0.52\Delta\rho^* + 0.24\Delta u^* + 0.81\Delta s$	-	ns
	$C_3 = \quad 0.18\Delta e_0^* + 0.71\Delta\rho^* + 0.60\Delta u^* + 0.31\Delta s$	-	ns
	$C_4 = 0.77\Delta e_0^* + 0.11\Delta\rho^* - 0.53\Delta u^* + 0.34\Delta s$	-0.023	0.007

System weighted $R^2 = 0.77$

The asterisk * indicates that variables are normalized; 'ns' means non-significant; C_i is the ith principal component; e_0, u, s, and ρ are abbreviated notations for $e_{0[t-5,t-1]}$, the life expectancy at birth from year $t - 5$ to year $t - 1$, $u(t)$, the urbanization rate at date t, $s_{[t-5,t-1]}$, the mean fraction of signatures on marriage certificates from year $t - 5$ to year $t - 1$, and $\rho_{[20-4,25,9][t-5,t-1]}$ the migration rate from 20–24 to 25–29 years old, from year $t - 5$ to year $t - 1$;
'non st.' means 'non stationary'.

may reflect the higher fertility of in-migrants. Change in mortality has a negligible effect, dominated by the other variables.

In Type 6, education is the dominant variable of the second component, with a very favourable effect on fertility change. Considering education in the other significant components reduces the magnitude of this effect, but not its sign. Urbanization dominating in the third component has a positive influence on fertility. Out-migration dominating in the fourth component suggests that an increase in out-migration favours fertility as well. A plausible scenario would be that access to land in rural areas is facilitated with population departure, thereby favouring higher fertility amongst the rural inhabitants who acceded to land ownership (typical of the old demographic regime, see Bonneuil, 1990). The out-migrants then arrived in Paris with relatively higher levels of fertility. This could explain therefore the positive effect on fertility of both in-migration and out-migration. Appearing as a second-order variable in the three significant components with comparable magnitude and with a negative sign, improving mortality has a negative influence on fertility.

In Type 7, mortality dominates for a depressing effect on fertility, while urbanization with a positive influence is the second-order variable. Out-migration plays no role. This result is very consistent to what was observed in this Type 7 for the whole century with no consideration for migration.

In summary, education appears as a stimulus to fertility in Type 6, but depressing in Paris and non-significant in the other geographical Types. Mortality has again a depressing effect in Types 6 and 7, but less obvious in Type 5. Urbanization is a secondary favouring factor in Types 1, 6 and 7. Migration plays a key role in improving fertility, as in-migration in Type 1 (Paris) or as out-migration in Type 6.

As before, the correlation matrix obtained from System 9.4 is presented in Table 9.7 and reveals the pattern of spatial interactions. This table

Table 9.7 Correlation matrix $\text{cov}(\epsilon_i(t), \epsilon_i(t+5))$ in Equation 9.4, when fertility is explained by mortality, urbanization, education, and migration (1856 to 1906).

Type	1	2	3	4	5	6	7
1	1						
2	0.598	1					
3	0.503	0.910	1				
4	0.527	0.934	0.978	1			
5	0.160	0.764	0.720	0.788	1		
6	0.153	0.779	0.744	0.766	0.764	1	
7	0.081	0.228	0.087	0.197	0.528	0.035	1

resembles Table 9.4 in some features: the geographical gradient emerges by the relatively high positive correlations along the diagonal of the correlation matrix, thus reflecting an important link between closest neighbours (with the exception of Types 6 and 7, but Type 5 is in fact a closer neighbour to Type 7 than Type 6). Paris is again poorly correlated with the rest of France, except slightly to the regional metropoles (Type 2), and now to the three poles (Type 3). This Type 2 and the three poles of Type 3 are remarkably positively correlated with almost the whole of France apart from Type 7, thus confirming the leading role played by the three poles in the diffusion of behaviours as well as the importance of the regional metropoles. In summary, three axes emerge from Table 9.4: (1) the relative isolation of Paris from the whole of the nation; (2) the driving influence of close neighbours, reflected by the heavy diagonal of the correlation matrices presented on Tables 9.4 and 9.7; (3) the leading role played by the three poles and the regional metropoles.

Thus, the addition of migration as a covariate alters the perception of the demographic dynamics above all for the *département* of Seine, where in-migration plays an important role in preventing a further decrease in fertility. This phenomenon takes place in the only geographical type where migration is a very important social fact that alters daily life.

In the other geographical types, migration seems to have been a secondary variable in the fertility process. For these other types, the process at work is thus better reflected in System 9.2, running over 15 period changes with migration neglected. We have seen how internal influences uncover a diffusion process originating from distinct poles and extending both to closest neighbours and via the second-rank urbanized *départements*.

In this section, I have paid attention to regional interaction on fertility behaviour. In order to continue my attempt at distinguishing adaptative mechanisms (adaptation to the improvement of mortality, to the rise of education or to urbanization) from the diffusion of an innovation, the analysis to come focuses on the search for a possible relationship between spatial trends of fertility. This treatment can highlight a long-term relationship between trends from various geographical types. If this is so, the hypothesis of the diffusion of an innovation wave would be favoured. Otherwise, if no such long-term relationship can be found, adaptationist arguments could be granted greater scope.

9.4   Inter-Related Trends: the Co-Integration Approach

In the previous section indeed, I considered interactions only among short-term fluctuations, managing to produce a spatial correlation matrix and to clarify the influence of certain covariates. Although viewing fertility responding to short-term changes of the environment makes sense, ignoring the levels of involved time-series is a waste of information. This is what Engle and Granger (1987) argued in the general case of economic time series analysis.

In the previous section, Tables 9.1 and 9.2 have shown that fertility, mortality, urbanization, and education are each non-stationary when taken crudely (except migration in Type 1), but that their first differences are stationary (these series are thus said to be 'integrated of order 1'). It is worth examining whether these four variables can be modelled through 'co-integration'. Co-integration is the property of several non-stationary time series having joint evolutions, such that they verify a long-term relationship defining an equilibrium. The concept was introduced by Engle and Granger (1987) and developed in the multidimensional case notably by Johansen and Juselius (1990). Applications in demography can be found in Abeysinghe (1993). Applications in macro-economics are numerous (see Perron and Campbell, 1992, for a review).

Here, searching for co-integration between demographic variables is another step towards entering the debate opposing adaptation to diffusion. Evidence for co-integration between fertility, mortality, urbanization, and education would indicate some long-term adaptation during the transition phase, and would favour the adaptationist point of view. Outside equilibrium, there would exist some adjusting scheme of a demographic variable to a so-called long-term target. For example, the decline of fertility here could be driven by the fall of mortality or by the rise of urbanization. Fertility would then adjust in the long term to these three exogenous variables. The change of fertility would depend on changes of mortality, education, and urbanization, but with some adjustment error. This error would reflect the instantaneous disequilibrium between the level of fertility at time t and its long-term target. We could thus describe precisely short-term changes associated with long-term relationships. This approach is typically that of the 'error correction models' suggested by Davidson et al. (1978).

9.4.1   *Long-Term Equilibrium between Environment and Fertility*

Tables 9.1 and 9.2 show that the four variables under study are separately integrated of order 1, that is to say they are stationary when differenced once. For p variables $X_t = (X_{1t}, \cdots, X_{pt})'$ which are integrated of order one, the basic idea of co-integration is based on the vector auto-regressive model (Johansen and Juselius, 1990):

$$X_t = \Pi_1 X_{t-1} + \ldots + \Pi_k X_{t-k} + \mu + \epsilon_t, \quad t = 1, \cdots, T \qquad (9.5)$$

where $\epsilon_1, \cdots, \epsilon_T$ are $ii\mathcal{N}_p(0, \Lambda)$ and $\mu \in I\!R^p$, $\Pi_1, \cdots, \Pi_{t-k}, \Lambda$ are $(p \times p)$ matrices.

Differencing this system 9.5 reads:

$$\Delta X_t = \Gamma_1 \Delta X_{t-1} + \ldots + \Gamma_{k-1} \Delta X_{t-k+1} + \Pi X_{t-k} + \mu + \epsilon_t, \quad t = 1, \cdots, T \tag{9.6}$$

where $\Gamma_i = (I - \Pi_1 - \cdots - \Pi_i)$, $(i = 1, \cdots, k - 1)$, and $\Pi = -(I - \Pi_1 - \cdots - \Pi_k)$. 'The coefficient matrix Π contains information about long-run relationships between the variables in the data vector' (Johansen and Juselius, 1990, p 170). If $0 < \text{rank}(\Pi) = r < p$, there exist $(p \times r)$ matrices α and β such that $\Pi = \alpha\beta'$, defining long-term relationships between the components of X_t, which are said to be co-integrated. Equation 9.6 is called error correction model, because it combines a dynamic adjustment with long-run relationships. The main hypothesis to be tested concerns then the value of r.

In my attempt to confront the spatially differentiated evolution of fertility together with the influence of environment (life expectancy, urbanization, education) in each of the seven selected geographical Types of Figure 9.2, the ideal data vector would consist of 7×4 variables. This is not possible with a maximum of 21 points in time. I suggest, therefore, to conduct two separate analyses: (1) in each geographical Type of Figure 9.2, check for co-integration between fertility, mortality, urbanization, and education; and (2) subsequently, check for co-integration among fertility indexes of homogeneous ensembles as regards fertility alone, that is to say among the 6 geographical Types of Figure 7.1.

I test for co-integration using Johansen's (1988, 1991) full information maximum likelihood method. This method permits testing the number r of co-integrating relations, not just the existence of co-integration. Normally, the lag length k is selected through minimizing the Schwarz criteria (Lütkepohl, 1991, see in Hamilton, 1994). The shortness of the time series however limits the study to $k = 2$, which is the minimum required to estimate error correction models. For each geographical Type, I construct a four-dimensional system of equations involving the same variables. Table 9.8 presents the 'trace' test, where the null hypothesis that there are at most r co-integrating vectors $(r = 0, \cdots, 3)$ is tested against a general alternative $(r = 4)$, and the 'maximum eigenvalue' test, where the null hypothesis of r co-integrating relations is tested against the alternative of $r+1$ co-integrating relations. Using these tests, I conclude that the numbers of co-integrating relations are one for Types 1, 4, and 5, two for Type 3, and three for Types 2, 6, and 7. No inference is possible on the coefficients of these relations. Their purpose lies thus not in looking for significant coefficients, but in producing linear combinations which are stationary and which can be incorporated into error correction models. Usually, the coefficients Γ_i of Equation 9.6 are obtained through OLS regressions. The scarcity of my demographic time-series creates multicollinearities between short-term fluctuations, which should vanish if the series were longer. This

Table 9.8 Testing for the dimension of the co-integrating space, for $X_t = (\tilde{I}_f(t), e_0([t-5, t-1], u(t), s([t-5, t-1]))$.

	(A) H_0: rank(Π) $\leq r$ against H_1: rank(Π)=4			
		Test Statistic		
Type	$r \leq 3$	$r \leq 2$	$r \leq 1$	$r = 0$
1^a	0.74	10.07	30.51	80.07
2^a	4.80	36.72	85.13	145.15
3^a	2.36	14.66	52.96	94.80
4^a	0.79	10.27	28.69	175.64
5^b	3.90	18.33	5.96	95.17
6^a	3.61	21.63	46.86	84.89
7^a	2.89	18.80	46.80	147.51

Critical values at the 5% level are (Johansen and Juselius (1990):
In ^{a}, the trend is tested to be present in the regressors:
       (8.08)   (17.84)   (31.26)   (48.42)
In ^{b}, the trend is tested to be present in the co-integration term:
       (9.09)   (20.17)   (35.07)   (53.35)

	(B) H_0: rank(Π) $= r$ against H_1: rank(Π) $= r+1$			
		Test Statistic		
Type	$r = 3 \mid r = 4$	$r = 2 \mid r = 3$	$r = 1 \mid r = 2$	$r = 0 \mid r = 1$
1^a	0.74	9.34	20.44	48.41
2^a	4.80	31.91	48.41	31.12
3^a	2.36	12.31	38.30	41.84
4^a	0.79	9.48	18.42	146.94
5^b	3.90	14.43	20.12	56.72
6^a	3.61	18.03	25.23	38.03
7^a	2.89	15.90	28.00	100.72

Critical values at the 5% level are (Johansen and Juselius, 1990):
In ^{a}, the trend is tested to be present in the regressors:
       (8.08)   (14.60)   (21.28)   (27.34)
In ^{b}, the trend is tested to be present in the co-integration term:
       (9.09)   (15.75)   (21.89)   (28.17)

warning leads me to use principal component regression instead of simple OLS to estimate the coefficients involved in the Γ_is. These coefficients are presented in Tables 9.9 to 9.11, and principal components in Tables 9.12 and 9.13.

Error-correction regressions presented on Table 9.9 show the correcting effect of the lagged short-term fluctuations of the environment: urbanization in Type 7 (through C_6 and C_7), education in Type 5 (through C_1 and C_5), life expectancy in Type 4 (through C_1 and C_5). In Type 1, C_4, mainly made of life expectancy and education, has a significant effect on fertility. This would suggest a slight negative effect of improving life expectancy and a slight positive effect of education. In Types 2, 3, and 6, no decisive interaction emerges.

As in the study of simultaneous short-term fluctuations presented on Table 9.3, the Types where environmental variables interact significantly with fertility belong to the most rural parts of France (Types 7 and 5). However, the effect of improvements in life expectancy is less obvious on Table 9.9 than on Table 9.3, though it appears now in Type 4. The sign of urbanization is changed in Type 7, which could suggest that urbanization had a double effect in time: positive immediately, then negative with time passing. Similarly, education seems to play a role in Type 5 only as a lagged effect. Finally, considering two lags in the co-integrating Equation 9.6 makes the introduction of the net migration time series with its nine points in time doubtful, and leads me regretfully to renounce doing it.

The adaptation hypothesis has thus been captured by the existence of co-integrating equations in any of the seven geographical Types considered, defining long-term relationships between environment and fertility. Short-term interactions appear only in the most rural parts of France (that is except in Types 2 and 3) and in Type 1, where important flows of rural in-migrants into the Paris metropolis produces a confused image of the influence of the environment on fertility changes.

9.4.2   *Long-Term Equilibrium among Typical Fertility Time Series*

Co-integration can also be searched for among the various geographical $\tilde{I}_f$ time series. Finding such co-integrating relationships would add further evidence to the diffusion argument, because a long-term joint evolution would be highlighted. Furthermore, an error correction model could link together short-term and long-term properties in a dynamic system.

Working on the sole $\tilde{I}_f$ series, I would rather use the typology of France shown in Figure 7.1, which concerns only the pattern of fertility through time. This map is divided into six types and three isolated *départements*, which I briefly describe approximately and enumerate as follows:

- Type (a): the 'three poles' of Figure 9.2: Normandy-Pays de Loire, Champagne-Burgundy, and the Garonne Valley;

Table 9.9 Multivariate error-correction regressions for $X_t = (\tilde{I}_f(t)$, $e_0([t-5, t-1])$, $u(t)$, $s([t-5, t-1]))$, by geographical Types (1831 to 1906, 15 observations).

Type	Regressors	Dependent variables: first difference in			
		$\tilde{I}_f(t)$	$e_{0[t-5,t-1]}$	$u(t)$	$s_{[t-5,t-1]}$
	μ	−0.016* (−2.38)	0.60 (0.94)	0.012* (2.34)	0.005 (1.37)
	C_1	0.006 (−1.24)	−0.18 (−0.40)	−0.007 (−1.98)	0.000 (0.18)
	C_2	0.006 (1.06)	−0.08 (−0.14)	−0.006 (−1.42)	−0.002 (−0.64)
1	C_3	0.009 (1.17)	−1.40 (−1.92)	0.014* (2.37)	−0.030* (−7.60)
	C_4	−0.068* (−4.75)	−1.48 (−1.06)	0.016 (1.36)	0.046* (5.97)
	C_5	0.015 (0.89)	−1.48 (−0.90)	−0.016 (−1.21)	−0.001 (−0.12)
	R^2	0.80	0.45	0.68	0.93
	J-B	0.56	1.31	0.86	0.67
	μ	−0.008* (−3.69)	0.40 (1.78)	0.017* (11.2)	0.043* (8.80)
	C_1	−0.003 (−2.06)	0.15 (1.07)	−0.005* (−4.87)	0.006 (2.02)
	C_2	0.002 (1.43)	−0.04 (−0.21)	0.009* (7.21)	−0.002 (−0.62)
2	C_3	−0.002 (−0.98)	−0.50* (−2.56)	−0.001 (−1.00)	0.006 (1.31)
	C_4	−0.019* (−6.00)	0.61 (1.84)	−0.014* (−6.16)	0.004 (0.53)
	C_5	−0.011* (−3.23)	0.46 (1.25)	0.003 (1.07)	−0.035* (−4.32)
	C_6	0.012* (2.93)	0.71 (1.62)	−0.006 (−2.03)	−0.013 (−1.32)
	C_7	−0.020* (−3.79)	−3.37* (−6.02)	0.000 (0.00)	−0.005 (−0.38)
	R^2	0.94	0.91	0.96	0.84
	J-B	0.13	0.24	1.01	0.98
	μ	−0.004 (−1.72)	0.25 (0.66)	0.009* (16.8)	0.041* (4.33)
3	C_1	−0.005* (−3.24)	0.21 (0.78)	0.000 (0.47)	0.013 (1.93)
	C_2	−0.004 (−2.29)	−0.31 (−1.11)	−0.000 (−0.24)	−0.006 (−0.85)

(continued...)

Table 9.10 Multivariate error-correction regressions for $X_t = (\tilde{I}_f(t),$ $e_0([t-5,t-1]), u(t), s([t-5,t-1]))$, by geographical Types (1831 to 1906, 15 observations).

Type	Regressors	Dependent variables: first difference in			
		$\tilde{I}_f(t)$	$e_{0[t-5,t-1]}$	$u(t)$	$s_{[t-5,t-1]}$
3	C_3	−0.005 (1.74)	0.20 (0.50)	0.000 (1.31)	−0.020 (−1.94)
	C_4	−0.005 (1.74)	0.58 (1.36)	0.000 (1.31)	−0.026* (−2.48)
	C_5	−0.021* (−2.82)	2.07 (1.70)	0.002 (−1.46)	0.041 (1.37)
	C_6	0.000 (0.05)	2.64 (1.82)	0.005 (2.30)	0.035 (0.97)
	R^2	0.82	0.63	0.65	0.74
	J-B	2.06	0.49	1.56	0.83
4	μ	−0.008 (−5.76)	0.56 (1.03)	0.010* (20.5)	0.042* (6.15)
	C_1	−0.004* (−4.19)	0.65 (1.72)	0.000 (0.41)	0.001 (0.21)
	C_2	−0.004* (−3.57)	−0.06 (−0.12)	0.000 (0.43)	0.007 (1.09)
	C_3	−0.001 (−0.59)	−1.06 (−1.67)	−0.000 (−0.55)	−0.005 (−0.67)
	C_4	0.005* (2.16)	−0.07 (−0.09)	−0.000 (−0.47)	0.019 (2.11)
	C_5	−0.041* (−9.86)	−0.78 (0.46)	−0.003 (−1.90)	0.000 (0.04)
	R^2	0.95	0.46	0.39	0.47
	J-B	1.27	2.25	0.52	0.53
5	μ	−0.010* (−2.17)	0.70 (1.23)	0.006* (8.90)	0.056* (6.45)
	C_1	−0.008 (−2.38)	0.75 (1.81)	−0.000 (−0.06)	−0.011 (−1.71)
	C_2	0.003 (0.79)	−0.80 (−1.58)	0.000 (0.83)	0.000 (0.04)
	C_3	−0.002 (−0.36)	0.91 (−1.63)	0.000 (1.13)	0.052* (6.17)
	C_4	−0.003* (−0.44)	−0.68 (−0.72)	0.000 (0.33)	−0.078* (−5.47)
	C_5	0.066 (−2.82)	4.53 (1.57)	0.005 (1.50)	−0.017* (−4.02)
	R^2	0.68	0.62	0.38	0.93
	J-B	1.00	1.55	0.23	0.55

(continued...)

Table 9.11 Multivariate error-correction regressions for $X_t = (\tilde{I}_f(t),$ $e_0([t-5,t-1]), u(t), s([t-5,t-1]))$, by geographical Types (1831 to 1906, 15 observations).

Type	Regressors	Dependent variables: first difference in			
		$\tilde{I}_f(t)$	$e_{0[t-5,t-1]}$	$u(t)$	$s_{[t-5,t-1]}$
	μ	−0.010* (−3.00)	0.55 (2.36)	0.012* (21.3)	0.047* (5.60)
	C_1	0.001 (0.56)	−0.40* ·(−2.68)	−0.000 (−1.07)	−0.004 (−0.67)
	C_2	0.002 (0.91)	−0.30 (−1.66)	0.000 (1.62)	0.009 (1.39)
6	C_3	0.004 (1.35)	0.37 (1.81)	0.000 (0.37)	0.009 (1.18)
	C_4	−0.010 (−2.28)	0.60 (1.88)	0.001 (−2.06)	−0.004 (−0.35)
	C_5	−0.012 (−2.26)	2.02* (5.06)	0.000 (−0.62)	0.026 (1.84)
	C_6	−0.014 (−1.83)	−1.39* (−2.58)	−0.001* (−2.54)	0.000 (0.00)
	C_7	−0.013 (−1.34)	−0.02 (0.03)	−0.000 (−0.45)	0.045 (1.89)
	R^2	0.79	0.91	0.75	0.68
	J-B	0.01	0.73	0.79	0.90
	μ	−0.015* (−3.74)	0.77 (1.20)	0.008* (10.4)	0.052* (3.32)
	C_1	−0.001 (−0.43)	−0.31 (−0.72)	0.000 (0.60)	0.007 (0.62)
	C_2	−0.002 (−0.82)	−0.11 (−0.21)	−0.003* (−4.74)	0.000 (0.07)
7	C_3	−0.006 (−1.61)	0.41 (0.70)	0.000 (0.98)	0.010 (−0.70)
	C_4	−0.002 (−0.49)	−1.57 (−2.18)	0.001 (1.51)	−0.012 (−0.69)
	C_5	−0.000 (−0.05)	1.05 (1.10)	0.001 (0.97)	0.004 (−0.16)
	C_6	−0.036* (−3.83)	−0.34 (−0.21)	−0.001 (−0.36)	0.047 (1.23)
	C_7	−0.030* (−2.63)	1.38 (0.72)	−0.004 (−1.71)	−0.105 (−2.26)
	R^2	0.83	0.60	0.86	0.61
	J-B	0.71	0.92	0.58	1.21

t-statistics in parentheses, '*' indicates significance at the 5% level, J-B is the Jarque-Bera test.

Table 9.12 Principal components used in the multivariate error-correction regressions (1831 to 1906, 15 observations).

Variables	Principal Components						
	C_1	C_2	C_3	C_4	C_5	C_6	C_7
Type 1							
$\Delta \tilde{I}_f(t-5)$	-0.60	-0.03	-0.41	-0.02	0.69		
$\Delta e_{[t-10,t-6]}$	-0.09	0.68	0.43	0.53	0.23		
$\Delta u(t-5)$	0.20	-0.61	0.57	0.14	0.49		
$\Delta s_{[t-10,t-6]}$	0.55	0.39	-0.03	-0.58	0.46		
$\beta' X_{t-2}$	0.54	-0.09	-0.56	0.60	0.15		
Type 2							
$\Delta \tilde{I}_f(t-5)$	-0.50	0.09	0.27	0.54	0.19	-0.33	0.47
$\Delta e_{[t-10,t-6]}$	-0.28	-0.42	-0.52	-0.21	-0.18	0.24	0.58
$\Delta u(t-5)$	-0.31	0.58	0.17	-0.17	0.12	0.70	0.11
$\Delta s_{[t-10,t-6]}$	0.04	-0.40	0.61	-0.53	0.36	-0.03	0.21
$(\beta' X_{t-2})_1$	0.44	0.43	0.14	-0.20	-0.45	-0.24	0.55
$(\beta' X_{t-2})_2$	0.42	-0.33	0.29	0.55	-0.16	0.53	0.15
$(\beta' X_{t-2})_3$	0.45	0.16	-0.37	0.09	0.75	0.00	0.26
Type 3							
$\Delta \tilde{I}_f(t-5)$	0.50	-0.15	-0.03	0.68	0.47	0.20	
$\Delta e_{[t-10,t-6]}$	-0.28	0.49	-0.25	0.58	-0.19	-0.49	
$\Delta u(t-5)$	0.27	0.33	0.81	-0.07	0.12	-0.36	
$\Delta s_{[t-10,t-6]}$	-0.47	-0.24	0.52	0.42	-0.34	0.40	
$(\beta' X_{t-2})_1$	-0.40	0.56	0.01	-0.10	0.56	0.44	
$(\beta' X_{t-2})_2$	0.47	0.50	-0.07	-0.00	-0.54	0.48	
Type 4							
$\Delta \tilde{I}_f(t-5)$	0.63	-0.02	-0.05	-0.26	0.73		
$\Delta e_{[t-10,t-6]}$	-0.21	0.71	0.22	-0.63	-0.01		
$\Delta u(t-5)$	0.37	0.34	0.69	0.50	-0.09		
$\Delta s_{[t-10,t-6]}$	0.24	0.59	-0.68	0.35	-0.11		
$\beta' X_{t-2}$	-0.60	0.18	0.03	0.40	0.67		

(continued...)

Table 9.13 Principal components used in the multivariate error-correction regressions (1831 to 1906, 15 observations).

Variables	Principal Components						
	C_1	C_2	C_3	C_4	C_5	C_6	C_7
Type 5							
$\Delta \tilde{I}_f(t-5)$	0.43	-0.38	0.46	0.68	0.00		
$\Delta e_{[t-10,t-6]}$	-0.12	0.77	-0.09	0.57	-0.24		
$\Delta u(t-5)$	0.08	0.44	0.77	-0.33	0.31		
$\Delta s_{[t-10,t-6]}$	0.59	0.21	-0.43	0.039	0.65		
$\beta' X_{t-2}$	-0.67	-0.14	0.03	0.33	0.65		
Type 6							
$\Delta \tilde{I}_f(t-5)$	-0.53	0.19	0.14	0.45	0.17	-0.35	0.56
$\Delta e_{[t-10,t-6]}$	0.46	-0.14	0.45	0.11	-0.53	0.11	0.51
$\Delta u(t-5)$	-0.22	0.52	0.46	0.25	-0.09	0.54	-0.33
$\Delta s_{[t-10,t-6]}$	0.42	0.42	-0.14	0.42	-0.20	-0.54	-0.32
$(\beta' X_{t-2})_1$	-0.04	-0.61	-0.14	0.71	-0.02	0.22	-0.22
$(\beta' X_{t-2})_2$	0.38	-0.13	0.54	0.05	0.72	-0.13	-0.07
$(\beta' X_{t-2})_3$	0.37	0.33	-0.49	0.18	0.34	0.46	0.39
Type 7							
$\Delta \tilde{I}_f(t-5)$	0.54	-0.04	-0.27	-0.24	0.53	0.39	0.37
$\Delta e_{[t-10,t-6]}$	-0.33	0.12	-0.61	0.42	0.23	0.36	-0.38
$\Delta u(t-5)$	0.46	-0.28	-0.10	0.40	-0.64	0.35	0.05
$\Delta s_{[t-10,t-6]}$	0.09	0.66	-0.11	0.45	-0.04	-0.28	0.51
$(\beta' X_{t-2})_1$	0.07	0.59	0.49	-0.10	-0.05	0.57	-0.27
$(\beta' X_{t-2})_2$	-0.61	-0.16	0.09	-0.05	-0.13	0.44	0.62
$(\beta' X_{t-2})_3$	0.03	-0.31	0.53	0.62	0.48	0.02	0.01

$(\beta' X_{t-2})_i$ is the ith row of $\beta' X_{t-2}$,
$\Delta \tilde{I}_f(t-5) = \tilde{I}_f(t-5) - \tilde{I}_f(t-10)$, and so on.

- Type (b): Picardy, Ile-de-France, Ardennes, Lorraine;
- Type (c): Poitou-Charentes, Centre-Loire, Provence;
- Type (d): Nord-Pas-de-Calais, Rennes Bassin, Jura, Ardèche, Bouches-du-Rhône, Aveyron, Dordogne, Pyrénées-Orientales;
- Type (e): Centre and Rhône-Alpes;
- Type (f): Middle Brittany, Corrèze, Hautes-Alpes, and Corsica;
- Type (g): Haute-Vienne;
- Type (h): Finistère;
- Type (i): Lozère.

An unpublished table similar to Table 9.1 shows that, with the exception of Lozère, the time series of the other eight geographical types of Figure 7.1 are integrated of order one.

The search for a co-integrating relationship is conducted as before, by estimating Equation 9.6 with $X_t = (\tilde{I}_f^{(a)}(t), \cdots, \tilde{I}_f^{(f)}(t))$. As the *départements* of Finistère and Haute-Vienne are not of first rank importance, let us focus our attention on the six other types, numerated (a) to (f). Table 9.14 shows

Table 9.14 Testing for the dimension of the co-integrating space, for $X_t = (\tilde{I}_f^{(a)}(t), ..., \tilde{I}_f^{(f)}(t))$.

(A) H_0: rank(Π) $\leq r$ against H_1: rank(Π)=6 Test Statistic				
$r \leq 5$	$r \leq 4$	$r \leq 3$	$r \leq 2$	$r \leq 1$
1.26	11.07	31.00	54.10	79.95
(8.08)	(17.84)	(35.07)	(53.35)	(69.98)

(B) H_0: rank(Π) $= r$ against H_1: rank(Π) $= r + 1$ Test Statistic				
$r = 5 \mid r = 6$	$r = 4 \mid r = 5$	$r = 3 \mid r = 4$	$r = 2 \mid r = 3$	$r = 1 \mid r = 2$
1.26	9.81	13.38	23.10	33.81
(8.08)	(14.60)	(21.89)	(28.17)	(33.26)

Critical values at the 5% level are in parentheses (Johansen and Juselius, 1990).

that null hypothesis $r \leq 2$ is rejected just at the five per cent level, but that $r = 2$ is accepted against $r = 3$. I thus conclude that there exist two co-integrating relations among the fertility times series of the six Types. To evaluate short-term corrections, I estimate Equation 9.6 for $X_t = (\tilde{I}_f^{(a)}(t), ..., \tilde{I}_f^{(f)}(t))$ by simple OLS and by principal component regression. No significant coefficient appears. The way fertility times series converge to a long run equilibrium is thus not portrayed by an error-correction mechanism.

Although no inference can be made on the coefficients of these relations, their magnitudes presented on Table 9.15 show that four ensembles can be distinguished: Types (a) and (b) go together with high coefficients of opposite signs, which means that, in the first order, a long-run equilibrium exists between the fertility time series of these two geographical Types; Types (c), (d), and (e) have coefficients comparable in magnitude, five-fold lower than the coefficients of Types (a) and (b) in both equations, but five-fold higher than the coefficient of Type (f) in the first equation. The comparison of the magnitudes of the coefficients in the second co-integrating equation suggests that (f) goes with (e), while (c) goes again with (d). Type (e) thus seems to play an intermediary role between the $\{(c),(d)\}$ group and Type (f).

The temporal advance of the three poles in the decline of fertility (Figure 7.2) suggests that Type (a) was the leader of the diffusion. This pattern of results would indicate that the diffusion would take place in four steps: (1) the three poles are accompanied by the Parisian Bassin in their pioneering decline; (2) the close periphery to this first ensemble follows with a delay. This close periphery is situated around the three poles as follows: Nord, Rennes Bassin, Poitou-Charentes, Jura-Vosges, Centre around the northern leaders of Normandy and Champagne; and, Ariège-Aude, the Dordogne, Aveyron, Puy-de-Dôme and Rhône Valley around the southern leader of the Garonne Valley (Types (c) and (d)); (3) the rest of France has its own way of catching up to the first two ensembles: Centre-Loire, which had a rapid take-off after mid-century, and Rhône-Alps (Type (e)) ; and (4) the rural enclaves: Brittany, Limousin, and Hautes-Alpes (Type (f)), finally joined the rest of France. These four ensembles described above are delineated on Figure 7.2 by four concentric circles, one circle around each of the three poles. This visual statement, finding a piece of econometric proof through Tables 9.14 and 9.15, contributes to point out a long-term joint evolution of fertility throughout a major part of French territory, thus rejoining the piece of evidence provided by the correlation matrices (Tables 9.4 and 9.7) of Systems 9.3 and 9.4.

Table 9.15 Co-integrating equations among the $(\tilde{I}_f^{(a)}(t), ..., \tilde{I}_f^{(f)}(t))$.

co-integrating vector	Geographical Type					
	(a)	(b)	(c)	(d)	(e)	(f)
$(\beta')_1$	476.3	-628.8	115.5	113.5	-114.4	24.1
$(\beta')_2$	-255.2	250.5	51.6	-59.1	75.0	-64.2

Short-term analysis and the co-integration approach thus yield some consistent results, that is to say a strong spatio-temporal pattern symptomatic of a diffusion process. Whether this process was triggered by adaptation to an exogenous diffused process is less clear, although the importance of mortality, education, and urbanization, and even of migration, have been emphasized in the short and the long terms. There is no doubt that the technical apparatus I have used is too rudimentary to capture the complexities of the historical case of the French fertility decline. However, in the next chapter which gathers the conclusions of this book, the consequences of the results found in the present analysis are put in the light of explanations brought by other authors to the French demographic transition of the nineteenth century.

10

Conclusion: The Feminine Population in the Nineteenth Century

10.1 Reconstructing and Correcting the Data are Essential Steps

A reexamination of the sources to guarantee their book-keeping coherence, and a preliminary correction of the censuses have enabled me to clear the *SGF* data of its most visible demographic inconsistencies. I then imagined a reconstruction which produced the three components of demography: fertility and mortality, as well as migration by age. In return, my method offers the opportunity to eventually correct most of the data: censuses, deaths by age, and births. I have suggested a method of estimating under-registration of births—the eternal Achilles heel of nineteenth-century French data.

The first strength of this method resides in the independence or the weak dependence of the estimation between each age and between each quinquennial period. Neither the imposition of a fixed migratory schedule by age (as is often the case in the literature), nor a condition of continuity from one period to another was necessary. The Ledermann model life tables are among the main foundations of my model; they could be superseded by others, probably producing slightly different results, especially for the estimation of under-registration at birth, and its corollary, those of corrected overall Coale indexes $\tilde{I}_f(t)$.

The second strength of my reconstruction is that populations are reconstructed with *départements*- and time-specific net migration age distributions.

Finally, the third strength of the reconstruction comes, like Van de Walle's method, from its capacity to correct the data: not only births, but also censuses in population sizes and age distributions, and the total number of deaths. The correction of births I have suggested could be disputed; it could also be accused of disturbing traditional beliefs about French de-

mography. The reader is invited to formulate his or her own opinion about
the validity of this exercise in the reconstruction of French demography,
bearing in mind the words of Dyson and Murphy (1985, p. 433): 'to reit-
erate, registration data must always be approached with caution'.

10.2   A Spatio-Temporal Portrayal of the French Transition

In addition to achieving a plausible reconstruction of the French population,
the above analysis has revealed a contrasting transition. Specifically, I have
offered a revision of the position of France in the fertility decline in Europe:
if, as seen, France remained less fertile in the nineteenth century than
England for instance, according to my results, the gap between France and
other European countries would diminish. Subsequently, the shift would be
smaller than has traditionally been thought. France would lose its claimed
position as 'pioneer' to adopt a position as simply one of the most advanced
countries in the decline (subject to the accuracy of estimates in the other
countries).

Another striking result accompanying the important revision of birth
registration is the erasing of the 'ski-jump', an image used by Van de Walle
to denote the baby-boom of the mid-century to the 1870s. My correction of
births supersedes the boom by a regular decline. The ups and downs of data
registration would be the sole factor responsible for the illusion. Although
all my following analysis has been based on a reevaluation of births, my
correction needs further confirmation before considering the ski-jump as a
real mirage.

On this basis, I have suggested a new panorama on mortality, fertility,
and migrations in time and space, by systematically using 'temporal maps':
instead of commenting upon numerous snapshots of the various variables
taken at successive dates, the typology of evolutions has been presented in
single maps. In this manner, evolutions become the object of study more
easily. The salient features emerging from the description have turned out
to support the idea of a diffusion process, be it sustained (innovation wave),
or governed by an adaptation mechanism to the diffused wave of another
system of covariates. This diffusion has revealed a specific pattern: the
existence of three regions, candidates to act as leaders or as diffusive poles,
the importance of an urban-rural order and the emergence of geographical
gradients.

As a consequence of these changing demographic forces, French demographic physiognomy has appeared in a contrasted light: pockets of ageing
people and stagnating populations alternated with compact zones of demographic renewals. This description achieved, the challenge consisted in
identifying and validating a dynamic process underlying the observed evolutions, where the part left to the local influence of various covariates could

be made out from a possible innovative wave running through the territory.

10.3 Improving Local Conditions Starts the Decline, before Innovation Takes its Own Rhythm

I have thus attempted a time series analysis of the transition, in extending my demographic data to markers of urbanization and education. The calculations have shown that the spatial partition of France into relatively homogeneous ensembles can be associated with a stratification in time, marking the following stages of the diffusion throughout the French spatial structure.

In the short term, the depressing influence of the mortality decline was moderated by the rises of education or urbanization in geographical types undertaking their transitions. The influence of these covariates seemed to vanish in a later stage of the decline. Thus, although no baby-boom can be found from my reconstruction, these results bring new evidence to Dyson and Murphy's (1985) statement, according to which the beginning of the decline is accompanied by reduced breastfeeding in urban areas, which in turn favours higher fertility. In France, however, evolutions look to have been very smooth, so that no prominent baby-boom has marked the start of the decline.

Migration played a significant role only in the *département* of Seine, where huge flows of in-migrants could have prevented fertility from falling further.

After these exogenous influences, the examination of the residuals has revealed a characteristic pattern of spatial interactions, bringing numerical precision to the idea of diffusion that could be inferred from the descriptive 'temporal' maps. The research for long-term equilibrium paths has confirmed the tight relationship bringing the various geographical evolutions together, as well as evidence for a long-term connection between fertility and local conditions. Short-term interactions never appeared in the most advanced geographical Types, while patterns are revealed in the rest of France.

The French transition could thus have unfolded as follows: the improvement of mortality provided an opportunity to undergo fewer pregnancies, simply because more children lived longer. A new behaviour was thus rendered possible, which could acquire its own autonomy. At the beginning, the inertia inherent in human behaviour led women to experience increased fertility due to a shorter breastfeeding period. After a while, the new deal imposed by new living conditions was integrated in people's perception of their environment. The wave of decline acquired its own rhythm, under the constraints imposed by mortality or the job market. The process thus became insensitive to constraints, reaction to the environment faded away with the disappearance of drastic conditions. The change then became more and more a question of culture, habit and opinion.

This means that another story would have been possible under the same constraints; only the diffusion of innovative behaviours delineated the particular one I have traced back. Adjustment would thus exist not as a one-to-one determinant, but as a limit to possibilities. At the beginning of the transition, we could say that people are unequivocally driven by these constraints, because their behaviour corresponds to the daily experience of these limits. The further these limits move away, the larger becomes the set of possible behaviours in store for people. Why should they unequivocally follow the change of such or such a variable, if the constraints remain far from the conditions of the moment? Conversely, keeping a large descent would push the demographic system to other limits, which are overcrowding, shortage in resources, joblessness, and so on. In between, there is room for an autonomous innovative wave to appear and to take its own rhythm. Why French people reacted with the speed they did in the context with which they were confronted is a difficult question to which no rigorous answer has ever been given, to my knowledge, and which I am unable to discuss in this monograph. In this present study, I have based my perception of the French area on the powerful tool of time series analysis, where notions such as causality, precedence, or temporal correlations have a precise meaning. This helped me to validate a dynamic system, within the limits of the data set available, which has fostered my present view of the diffusive nature of demographic change.

A

Some Other Examples of Smoothing Operations

Another Example of Female Cohort Age Distributions

Figures A.1, A.2, and A.3 show another example in addition to the example of Figures 4.1, 4.2, and 4.3. This could help the reader to visualize the operation of preliminary smoothing of the censuses used in the reconstruction.

Other Examples of Directly Estimated Probabilities of Dying within a Calendar Quinquennial Period and Fitted Ledermann Probabilities.

The examples presented here have been selected to represent a very urban *département*, Seine, an intermediate urban *département*, Gironde, and a rural one, Creuse, in addition to Finistère on Figure 5.2. The reader can then vizualize the quality of the fit.

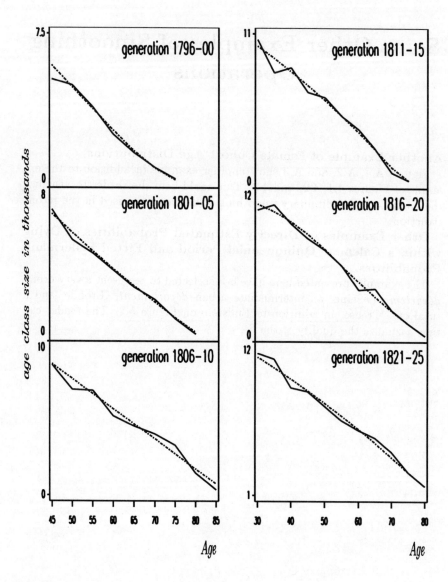

Figure A.1 Example of least squares smoothing by cohorts: *département* of Creuse.

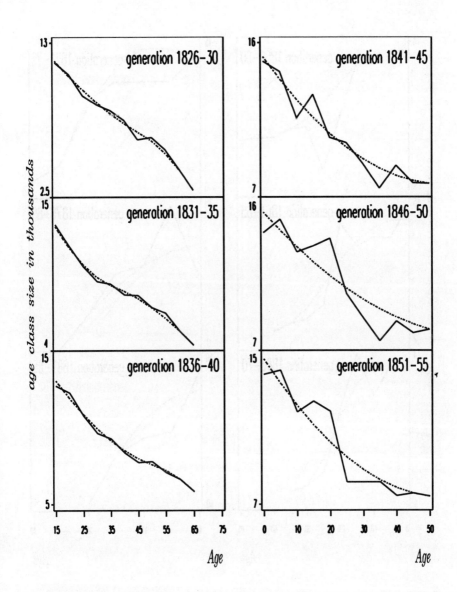

Figure A.2 Example of least squares smoothing by cohorts: *département* of Creuse.

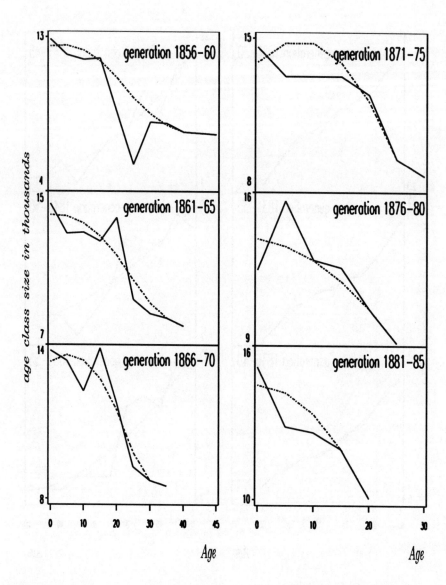

Figure A.3 Example of least squares smoothing by cohorts: *département* of Creuse.

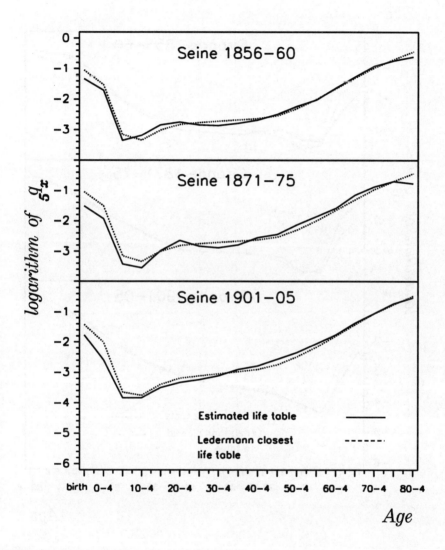

Figure A.4 Example of fit to a Ledermann model life table: *département* of Seine.

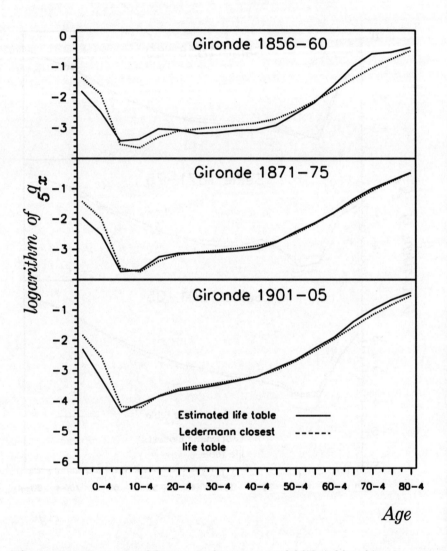

Figure A.5 Example of fit to a Ledermann model life table: *département* of Gironde (city of Bordeaux).

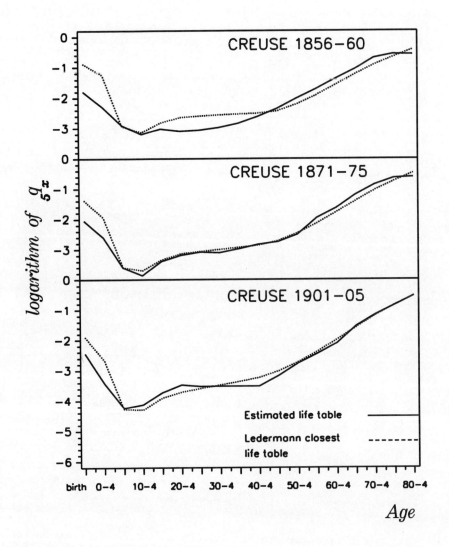

Figure A.6 Example of fit to a Ledermann model life table: *département* of Creuse.

B

References of the Data

Table B.1 References of the census data.

(1) Ministre de l'Agriculture du Commerce et des Travaux Publics. – *Statistique de la France.* – Paris, Imprimerie Impériale, 1855.

(2) Statistique de la France. – *Résultats du dénombrement de la population en 1856.* – Strasbourg, Imprimerie administrative de Vve Berger-Levrault, 1859.

(3) Statistique de la France. – *Résultats généraux du dénombrement de 1861 comparé aux cinq dénombrements antérieurs.* – Strasbourg, Imprimerie administrative de Vve Berger-Levrault, 1864.

(4) Statistique de la France. – *Résultats généraux du dénombrement de 1866.* – Strasbourg, Imprimerie administrative de Vve Berger-Levrault, 1869.

(5) Statistique de la France. – *Résultats généraux du dénombrement de 1872.* – Paris, Imprimerie Nationale, 1873.

(6) Statistique de la France. – *Résultats généraux du dénombrement de 1876.* – Paris, Imprimerie Nationale, 1878.

(7) Ministère du Commerce (Service de la Statistique Générale). – *Résultats statistiques du dénombrement de 1881.* – Paris, Imprimerie Nationale, 1883.

(8) Statistique Générale de la France. – *Résultats statistiques du dénombrement de 1886.* – Paris, Nancy, Berger-Levrault et Cie, 1888.

(9) Statistique Générale de la France. – *Résultats statistiques du dénombrement de 1891.* – Paris, Imprimerie Nationale, 1894.

(10) Statistique Générale de la France. – *Résultats statistiques du dénombrement de 1896.* – Paris, Imprimerie Nationale, 1899.

(11) Ministère du Commerce (Service du Recensement). – *Résultats statistiques du recensement général de la population effectué le 24 mars 1901 (Tome IV).* – Paris, Imprimerie Nationale, 1906.

(12) Ministère du Travail et de la Prévoyance Sociale. – *Résultats statistiques du recensement général de la population effectué le 4 mars 1906 (Tome I).* – Paris, Imprimerie Nationale, 1910.

Table B.2 References of the vital statistics.

(1) Ministre des Travaux Publics de l'Agriculture et du Commerce. – *Statistique de la France : territoire et population.* – Paris, Imprimerie Royale, 1837.

(2) Ministre de l'Agriculture du Commerce et des Travaux Publics. – *Statistique de la France.* – Paris, Imprimerie Impériale, 1855.

(3) Statistique de la France. – *Mouvement de la population pendant les années 1858, 1859, 1860.* – Strasbourg, Imprimerie administrative de Vve Berger-Levrault, 1863. (Ce volume contient un récapitulatif pour les années 1806 à 1859).

(4) Statistique de la France. – *Mouvement de la population en 1851, 1852 et 1853 et pendant l'année 1854.* – Strasbourg, Imprimerie administrative de Vve Berger-Levrault, 1856 *et* 1857.

(5) Statistique de la France. – *Mouvement de la population pendant les années 1861, 1862, 1863, 1864 et 1865.* – Strasbourg, Imprimerie administrative de Vve Berger-Levrault, 1870
Statistique de la France. – *Mouvement de la population pendant les années 1866, 1867 et 1868.* – Paris, Imprimerie Nationale, 1872.

(6) Statistique de la France. – *Nouvelle série, Tome I, Statistique annuelle année 1871.* – Paris, Imprimerie nationale 1874.

(7) Statistique de la France. – *Nouvelle série, Tome II, Statistique annuelle, année 1872.* – Paris, Imprimerie Nationale, 1875. (Et ainsi de suite : *Tome III, [...], année 1873.* – [...] 1876. à *Tome XIV, [...], année 1884.* – [...] 1887.).

(8) Statistique Générale de la France. – *Tome XV, statistique annuelle, année 1885.* Paris, Nancy, Berger-Levrault et Cie, 1888.

(9) Statistique Générale de la France. – *Tomes XVI et XVII, statistique annuelle, années 1886 et 1887.* Paris, Nancy, Berger-Levrault et Cie, 1889.

(10) Statistique Générale de la France. – *Tomes XVIII et XIX, statistique annuelle, années 1888 et 1889.* Paris, Imprimerie Nationale, 1890.
Statistique Générale de la France. – *Tome XX, statistique annuelle, année 1890.* Paris, Imprimerie Nationale, 1891.

(11) Statistique Générale de la France. – *Tomes XXI et XXII, statistique annuelle, années 1891 et 1892.* Paris, Imprimerie Nationale, 1895.
Statistique Générale de la France. – *Tome XXIII, Statistique annuelle, année 1893.* – Paris, Imprimerie Nationale, 1896. (Et ainsi de suite : *Tome XXIV, [...], année 1894.* – [...] 1897. à *Tome XXVI, [...], année 1896.* – [...] 1898.).

(12) Statistique Générale de la France. – *Tome XXVII* et *Tome XXVIII, statistique annuelle, année 1897* et *année 1898.* Paris, Imprimerie Nationale, 1899 *et* 1900.
Statistique Générale de la France. – *Mouvement de la population en 1899-1900.* Paris, Imprimerie Nationale, 1901.
Statistique Générale de la France. – *Mouvement de la population en 1901.* Paris, Imprimerie Nationale, 1902. (and so on: 1902 to 1906)

C

Some Numerical Results

Fertility, Mortality and Migration from 20-24 to 25-29 by *Départements*, 1806-1906.

Table C.1 Data for the seven Types considered.

Type	date t	Coale index at t	Life expect. $[t-5, t-1]$	Migration 20-24 to 25-29 $[t-5, t-1]$	urbaniza-tion at t	% of signed marriage certificates women $[t-5, t-1]$
	1806	0.436	.	.	.	0.750
	1811	0.416	33.0	.	.	0.800
	1816	0.382	33.1	.	.	0.833
	1821	0.380	32.4	.	.	0.500
	1826	0.412	31.8	.	.	0.750
	1831	0.405	32.2	.	0.799	0.933
	1836	0.408	31.0	.	0.904	0.938
	1841	0.366	35.1	.	0.832	0.880
	1846	0.358	35.2	.	0.967	0.900
	1851	0.281	30.9	.	0.979	0.857
1	1856	0.301	30.8	.	0.992	0.844
	1861	0.315	34.7	0.258	1.011	0.852
	1866	0.284	33.3	0.294	1.008	0.947
	1871	0.202	36.7	0.063	1.017	0.925
	1876	0.270	34.5	0.184	0.988	0.931
	1881	0.288	36.9	0.140	1.025	0.947
	1886	0.262	35.9	0.173	1.020	0.978
	1891	0.241	38.2	0.181	0.979	0.984
	1896	0.210	40.2	0.198	0.981	0.995
	1901	0.200	42.2	0.193	1.019	1.000
	1906	0.162	42.9	0.151	1.026	1.000
	1806	0.398	.	.	.	0.284
	1811	0.384	39.1	.	.	0.321
	1816	0.371	39.8	.	.	0.277
	1821	0.333	40.6	.	.	0.340
	1826	0.331	40.3	.	.	0.379
	1831	0.319	39.9	.	0.339	0.412
	1836	0.319	37.5	.	0.339	0.399
	1841	0.289	39.8	.	0.334	0.474
	1846	0.289	40.1	.	0.390	0.497
	1851	0.298	39.4	.	0.443	0.483
2	1856	0.294	38.8	.	0.475	0.543
	1861	0.306	42.3	0.042	0.506	0.590
	1866	0.320	40.1	0.051	0.515	0.660
	1871	0.275	38.0	0.039	0.526	0.725

(continued...)

Numerical Results
Numerical Results

185

Table C.2 Data for the seven Types considered, continuing previous Table.

	1876	0.296	38.2	0.069	0.522	0.785
	1881	0.282	39.5	0.054	0.534	0.848
	1886	0.259	38.2	0.078	0.533	0.905
2	1891	0.232	40.2	0.076	0.546	0.936
	1896	0.225	42.3	0.089	0.553	0.959
	1901	0.220	44.2	0.070	0.551	0.955
	1906	0.189	45.0	0.074	0.553	0.951
	1806	0.330	.	.	.	0.327
	1811	0.321	43.2	.	.	0.360
	1816	0.311	44.1	.	.	0.302
	1821	0.299	46.8	.	.	0.361
	1826	0.286	47.1	.	.	0.356
	1831	0.276	46.4	.	0.135	0.379
	1836	0.259	44.8	.	0.139	0.441
	1841	0.250	47.0	.	0.141	0.472
	1846	0.244	47.4	.	0.157	0.515
	1851	0.255	45.5	.	0.166	0.540
3	1856	0.233	45.4	.	0.176	0.632
	1861	0.234	46.5	-0.020	0.183	0.604
	1866	0.234	47.7	-0.008	0.190	0.696
	1871	0.206	45.8	0.002	0.199	0.739
	1876	0.232	44.6	0.004	0.208	0.852
	1881	0.222	48.5	-0.019	0.225	0.808
	1886	0.216	48.4	-0.015	0.232	0.888
	1891	0.204	48.8	-0.016	0.238	0.948
	1896	0.207	48.6	-0.037	0.246	0.958
	1901	0.212	50.5	-0.052	0.255	0.971
	1906	0.197	50.2	-0.026	0.258	0.984
	1806	0.374	.	.	.	0.351
	1811	0.379	40.6	.	.	0.382
	1816	0.394	40.8	.	.	0.350
	1821	0.364	43.1	.	.	0.369
	1826	0.365	42.1	.	.	0.370
4	1831	0.350	41.0	.	0.150	0.414
	1836	0.335	40.4	.	0.157	0.437
	1841	0.317	42.3	.	0.155	0.450
	1846	0.301	44.0	.	0.176	0.448
	1851	0.317	42.1	.	0.181	0.455
	1856	0.287	41.8	.	0.192	0.498

(continued...)

Appendices

Table C.3 Data for the seven Types considered, continuing previous Table.

	1861	0.287	41.7	-0.017	0.201	0.558
	1866	0.288	44.3	-0.011	0.209	0.594
	1871	0.260	42.3	-0.005	0.218	0.680
	1876	0.284	40.4	-0.001	0.229	0.736
4	1881	0.270	45.7	-0.019	0.245	0.795
	1886	0.256	45.9	-0.022	0.252	0.854
	1891	0.239	46.8	-0.027	0.262	0.878
	1896	0.235	47.3	-0.032	0.271	0.920
	1901	0.240	49.3	-0.053	0.284	0.986
	1906	0.217	49.6	-0.030	0.288	1.000
	1806	0.378	.	.	.	0.194
	1811	0.373	41.2	.	.	0.189
	1816	0.387	42.6	.	.	0.186
	1821	0.379	42.6	.	.	0.210
	1826	0.379	41.9	.	.	0.141
	1831	0.371	41.9	.	0.110	0.182
	1836	0.361	40.4	.	0.120	0.235
	1841	0.356	40.7	.	0.117	0.189
	1846	0.303	43.5	.	0.130	0.316
	1851	0.329	41.2	.	0.124	0.402
5	1856	0.296	40.9	.	0.131	0.294
	1861	0.294	37.6	-0.053	0.137	0.452
	1866	0.302	41.1	-0.039	0.144	0.435
	1871	0.292	42.9	-0.036	0.150	0.548
	1876	0.305	40.8	-0.016	0.157	0.586
	1881	0.285	46.0	-0.051	0.171	0.684
	1886	0.264	44.2	-0.067	0.173	0.880
	1891	0.232	46.8	-0.092	0.180	0.877
	1896	0.239	47.5	-0.121	0.184	0.963
	1901	0.246	48.7	-0.178	0.194	0.960
	1906	0.225	49.8	-0.094	0.199	0.957
	1806	0.441	.	.	.	0.300
	1811	0.426	38.6	.	.	0.274
	1816	0.441	39.5	.	.	0.306
	1821	0.418	38.4	.	.	0.303
6	1826	0.405	39.3	.	.	0.287
	1831	0.404	38.1	.	0.172	0.336
	1836	0.391	37.6	.	0.179	0.344
	1841	0.366	39.0	.	0.179	0.382
	1846	0.353	39.5	.	0.202	0.388

(continued...)

Table C.4 Data for the seven Types considered, continuing previous Table.

	1851	0.361	38.9	.	0.205	0.476
6	1856	0.334	38.6	.	0.218	0.460
	1861	0.337	36.9	-0.016	0.233	0.484
	1866	0.326	38.9	-0.011	0.246	0.571
	1871	0.317	39.7	-0.015	0.261	0.618
	1876	0.341	36.6	0.001	0.273	0.719
	1881	0.319	40.5	-0.025	0.290	0.792
	1886	0.298	40.8	-0.028	0.296	0.834
	1891	0.272	41.7	-0.029	0.304	0.899
	1896	0.271	42.7	-0.044	0.315	0.940
	1901	0.271	45.5	-0.061	0.328	0.953
	1906	0.235	46.2	-0.032	0.334	0.966
	1806	0.543	.	.	.	0.158
	1811	0.539	33.5	.	.	0.154
	1816	0.588	34.0	.	.	0.139
	1821	0.562	32.9	.	.	0.156
	1826	0.552	34.1	.	.	0.141
	1831	0.558	33.4	.	0.111	0.154
	1836	0.516	32.5	.	0.123	0.209
	1841	0.464	33.5	.	0.117	0.185
	1846	0.435	35.9	.	0.137	0.226
	1851	0.464	34.1	.	0.159	0.320
7	1856	0.427	33.5	.	0.164	0.313
	1861	0.410	29.5	-0.034	0.173	0.272
	1866	0.395	32.6	-0.037	0.185	0.378
	1871	0.392	35.0	-0.035	0.190	0.430
	1876	0.408	33.0	-0.010	0.193	0.504
	1881	0.396	36.2	-0.052	0.200	0.531
	1886	0.355	35.9	-0.058	0.203	0.714
	1891	0.331	39.0	-0.071	0.213	0.757
	1896	0.329	39.5	-0.097	0.208	0.832
	1901	0.324	42.5	-0.138	0.225	0.887
	1906	0.274	43.6	-0.070	0.225	0.946

Table C.5 Life Expectancy at Birth.

département	period						
	1806-10	11-15	16-20	21-25	26-30	31-35	36-40
Ain	31.4	34.9	33.1	36.7	33.0	32.6	36.1
Aisne	41.8	41.9	44.9	45.7	44.2	41.9	46.2
Allier	32.8	34.2	37.7	31.4	32.0	34.8	33.8
Alpes(Basses-)	31.5	31.9	32.3	31.1	31.9	29.1	32.3
Alpes(Hautes-)	31.2	29.0	30.8	30.6	29.7	29.1	29.3
Alpes Marit.	.	.	.	.	.	.	.
Ardèche	44.5	44.4	42.5	47.0	42.4	40.6	40.5
Ardennes	43.5	45.0	45.7	48.9	47.5	46.7	48.7
Ariège	43.7	42.3	40.8	43.4	42.0	41.5	42.6
Aube	40.3	42.4	47.2	48.2	46.1	43.7	48.2
Aude	43.8	41.6	40.3	42.1	42.0	40.1	41.4
Aveyron	42.7	44.8	41.4	43.6	44.7	41.4	42.8
Bouches-du-Rh.	37.1	37.8	37.3	36.3	36.9	35.2	38.2
Calvados	47.5	48.1	48.7	47.0	47.3	47.8	49.1
Cantal	37.0	41.6	39.5	41.1	42.0	38.2	40.9
Charente	41.9	39.6	42.5	40.0	40.8	36.8	43.0
Charente-Inf.	42.5	39.3	43.3	41.9	43.5	39.7	44.9
Cher	35.1	35.2	37.8	33.4	29.2	36.4	30.2
Correze	31.3	34.0	34.0	31.9	32.7	29.1	28.5
Corse	32.9	32.5	33.5	36.3	38.1	40.6	42.5
Côte d'Or	43.6	44.4	46.1	46.4	44.4	44.4	48.2
Côtes du Nord	37.1	35.4	32.0	36.9	32.7	32.5	34.9
Creuse	31.1	37.1	38.3	32.3	34.9	36.1	33.1
Dordogne	40.3	40.3	38.9	39.2	40.9	34.6	38.9
Doubs	42.6	40.1	38.8	40.4	39.7	38.9	40.4
Drome	40.4	41.3	40.4	38.9	39.3	38.0	39.8
Eure	46.3	47.7	48.1	46.7	46.8	46.1	47.3
Eure-et-Loir	40.6	43.6	47.6	46.5	45.1	44.2	44.7
Finistère	28.7	30.8	28.7	32.9	29.1	29.5	30.6

Table C.6 Life Expectancy at Birth.

département	period						
	1841-45	46-50	51-55	56-60	61-65	66-70	71-75
Ain	36.2	36.3	36.2	33.6	36.9	40.9	33.9
Aisne	46.2	43.6	42.9	45.5	47.3	45.0	43.9
Allier	38.8	34.5	39.7	32.9	40.2	42.9	41.5
Alpes(Basses-)	32.3	32.3	32.3	29.4	29.8	38.4	35.4
Alpes(Hautes-)	32.3	31.2	30.8	25.5	25.2	33.6	29.9
Alpes Marit.	.	.	.	.	36.8	37.5	35.4
Ardèche	40.9	40.7	38.2	38.2	37.7	38.1	35.4
Ardennes	49.3	46.7	46.1	46.5	49.9	44.7	43.9
Ariège	43.4	41.9	34.8	37.8	40.1	43.0	39.6
Aube	48.8	45.8	44.0	47.3	51.2	47.1	47.2
Aude	42.5	41.7	41.8	39.8	42.0	37.3	38.8
Aveyron	43.7	43.3	40.8	36.4	42.7	43.7	38.4
Bouches-du-Rh.	38.7	38.4	37.6	43.9	38.8	35.7	34.8
Calvados	48.9	47.0	44.9	46.5	44.4	42.9	36.7
Cantal	43.3	42.4	42.4	37.1	39.5	42.3	42.6
Charente	45.3	43.3	39.5	39.1	39.7	36.3	35.8
Charente-Inf.	45.9	41.8	45.4	43.8	45.9	40.7	35.2
Cher	37.8	34.5	38.3	32.8	40.7	39.8	39.2
Correze	33.2	28.1	31.6	26.0	29.1	30.8	29.4
Corse	39.4	39.6	35.0	33.1	33.7	33.9	33.1
Côte d'Or	47.1	45.6	44.1	47.1	50.7	47.7	43.2
Côtes du Nord	37.2	36.4	35.1	32.1	36.8	34.9	33.2
Creuse	40.4	37.5	38.9	30.2	38.9	44.4	41.9
Dordogne	39.5	38.8	40.0	36.5	38.6	37.1	36.3
Doubs	39.4	40.4	36.8	39.8	39.5	38.6	34.9
Drome	40.1	39.2	37.0	36.2	38.0	38.6	36.4
Eure	47.8	46.7	45.5	49.7	50.7	45.6	46.0
Eure-et-Loir	46.1	44.4	46.2	47.0	50.1	45.3	44.2
Finistère	33.8	30.5	30.3	27.6	31.1	26.6	30.1

Appendices

Table C.7 Life Expectancy at Birth.

département	period					
	1876-80	81-85	86-90	91-95	96-1900	01-05
Ain	38.8	40.6	42.5	43.6	45.1	46.1
Aisne	46.4	45.7	46.9	47.0	47.7	48.5
Allier	47.5	49.0	48.3	48.6	51.2	51.3
Alpes(Basses-)	37.0	34.7	37.2	37.9	41.8	43.3
Alpes(Hautes-)	31.0	32.9	34.8	33.8	39.2	42.6
Alpes Marit.	35.0	31.7	36.9	40.5	44.4	45.6
Ardèche	37.3	39.1	39.4	39.9	41.6	43.6
Ardennes	47.8	47.1	48.8	48.7	49.9	49.9
Ariège	46.6	43.2	46.5	45.7	47.4	50.6
Aube	47.6	47.2	47.6	46.7	49.2	49.1
Aude	45.0	42.6	43.8	45.7	47.8	49.5
Aveyron	45.7	40.1	43.2	45.8	47.1	49.5
Bouches-du-Rh.	36.4	33.6	35.6	37.9	39.8	41.9
Calvados	43.9	43.9	43.6	43.7	45.3	45.8
Cantal	48.0	47.6	46.3	49.0	50.2	50.3
Charente	41.0	41.0	47.2	46.8	49.4	50.6
Charente-Infér.	45.7	45.7	48.6	47.8	51.4	50.8
Cher	44.8	46.6	46.8	48.8	49.9	49.5
Correze	36.8	33.2	42.9	43.7	47.9	49.0
Corse	31.9	31.0	39.1	37.2	38.4	41.8
Côte d'Or	49.8	49.5	49.7	49.4	50.7	50.8
Côtes du Nord	39.6	40.4	38.4	39.9	40.4	39.3
Creuse	47.9	49.3	49.1	49.8	51.5	52.2
Dordogne	44.0	44.7	43.1	45.0	49.3	50.0
Doubs	39.1	38.5	41.7	41.7	42.3	42.2
Drome	39.5	38.7	40.2	40.9	44.7	45.6
Eure	49.6	49.3	48.1	45.3	48.8	48.4
Eure-et-Loir	48.9	48.9	48.5	47.2	49.1	49.1
Finistère	32.4	29.8	32.4	35.0	38.4	39.5

Table C.8 Life Expectancy at Birth.

département	period						
	1806-10	11-15	16-20	21-25	26-30	31-35	36-40
Gard	43.7	43.1	42.6	43.0	45.7	48.5	42.8
Garonne(Haute-)	42.7	44.4	42.3	44.7	45.9	45.4	46.0
Gers	41.9	41.9	44.1	44.2	45.8	40.7	43.2
Gironde	35.7	36.7	43.8	43.4	42.9	36.7	42.3
Hérault	45.5	44.8	42.5	42.7	40.3	39.3	39.7
Ille-et-Vilaine	37.8	39.9	35.5	36.8	33.4	33.2	37.7
Indre	32.9	36.1	37.8	33.1	33.7	37.8	31.1
Indre-et-Loire	42.3	46.5	48.0	45.8	42.7	44.3	45.5
Isère	34.8	35.6	34.3	33.9	33.3	34.2	34.1
Jura	34.7	36.2	33.4	37.4	34.4	33.8	35.2
Landes	32.5	34.5	34.2	36.7	36.7	32.8	31.1
Loire-et-Cher	37.9	40.1	44.6	40.5	38.2	40.6	40.7
Loire	35.4	37.5	35.1	36.0	34.9	36.0	36.3
Loire(Haute-)	35.4	35.9	32.8	33.6	36.2	34.7	37.0
Loire-Infér.	44.0	42.8	46.4	45.6	39.9	37.1	44.4
Loiret	35.6	37.6	39.8	40.7	38.5	39.4	38.2
Lot	48.4	48.2	46.0	45.9	46.3	39.8	43.9
Lot-et-Garonne	45.6	44.2	47.2	48.5	49.5	45.3	46.7
Lozère	40.2	39.6	34.7	37.6	39.8	36.1	37.7
Maine-et-Loire	42.3	41.4	44.7	42.7	39.8	38.9	42.6
Manche	40.3	41.3	42.6	43.0	40.2	42.4	44.2
Marne	41.5	40.5	43.3	45.2	44.8	40.7	45.8
Marne(Haute-)	45.0	40.9	50.1	51.2	49.6	45.0	49.1
Mayenne	32.2	36.0	37.3	37.8	33.9	36.1	36.8
Meurthe	41.2	39.4	41.5	43.4	42.8	40.8	43.1
Meurthe-et-Mos.	.	.	.	.	.	.	.
Meuse	41.4	39.6	42.2	46.0	45.3	42.3	45.9
Morbihan	28.4	30.2	27.4	32.1	29.2	30.2	32.3
Moselle	42.4	39.3	43.6	49.1	45.9	43.8	44.3
Nièvre	33.4	36.0	36.9	36.4	30.9	35.0	34.7

Table C.9 Life Expectancy at Birth.

département	period						
	1841-45	46-50	51-55	56-60	61-65	66-70	71-75
Gard	42.4	41.8	39.0	39.8	40.8	40.8	38.3
Garonne(Haute-)	46.3	41.7	41.0	41.7	42.8	45.1	45.1
Gers	44.3	40.9	46.6	43.1	42.2	42.8	41.7
Gironde	42.0	40.7	44.0	41.1	41.9	43.3	42.6
Hérault	39.4	38.6	35.8	47.0	45.7	34.7	37.7
Ille-et-Vilaine	39.3	40.2	38.2	36.9	38.1	40.4	34.7
Indre	38.7	37.0	37.6	32.9	42.8	41.4	41.1
Indre-et-Loire	46.7	43.3	47.0	44.5	46.4	44.3	43.3
Isère	35.3	36.2	36.0	26.5	32.4	40.1	35.1
Jura	34.5	35.5	31.9	34.0	33.6	37.3	37.4
Landes	32.9	33.2	39.5	31.7	38.5	42.0	33.0
Loire-et-Cher	45.9	43.3	45.9	41.8	46.5	43.8	41.3
Loire	37.4	36.2	38.1	30.2	36.6	39.4	36.3
Loire(Haute-)	37.7	35.0	36.3	33.5	32.5	39.0	36.3
Loire-Infér.	44.1	41.8	42.6	41.5	45.5	41.4	44.4
Loiret	44.0	41.4	42.0	40.1	44.1	41.7	41.2
Lot	44.8	43.5	43.3	44.9	43.0	45.9	41.7
Lot-et-Garonne	45.9	45.9	48.7	47.3	47.4	43.8	46.2
Lozère	39.7	39.1	38.1	33.8	36.7	37.9	35.1
Maine-et-Loire	42.0	40.7	43.6	40.8	43.0	41.3	37.1
Manche	44.6	42.2	41.8	40.4	43.8	40.9	38.1
Marne	44.8	44.3	40.7	47.7	48.1	44.4	36.4
Marne(Haute-)	49.3	48.9	39.1	49.2	49.2	45.8	42.3
Mayenne	40.1	41.0	39.6	36.5	37.3	38.1	35.0
Meurthe	42.8	42.9	38.7	45.7	45.1	.	.
Meurthe-et-Mos.	.	.	.	.	.	.	43.4
Meuse	45.2	44.9	40.1	48.1	50.7	44.0	45.0
Morbihan	36.7	33.8	32.9	26.7	36.5	34.8	33.2
Moselle	45.8	46.1	43.1	45.4	44.4	.	.
Nièvre	39.3	35.2	40.0	36.6	39.4	38.2	38.3

Table C.10 Life Expectancy at Birth.

département	period					
	1876-80	81-85	86-90	91-95	96-1900	01-05
Gard	39.7	43.2	41.6	41.9	44.1	45.4
Garonne(Haute-)	45.9	45.9	45.7	47.0	48.9	49.0
Gers	47.4	47.6	47.4	48.5	52.0	53.0
Gironde	45.1	42.6	44.7	47.4	50.0	50.8
Hérault	40.0	41.7	42.4	44.3	45.7	46.1
Ille-et-Vilaine	41.4	39.0	39.2	39.9	42.9	43.4
Indre	45.8	47.0	48.6	48.6	50.1	51.2
Indre-et-Loire	48.6	49.3	49.3	49.5	52.1	51.3
Isère	39.0	42.9	39.8	40.2	45.4	46.5
Jura	38.9	38.8	38.3	40.2	43.0	43.1
Landes	35.1	37.0	39.8	46.6	51.5	51.5
Loire-et-Cher	49.8	50.0	51.7	50.8	53.5	53.5
Loire	39.4	40.0	42.3	42.4	43.3	44.4
Loire(Haute-)	41.6	39.9	40.0	41.9	44.6	44.6
Loire-Infér.	42.2	44.2	42.4	44.8	48.3	48.2
Loiret	47.8	49.2	49.3	49.3	51.9	51.3
Lot	44.3	38.8	48.4	46.2	45.8	47.9
Lot-et-Gar.	49.0	50.2	51.6	51.3	52.8	52.1
Lozère	26.2	28.2	41.8	43.1	44.5	45.0
Maine-et-Loire	43.3	44.0	44.2	46.2	49.4	48.6
Manche	42.7	39.0	38.8	39.6	43.4	45.6
Marne	46.8	46.2	46.7	46.7	47.9	47.6
Marne(Haute-)	47.9	46.0	48.0	50.3	50.4	50.0
Mayenne	40.7	39.5	42.7	41.7	44.2	44.2
Meurthe	.	.	.	.	.	.
Meurthe-et-Moselle	.	.	.	.	.	43.4
Meuse	46.1	44.9	45.4	46.4	48.7	49.4
Morbihan	41.9	41.6	40.3	40.5	44.7	45.1
Moselle	.	.	.	.	.	.
Nièvre	44.4	43.7	46.9	48.1	49.2	49.4

Table C.11 Life Expectancy at Birth.

département	period						
	1806-10	11-15	16-20	21-25	26-30	31-35	36-40
Nord	43.0	43.1	42.3	43.0	41.0	38.9	42.1
Oise	40.4	40.7	44.4	44.7	44.1	42.6	45.4
Orne	42.9	46.0	48.3	49.4	48.5	49.1	49.8
Pas-de-Calais	43.3	44.4	45.0	45.0	42.3	39.4	43.7
Puy-de-Dome	33.6	37.0	36.0	36.0	35.8	35.8	37.6
Pyr.(Basses-)	43.6	41.9	46.9	42.6	44.2	44.0	41.8
Pyr.(Hautes-)	50.0	48.7	51.3	49.9	50.5	47.3	45.6
Pyr.-Orient.	40.0	41.4	39.2	39.4	38.2	39.7	39.5
Rhin(Bas-)	37.1	36.2	40.5	41.9	39.7	38.0	38.7
Rhin(Haut-)	42.8	38.9	42.7	41.6	39.7	39.6	38.3
Rhône	32.9	33.2	32.2	31.0	29.8	31.8	31.4
Saône(Haute-)	38.1	39.1	41.5	40.6	41.2	40.6	42.9
Saône-et-Loire	35.2	37.6	38.2	39.3	34.6	37.5	39.5
Sarthe	37.1	40.9	46.2	43.4	37.9	42.3	43.6
Savoie	.	.	.	.	.	.	.
Savoie(Haute-)	.	.	.	.	.	.	.
Seine	33.0	33.1	32.4	31.8	32.2	31.0	35.1
Seine-et-Marne	40.1	40.9	46.1	43.2	42.7	39.2	44.9
Seine-et-Oise	43.3	45.2	46.3	44.7	45.4	42.6	45.6
Seine-Infér.	48.0	46.5	46.6	46.6	46.0	44.2	43.8
Sèvres(Deux-)	43.7	42.2	44.5	42.4	41.8	40.9	44.0
Somme	43.9	42.4	44.1	46.2	44.9	42.3	44.8
Tarn	45.5	42.9	41.9	44.7	44.6	42.0	44.7
Tarn-et-Gar.	46.6	45.4	45.9	47.6	48.6	44.9	47.5
Var	40.2	40.8	41.5	43.8	44.2	39.4	41.6
Vaucluse	43.5	41.5	40.3	40.0	41.2	40.3	39.7
Vendée	36.9	37.6	34.0	35.2	34.3	34.6	38.9
Vienne	46.8	48.9	50.7	45.6	44.7	42.0	41.5
Vienne(Haute-)	29.1	31.9	32.6	24.6	28.8	28.4	26.8
Vosges	38.9	40.6	41.3	43.4	40.8	38.5	40.6
Yonne	40.3	42.0	46.9	45.6	43.5	43.9	47.2
Terr. de Belfort	.	.	.	.	.	.	.
France	36.0	40.0	40.8	41.0	39.9	38.8	40.6

Table C.12 Life Expectancy at Birth.

département	period						
	1841-45	46-50	51-55	56-60	61-65	66-70	71-75
Nord	42.5	39.4	41.4	42.1	43.0	37.9	38.4
Oise	46.7	42.8	42.1	45.1	46.9	43.8	44.3
Orne	51.2	51.8	48.7	46.4	44.9	46.0	42.1
Pas-de-Calais	43.8	41.7	43.4	44.1	44.1	39.9	40.4
Puy-de-Dome	38.4	36.5	37.5	33.7	36.5	39.7	38.2
Pyr.(Basses-)	44.8	40.2	40.1	37.9	42.1	43.1	40.6
Pyr.(Hautes-)	48.2	45.3	47.1	40.1	42.9	42.6	43.5
Pyr.-Orient.	39.0	39.0	37.4	38.3	37.2	40.1	38.6
Rhin(Bas-)	40.0	39.8	39.3	39.3	37.7	.	.
Rhin(Haut-)	39.8	40.6	38.0	41.3	37.6	.	.
Rhône	32.4	33.1	31.4	30.1	32.8	33.8	35.3
Saône(Haute-)	42.3	43.2	34.0	43.9	44.4	44.5	40.5
Saône-et-Loire	39.9	39.1	41.7	36.0	40.7	42.3	37.3
Sarthe	43.6	43.4	43.2	42.9	45.2	42.9	38.7
Savoie	.	.	.	.	31.0	37.4	35.6
Savoie(Haute-)	.	.	.	.	33.8	41.3	35.2
Seine	35.2	30.9	30.8	34.7	33.3	36.7	34.5
Seine-et-Marne	45.7	45.3	42.8	49.0	49.3	44.5	44.8
Seine-et-Oise	45.8	43.9	44.8	47.7	44.1	42.6	41.1
Seine-Infér.	43.2	41.8	40.4	43.2	43.4	39.3	34.6
Sèvres(Deux-)	44.2	41.5	43.4	39.8	41.1	42.2	38.9
Somme	43.8	43.0	43.4	44.8	45.2	40.9	41.5
Tarn	45.7	45.1	43.4	42.0	43.0	46.1	42.0
Tarn-et-Gar.	48.3	45.8	48.8	45.7	45.3	47.3	45.9
Var	42.0	41.8	39.2	44.2	40.9	38.2	40.8
Vaucluse	40.9	42.6	39.3	42.6	42.1	40.5	39.8
Vendée	39.6	36.2	39.8	35.3	39.7	38.0	36.2
Vienne	45.6	42.1	43.2	39.1	41.2	42.9	39.1
Vienne(Haute-)	33.8	28.9	31.0	22.6	29.3	32.4	30.3
Vosges	41.6	40.5	36.0	38.3	39.4	42.5	38.5
Yonne	46.9	45.3	45.0	48.4	51.2	49.0	47.8
Terr. de Belfort	.	.	.	.	.	.	34.0
France	41.6	40.0	39.7	38.9	41.0	39.9	38.5

Table C.13 Life Expectancy at Birth.

département	period					
	76-80	81-85	86-90	91-95	96-1900	01-05
Nord	42.3	42.8	44.3	44.8	47.0	46.5
Oise	46.5	44.9	46.3	45.6	46.0	47.5
Orne	45.7	46.1	48.3	46.0	48.2	46.6
Pas-de-Calais	41.8	39.9	44.3	45.6	46.6	47.3
Puy-de-Dome	41.6	42.2	44.7	45.8	49.4	50.1
Pyr.(Basses-)	45.0	43.7	46.5	48.1	50.4	50.9
Pyr.(Hautes-)	46.3	47.0	47.9	47.0	47.9	47.8
Pyrénées-Orient.	39.6	36.6	43.7	44.0	46.0	46.9
Rhin(Bas-)	.	.	.	.	.	.
Rhin(Haut-)	.	.	.	.	.	.
Rhône	36.9	37.6	39.5	39.9	42.8	43.1
Saône(Haute-)	46.5	46.0	45.0	46.6	47.0	47.3
Saône-et-Loire	45.0	45.8	44.4	45.2	47.2	48.1
Sarthe	45.9	47.2	48.0	46.8	49.0	48.2
Savoie	40.2	36.9	40.1	40.9	44.8	44.5
Savoie(Haute-)	40.4	40.4	38.3	39.3	42.7	41.8
Seine	36.9	35.9	38.2	40.2	42.2	42.9
Seine-et-Marne	48.2	47.6	48.5	48.4	49.4	49.9
Seine-et-Oise	43.4	42.7	43.1	42.1	43.7	43.6
Seine-Infér.	38.6	40.9	41.3	40.5	43.3	45.1
Sèvres(Deux-)	45.8	45.3	46.7	47.8	50.3	51.3
Somme	44.8	44.7	45.4	45.6	46.8	47.7
Tarn	48.6	49.8	47.9	49.3	51.1	52.0
Tarn-et-Gar.	50.6	50.7	50.1	51.8	53.3	51.6
Var	39.9	37.8	39.4	43.8	42.8	43.6
Vaucluse	39.9	40.0	38.7	42.2	45.1	44.9
Vendée	41.1	45.1	44.4	44.3	48.5	49.4
Vienne	45.3	47.9	48.1	48.6	50.8	51.2
Vienne(Haute-)	40.0	42.1	43.1	42.9	45.2	47.6
Vosges	42.9	43.9	43.8	43.5	47.0	48.6
Yonne	50.9	49.9	50.8	50.1	51.0	51.2
Terr. de Belfort	31.5	34.2	41.7	42.9	46.1	46.9
France	42.6	42.3	43.9	44.6	46.6	46.9

Table C.14 Overall Coale Index $\tilde{I}_f$.

département	date						
	1806	1811	1816	1821	1826	1831	1836
Ain	0.524	0.443	0.500	0.540	0.475	0.471	0.418
Aisne	0.318	0.367	0.378	0.347	0.350	0.330	0.298
Allier	0.534	0.540	0.562	0.511	0.614	0.559	0.441
Alpes(Basses-)	0.498	0.490	0.598	0.474	0.494	0.487	0.493
Alpes(Hautes-)	0.495	0.558	0.628	0.573	0.568	0.591	0.588
Alpes Maritimes	.	.	.	.	.	.	.
Ardèche	0.329	0.311	0.373	0.350	0.372	0.393	0.412
Ardennes	0.322	0.363	0.322	0.326	0.346	0.310	0.306
Ariège	0.316	0.334	0.343	0.396	0.407	0.397	0.380
Aube	0.334	0.321	0.307	0.332	0.318	0.281	0.275
Aude	0.350	0.376	0.430	0.403	0.358	0.365	0.338
Aveyron	0.357	0.323	0.391	0.359	0.349	0.336	0.334
Bouches-du-Rhône	0.391	0.369	0.350	0.348	0.349	0.319	0.367
Calvados	0.246	0.239	0.194	0.242	0.233	0.244	0.254
Cantal	0.343	0.332	0.342	0.349	0.332	0.346	0.357
Charente	0.368	0.379	0.447	0.359	0.330	0.303	0.338
Charente-Infér.	0.344	0.323	0.400	0.358	0.359	0.321	0.309
Cher	0.593	0.495	0.574	0.507	0.540	0.520	0.487
Correze	0.662	0.592	0.608	0.641	0.514	0.544	0.634
Corse	0.606	0.502	0.561	0.475	0.640	0.574	0.439
Côte d'Or	0.298	0.322	0.310	0.305	0.302	0.296	0.294
Côtes du Nord	0.425	0.439	0.537	0.522	0.460	0.531	0.397
Creuse	0.528	0.568	0.550	0.517	0.526	0.501	0.449
Dordogne	0.410	0.390	0.445	0.385	0.380	0.351	0.406
Doubs	0.402	0.406	0.419	0.418	0.383	0.352	0.374
Drome	0.404	0.378	0.425	0.374	0.352	0.331	0.415
Eure	0.306	0.259	0.251	0.246	0.246	0.234	0.229
Eure-et-Loir	0.296	0.291	0.313	0.307	0.292	0.292	0.263
Finistère	0.649	0.709	0.749	0.723	0.781	0.664	0.613

Table C.15 Overall Coale Index $\tilde{I}_f$.

département	date						
	1806	1811	1816	1821	1826	1831	1836
Gard	0.370	0.379	0.383	0.361	0.359	0.337	0.310
Garonne(Haute-)	0.408	0.382	0.358	0.384	0.325	0.315	0.267
Gers	0.344	0.322	0.351	0.311	0.278	0.294	0.233
Gironde	0.351	0.315	0.326	0.294	0.274	0.289	0.286
Hérault	0.380	0.354	0.316	0.255	0.256	0.241	0.245
Ille-et-Vilaine	0.510	0.428	0.439	0.458	0.434	0.430	0.372
Indre	0.507	0.570	0.531	0.464	0.478	0.468	0.449
Indre-et-Loire	0.379	0.341	0.360	0.299	0.290	0.294	0.260
Isère	0.482	0.455	0.487	0.498	0.523	0.542	0.505
Jura	0.492	0.414	0.421	0.426	0.371	0.372	0.416
Landes	0.690	0.674	0.586	0.567	0.464	0.458	0.422
Loire-et-Cher	0.378	0.384	0.390	0.343	0.350	0.351	0.352
Loire	0.519	0.532	0.548	0.554	0.574	0.568	0.493
Loire(Haute-)	0.436	0.438	0.481	0.509	0.448	0.453	0.465
Loire-Infér.	0.369	0.387	0.421	0.381	0.369	0.372	0.329
Loiret	0.384	0.423	0.415	0.362	0.368	0.379	0.357
Lot	0.329	0.301	0.326	0.276	0.276	0.278	0.294
Lot-et-Gar.	0.313	0.310	0.312	0.267	0.263	0.239	0.240
Lozère	0.293	0.323	0.395	0.390	0.364	0.363	0.398
Maine-et-Loire	0.365	0.374	0.379	0.337	0.340	0.377	0.323
Manche	0.313	0.331	0.327	0.283	0.279	0.300	0.262
Marne	0.340	0.358	0.322	0.318	0.323	0.307	0.295
Marne(Haute-)	0.319	0.335	0.323	0.304	0.301	0.283	0.287
Mayenne	0.440	0.426	0.450	0.383	0.390	0.424	0.392
Meurthe	0.367	0.366	0.344	0.330	0.321	0.306	0.305
Meurthe-et-Moselle	.	.	.	.	.	.	.
Meuse	0.361	0.389	0.352	0.341	0.331	0.277	0.318
Morbihan	0.641	0.598	0.654	0.652	0.571	0.689	0.519
Moselle	0.353	0.397	0.345	0.375	0.356	0.345	0.350
Nièvre	0.546	0.513	0.509	0.507	0.512	0.532	0.476

Table C.16 Overall Coale Index $\tilde{I}_f$.

département	date						
	1806	1811	1816	1821	1826	1831	1836
Nord	0.364	0.370	0.400	0.367	0.375	0.375	0.395
Oise	0.324	0.319	0.327	0.288	0.284	0.277	0.267
Orne	0.330	0.345	0.266	0.249	0.232	0.233	0.232
Pas-de-Calais	0.338	0.329	0.346	0.332	0.333	0.338	0.343
Puy-de-Dome	0.379	0.361	0.411	0.407	0.409	0.412	0.410
Pyrénées(Basses-)	0.318	0.328	0.311	0.317	0.312	0.298	0.307
Pyrénées(Hautes-)	0.291	0.282	0.329	0.315	0.318	0.280	0.289
Pyrénées-Orient.	0.454	0.477	0.449	0.397	0.397	0.409	0.386
Rhin(Bas-)	0.407	0.452	0.381	0.383	0.368	0.379	0.368
Rhin(Haut-)	0.432	0.440	0.397	0.402	0.409	0.372	0.405
Rhône	0.569	0.553	0.536	0.515	0.525	0.465	0.448
Saône(Haute-)	0.375	0.361	0.376	0.501	0.378	0.344	0.336
Saône-et-Loire	0.423	0.409	0.439	0.362	0.419	0.444	0.413
Sarthe	0.367	0.359	0.356	0.309	0.346	0.307	0.284
Savoie	.	.	.	.	.	.	.
Savoie(Haute-)	.	.	.	.	.	.	.
Seine	0.436	0.416	0.382	0.380	0.412	0.405	0.408
Seine-et-Marne	0.354	0.340	0.361	0.334	0.314	0.316	0.299
Seine-et-Oise	0.305	0.322	0.306	0.270	0.271	0.266	0.247
Seine-Infér.	0.324	0.315	0.327	0.316	0.338	0.320	0.286
Sèvres(Deux-)	0.380	0.352	0.428	0.333	0.367	0.331	0.340
Somme	0.329	0.335	0.338	0.303	0.307	0.301	0.284
Tarn	0.346	0.348	0.355	0.335	0.345	0.332	0.325
Tarn-et-Gar.	0.304	0.283	0.273	0.252	0.260	0.260	0.239
Var	0.392	0.389	0.392	0.316	0.311	0.337	0.321
Vaucluse	0.455	0.394	0.423	0.383	0.367	0.356	0.320
Vendée	0.528	0.566	0.570	0.489	0.480	0.484	0.434
Vienne	0.346	0.364	0.390	0.336	0.317	0.306	0.311
Vienne(Haute-)	0.836	0.871	0.776	0.820	0.759	0.743	0.666
Vosges	0.387	0.386	0.407	0.378	0.358	0.365	0.386
Yonne	0.332	0.340	0.311	0.337	0.323	0.289	0.294
Terr. de Belfort	.	.	.	.	.	.	.
France	0.393	0.396	0.389	0.370	0.383	0.369	0.341

Table C.17 Overall Coale Index $\tilde{I}_f$.

département	date						
	1841	1846	1851	1856	1861	1866	1871
Ain	0.393	0.371	0.369	0.304	0.303	0.288	0.311
Aisne	0.289	0.281	0.298	0.259	0.280	0.275	0.241
Allier	0.447	0.355	0.418	0.371	0.348	0.332	0.288
Alpes(Basses-)	0.404	0.413	0.451	0.388	0.398	0.354	0.344
Alpes(Hautes-)	0.456	0.496	0.522	0.464	0.467	0.380	0.445
Alpes Maritimes	.	.	.	.	0.326	0.362	0.355
Ardèche	0.398	0.373	0.380	0.353	0.362	0.356	0.369
Ardennes	0.294	0.275	0.282	0.253	0.270	0.280	0.243
Ariège	0.365	0.299	0.356	0.318	0.313	0.300	0.299
Aube	0.250	0.257	0.248	0.246	0.230	0.217	0.186
Aude	0.293	0.280	0.288	0.287	0.304	0.347	0.260
Aveyron	0.332	0.311	0.322	0.355	0.330	0.344	0.340
Bouches-du-Rhône	0.333	0.353	0.385	0.349	0.374	0.385	0.347
Calvados	0.230	0.216	0.218	0.217	0.224	0.234	0.232
Cantal	0.334	0.291	0.305	0.281	0.279	0.299	0.306
Charente	0.229	0.295	0.284	0.279	0.277	0.270	0.263
Charente-Infér.	0.249	0.249	0.275	0.245	0.268	0.263	0.246
Cher	0.506	0.452	0.506	0.413	0.376	0.370	0.303
Correze	0.492	0.496	0.513	0.451	0.478	0.412	0.428
Corse	0.442	0.403	0.431	0.408	0.375	0.415	0.369
Côte d'Or	0.273	0.270	0.275	0.253	0.246	0.235	0.212
Côtes du Nord	0.405	0.385	0.419	0.380	0.389	0.415	0.378
Creuse	0.468	0.313	0.343	0.291	0.277	0.284	0.313
Dordogne	0.335	0.321	0.347	0.303	0.331	0.327	0.303
Doubs	0.350	0.337	0.349	0.304	0.324	0.336	0.297
Drome	0.396	0.373	0.337	0.325	0.317	0.302	0.302
Eure	0.220	0.223	0.240	0.215	0.230	0.234	0.213
Eure-et-Loir	0.273	0.277	0.282	0.277	0.269	0.264	0.240
Finistère	0.544	0.500	0.535	0.472	0.463	0.531	0.500

Table C.18 Overall Coale Index $\tilde{I}_f$.

département	date						
	1841	1846	1851	1856	1861	1866	1871
Gard	0.350	0.364	0.332	0.341	0.330	0.326	0.293
Garonne(Haute-)	0.270	0.245	0.276	0.235	0.228	0.224	0.175
Gers	0.258	0.234	0.251	0.210	0.231	0.230	0.210
Gironde	0.225	0.245	0.242	0.237	0.249	0.250	0.227
Hérault	0.246	0.253	0.255	0.276	0.274	0.336	0.242
Ille-et-Vilaine	0.313	0.348	0.351	0.313	0.323	0.310	0.329
Indre	0.460	0.369	0.413	0.375	0.331	0.341	0.295
Indre-et-Loire	0.249	0.236	0.245	0.235	0.230	0.247	0.219
Isère	0.465	0.408	0.401	0.400	0.389	0.295	0.309
Jura	0.390	0.368	0.405	0.318	0.342	0.315	0.309
Landes	0.374	0.388	0.428	0.381	0.354	0.342	0.332
Loire-et-Cher	0.319	0.329	0.340	0.285	0.291	0.292	0.250
Loire	0.444	0.412	0.406	0.467	0.387	0.355	0.336
Loire(Haute-)	0.446	0.383	0.401	0.360	0.374	0.350	0.346
Loire-Infér.	0.300	0.294	0.297	0.299	0.312	0.309	0.277
Loiret	0.357	0.321	0.345	0.333	0.302	0.306	0.263
Lot	0.260	0.261	0.268	0.237	0.257	0.252	0.227
Lot-et-Gar.	0.206	0.208	0.213	0.199	0.209	0.216	0.189
Lozère	0.410	0.385	0.405	0.429	0.400	0.397	0.418
Maine-et-Loire	0.298	0.309	0.286	0.258	0.256	0.260	0.253
Manche	0.276	0.269	0.289	0.281	0.275	0.281	0.278
Marne	0.280	0.281	0.300	0.276	0.264	0.263	0.297
Marne(Haute-)	0.247	0.242	0.269	0.255	0.242	0.247	0.215
Mayenne	0.354	0.333	0.339	0.306	0.308	0.308	0.309
Meurthe	0.298	0.279	0.312	0.255	0.271	.	.
Meurthe-et-Moselle	.	.	.	.	.	.	0.224
Meuse	0.302	0.273	0.306	0.253	0.245	0.249	0.212
Morbihan	0.475	0.422	0.457	0.424	0.383	0.371	0.368
Moselle	0.336	0.320	0.337	0.302	0.314	.	.
Nièvre	0.480	0.434	0.453	0.346	0.353	0.362	0.308

Table C.19 Overall Coale Index $\tilde{I}_f$.

département	\multicolumn{7}{c}{date}
	1841	1846	1851	1856	1861	1866	1871
Nord	0.351	0.350	0.393	0.364	0.377	0.424	0.384
Oise	0.281	0.269	0.291	0.252	0.260	0.260	0.240
Orne	0.220	0.209	0.221	0.205	0.205	0.206	0.199
Pas-de-Calais	0.323	0.325	0.335	0.318	0.336	0.371	0.342
Puy-de-Dome	0.401	0.355	0.349	0.306	0.296	0.276	0.270
Pyrénées(Basses-)	0.323	0.278	0.318	0.280	0.289	0.316	0.294
Pyrénées(Hautes-)	0.284	0.238	0.270	0.263	0.251	0.263	0.245
Pyrénées-Orient.	0.391	0.410	0.358	0.351	0.385	0.357	0.341
Rhin(Bas-)	0.385	0.361	0.402	0.339	0.371	.	.
Rhin(Haut-)	0.393	0.352	0.408	0.362	0.391	.	.
Rhône	0.389	0.348	0.351	0.362	0.339	0.317	0.249
Saône(Haute-)	0.317	0.277	0.311	0.263	0.277	0.272	0.274
Saône-et-Loire	0.391	0.359	0.381	0.349	0.328	0.339	0.336
Sarthe	0.265	0.267	0.279	0.243	0.237	0.255	0.234
Savoie	.	.	.	.	0.399	0.366	0.337
Savoie(Haute-)	.	.	.	.	0.371	0.349	0.365
Seine	0.366	0.358	0.281	0.301	0.315	0.284	0.202
Seine-et-Marne	0.304	0.288	0.326	0.294	0.291	0.285	0.234
Seine-et-Oise	0.250	0.257	0.268	0.267	0.272	0.283	0.218
Seine-Infér.	0.262	0.269	0.268	0.273	0.306	0.303	0.314
Sèvres(Deux-)	0.295	0.311	0.291	0.272	0.325	0.299	0.289
Somme	0.289	0.299	0.321	0.268	0.258	0.287	0.238
Tarn	0.309	0.276	0.294	0.263	0.284	0.284	0.254
Tarn-et-Gar.	0.233	0.231	0.238	0.214	0.233	0.240	0.205
Var	0.291	0.275	0.287	0.274	0.308	0.310	0.290
Vaucluse	0.334	0.329	0.336	0.325	0.316	0.295	0.287
Vendée	0.403	0.389	0.413	0.342	0.339	0.316	0.328
Vienne	0.290	0.297	0.299	0.329	0.311	0.294	0.279
Vienne(Haute-)	0.612	0.478	0.525	0.496	0.435	0.390	0.379
Vosges	0.338	0.306	0.340	0.285	0.330	0.307	0.267
Yonne	0.299	0.304	0.310	0.247	0.251	0.247	0.214
Terr. de Belfort	.	.	.	.	.	.	0.365
France	0.329	0.336	0.316	0.307	0.311	0.309	0.281

Table **C.20** Overall Coale Index $\tilde{I}_f$.

département	date						
	1876	1881	1886	1891	1896	1901	1906
Ain	0.318	0.285	0.265	0.249	0.256	0.263	0.221
Aisne	0.285	0.277	0.260	0.263	0.263	0.270	0.249
Allier	0.309	0.267	0.241	0.229	0.224	0.220	0.184
Alpes(Basses-)	0.348	0.363	0.313	0.287	0.293	0.302	0.256
Alpes(Hautes-)	0.444	0.404	0.374	0.356	0.326	0.317	0.275
Alpes Maritimes	0.367	0.382	0.339	0.258	0.235	0.203	0.193
Ardèche	0.358	0.359	0.337	0.319	0.312	0.296	0.265
Ardennes	0.289	0.282	0.255	0.236	0.239	0.250	0.233
Ariège	0.306	0.293	0.268	0.237	0.247	0.243	0.215
Aube	0.229	0.221	0.227	0.229	0.221	0.219	0.199
Aude	0.315	0.320	0.294	0.231	0.223	0.230	0.202
Aveyron	0.370	0.363	0.335	0.264	0.270	0.278	0.264
Bouches-du-Rh.	0.326	0.322	0.284	0.276	0.270	0.242	0.209
Calvados	0.235	0.243	0.240	0.236	0.238	0.246	0.220
Cantal	0.290	0.257	0.274	0.234	0.253	0.263	0.255
Charente	0.304	0.276	0.236	0.231	0.228	0.222	0.206
Charente-Infér.	0.268	0.259	0.234	0.207	0.210	0.214	0.207
Cher	0.347	0.299	0.282	0.251	0.232	0.237	0.210
Correze	0.402	0.429	0.322	0.287	0.287	0.293	0.257
Corse	0.393	0.381	0.344	0.347	0.338	0.307	0.256
Côte d'Or	0.231	0.220	0.217	0.215	0.211	0.216	0.192
Côtes du Nord	0.371	0.333	0.326	0.330	0.361	0.366	0.298
Creuse	0.303	0.261	0.267	0.235	0.240	0.242	0.214
Dordogne	0.333	0.321	0.335	0.239	0.246	0.249	0.241
Doubs	0.351	0.348	0.312	0.282	0.283	0.301	0.248
Drome	0.296	0.276	0.271	0.250	0.254	0.243	0.203
Eure	0.230	0.216	0.228	0.233	0.235	0.247	0.223
Eure-et-Loir	0.273	0.259	0.259	0.250	0.243	0.248	0.236
Finistère	0.523	0.510	0.479	0.446	0.436	0.416	0.332

Table C.21 Overall Coale Index $\tilde{I}_f$.

département	date						
	1876	1881	1886	1891	1896	1901	1906
Gard	0.328	0.291	0.272	0.256	0.250	0.240	0.201
Garonne(Haute-)	0.225	0.207	0.230	0.180	0.190	0.189	0.176
Gers	0.226	0.211	0.193	0.160	0.176	0.184	0.178
Gironde	0.225	0.236	0.238	0.194	0.195	0.188	0.161
Hérault	0.320	0.249	0.222	0.222	0.218	0.229	0.191
Ille-et-Vilaine	0.350	0.336	0.327	0.295	0.278	0.276	0.226
Indre	0.321	0.293	0.289	0.256	0.248	0.252	0.217
Indre-et-Loire	0.240	0.234	0.230	0.207	0.204	0.207	0.187
Isère	0.344	0.247	0.240	0.228	0.231	0.226	0.196
Jura	0.333	0.313	0.304	0.270	0.271	0.291	0.235
Landes	0.392	0.369	0.323	0.227	0.252	0.265	0.234
Loire-et-Cher	0.277	0.259	0.253	0.237	0.226	0.232	0.217
Loire	0.372	0.353	0.272	0.260	0.249	0.252	0.202
Loire(Haute-)	0.352	0.317	0.309	0.294	0.290	0.273	0.243
Loire-Infér.	0.274	0.286	0.289	0.260	0.247	0.248	0.201
Loiret	0.292	0.274	0.268	0.249	0.230	0.234	0.216
Lot	0.250	0.277	0.221	0.190	0.195	0.207	0.197
Lot-et-Gar.	0.208	0.195	0.173	0.165	0.174	0.179	0.166
Lozère	0.585	0.566	0.407	0.355	0.372	0.352	0.293
Maine-et-Loire	0.251	0.240	0.227	0.210	0.207	0.215	0.192
Manche	0.278	0.285	0.279	0.288	0.274	0.268	0.235
Marne	0.279	0.271	0.270	0.258	0.249	0.256	0.236
Marne(Haute-)	0.259	0.248	0.235	0.224	0.228	0.236	0.217
Mayenne	0.318	0.312	0.277	0.266	0.265	0.269	0.238
Meurthe	.	.	.	.	.	.	.
Meurthe-et-Moselle	0.295	0.272	0.266	0.263	0.267	0.273	0.265
Meuse	0.270	0.265	0.252	0.258	0.255	0.257	0.240
Morbihan	0.384	0.364	0.362	0.357	0.347	0.340	0.291
Moselle	.	.	.	.	.	.	.
Nièvre	0.327	0.278	0.267	0.241	0.232	0.242	0.209

Table C.22 Overall Coale Index $\tilde{I}_f$.

département	date						
	1876	1881	1886	1891	1896	1901	1906
Nord	0.392	0.374	0.329	0.309	0.297	0.292	0.242
Oise	0.264	0.266	0.251	0.250	0.252	0.261	0.236
Orne	0.201	0.222	0.195	0.198	0.202	0.216	0.208
Pas-de-Calais	0.399	0.387	0.366	0.357	0.352	0.369	0.316
Puy-de-Dome	0.278	0.267	0.250	0.213	0.215	0.216	0.186
Pyrénées(Basses-)	0.314	0.307	0.271	0.256	0.259	0.267	0.248
Pyrénées(Hautes-)	0.275	0.245	0.211	0.196	0.214	0.225	0.201
Pyrénées-Orient.	0.382	0.376	0.317	0.281	0.282	0.261	0.238
Rhin(Bas-)	.	.	.	.	.	.	.
Rhin(Haut-)	.	.	.	.	.	.	.
Rhône	0.276	0.255	0.225	0.214	0.200	0.202	0.167
Saône(Haute-)	0.296	0.281	0.283	0.251	0.256	0.275	0.241
Saône-et-Loire	0.354	0.319	0.285	0.259	0.265	0.278	0.232
Sarthe	0.234	0.223	0.234	0.217	0.227	0.241	0.223
Savoie	0.343	0.349	0.322	0.286	0.280	0.295	0.252
Savoie(Haute-)	0.340	0.349	0.338	0.303	0.297	0.316	0.260
Seine	0.270	0.288	0.262	0.241	0.210	0.200	0.162
Seine-et-Marne	0.273	0.260	0.247	0.240	0.239	0.242	0.218
Seine-et-Oise	0.276	0.265	0.245	0.245	0.241	0.241	0.198
Seine-Infér.	0.341	0.314	0.327	0.301	0.295	0.298	0.270
Sèvres(Deux-)	0.306	0.294	0.270	0.256	0.241	0.230	0.212
Somme	0.254	0.263	0.247	0.250	0.245	0.256	0.223
Tarn	0.274	0.244	0.213	0.207	0.219	0.229	0.210
Tarn-et-Gar.	0.227	0.216	0.196	0.181	0.193	0.202	0.187
Var	0.284	0.262	0.261	0.215	0.218	0.236	0.202
Vaucluse	0.260	0.248	0.243	0.220	0.236	0.234	0.207
Vendée	0.358	0.336	0.327	0.303	0.280	0.271	0.242
Vienne	0.311	0.280	0.259	0.237	0.233	0.234	0.221
Vienne(Haute-)	0.402	0.348	0.333	0.304	0.302	0.292	0.250
Vosges	0.316	0.293	0.285	0.271	0.283	0.279	0.258
Yonne	0.237	0.217	0.211	0.201	0.207	0.206	0.194
Terr. de Belfort	0.460	0.386	0.351	0.299	0.277	0.286	0.249
France	0.305	0.294	0.274	0.254	0.250	0.251	0.217

Appendices

Table C.23 Net migration from [20-24] to [25-29] years old.

département	period				
	56-60	61-65	66-70	71-75	76-80
Ain	-0.020	-0.010	-0.027	0.003	-0.048
Aisne	-0.029	-0.016	-0.013	-0.013	-0.043
Allier	0.025	0.017	0.017	-0.004	-0.025
Alpes(Basses-)	-0.033	-0.054	-0.040	-0.029	-0.062
Alpes(Hautes-)	-0.039	-0.017	-0.054	-0.008	-0.059
Alpes Marit.	.	-0.038	-0.058	0.062	0.102
Ardèche	-0.062	-0.056	-0.048	-0.019	-0.087
Ardennes	-0.035	-0.023	-0.016	-0.018	-0.016
Ariège	-0.070	-0.053	-0.045	-0.041	-0.058
Aube	-0.004	-0.008	-0.005	0.016	0.005
Aude	-0.031	-0.033	0.003	0.021	-0.004
Aveyron	-0.047	-0.018	-0.018	0.003	-0.077
Bouches-du-Rh.	0.062	0.095	0.083	0.085	0.067
Calvados	0.004	0.020	0.018	0.020	-0.016
Cantal	-0.084	-0.061	-0.060	-0.030	-0.061
Charente	0.002	0.010	0.010	0.019	0.007
Charente-Inf.	-0.003	0.010	0.023	-0.012	-0.011
Cher	-0.029	-0.017	-0.015	-0.017	-0.025
Correze	0.027	-0.027	-0.007	0.009	-0.054
Corse	-0.018	-0.036	-0.022	0.015	-0.063
Côte d'Or	-0.055	-0.032	-0.007	-0.002	-0.023
Côtes du Nord	-0.086	-0.048	-0.030	-0.011	-0.068
Creuse	-0.065	-0.048	-0.045	-0.019	-0.049
Dordogne	-0.025	-0.034	-0.011	-0.002	-0.026
Doubs	-0.047	-0.009	0.001	0.001	-0.006
Drome	-0.070	-0.029	-0.017	0.013	-0.031
Eure	-0.023	-0.004	-0.013	-0.004	-0.033
Eure-et-Loir	-0.046	-0.018	-0.006	0.011	-0.023
Finistère	-0.010	-0.011	-0.025	-0.014	-0.009

Table C.24 Net migration from [20-24] to [25-29] years old.

département	period				
	81-85	86-90	91-95	96-00	01-05
Ain	-0.009	-0.019	-0.041	-0.117	-0.036
Aisne	-0.029	-0.016	-0.039	-0.060	-0.018
Allier	-0.032	-0.036	-0.064	-0.093	-0.065
Alpes(Basses-)	-0.084	-0.091	-0.114	-0.152	-0.043
Alpes(Hautes-)	-0.073	-0.077	-0.116	-0.136	-0.056
Alpes Marit.	0.101	0.142	0.172	0.109	0.184
Ardèche	-0.077	-0.079	-0.104	-0.163	-0.102
Ardennes	-0.014	-0.024	-0.042	-0.078	-0.031
Ariège	-0.081	-0.078	-0.131	-0.108	-0.044
Aube	0.008	0.015	0.012	-0.007	-0.021
Aude	-0.003	0.030	0.015	-0.033	-0.039
Aveyron	-0.072	-0.102	-0.133	-0.201	-0.100
Bouches-du-Rh.	0.113	0.099	0.145	0.129	0.115
Calvados	-0.017	-0.007	-0.014	-0.010	-0.027
Cantal	-0.096	-0.137	-0.140	-0.195	-0.173
Charente	-0.010	-0.012	-0.002	-0.008	-0.024
Charente-Inf.	-0.013	-0.071	-0.062	-0.018	-0.013
Cher	-0.053	-0.041	-0.078	-0.103	-0.048
Correze	-0.053	-0.087	-0.151	-0.146	-0.115
Corse	-0.008	-0.039	-0.076	-0.177	-0.083
Côte d'Or	-0.024	-0.033	-0.042	-0.054	-0.037
Côtes du Nord	-0.090	-0.092	-0.112	-0.151	-0.084
Creuse	-0.083	-0.080	-0.119	-0.195	-0.119
Dordogne	-0.031	-0.003	-0.110	-0.157	-0.060
Doubs	0.003	-0.014	-0.056	-0.063	-0.015
Drome	-0.054	-0.008	-0.010	-0.073	-0.042
Eure	-0.021	-0.015	-0.002	-0.017	-0.004
Eure-et-Loir	-0.017	-0.012	-0.032	-0.035	-0.018
Finistère	-0.047	-0.066	-0.069	-0.039	-0.058

Table C.25 Net migration from [20-24] to [25-29] years old.

département	period				
	56-60	61-65	66-70	71-75	76-80
Gard	0.001	0.003	-0.004	0.011	-0.014
Garonne(Hte-)	0.026	0.022	0.015	0.020	-0.043
Gers	-0.035	-0.015	0.004	0.009	0.020
Gironde	0.053	0.068	0.062	0.070	0.041
Hérault	0.030	0.066	0.085	0.080	0.053
Ille-et-Vilaine	-0.003	-0.000	-0.027	-0.005	-0.021
Indre	-0.047	-0.021	-0.023	-0.014	-0.023
Indre-et-Loire	-0.016	-0.002	0.037	0.024	0.011
Isère	-0.034	-0.070	-0.049	-0.006	-0.031
Jura	-0.041	-0.024	-0.021	-0.006	-0.056
Landes	0.037	0.018	-0.046	-0.022	-0.002
Loire-et-Cher	-0.042	-0.015	-0.032	-0.018	-0.025
Loire	0.030	0.020	-0.004	0.016	0.001
Loire(Haute-)	-0.025	-0.039	-0.015	-0.002	-0.063
Loire-Infér.	0.031	0.004	0.015	0.007	0.006
Loiret	-0.018	-0.012	-0.001	-0.007	-0.037
Lot	-0.024	-0.016	-0.020	-0.009	-0.023
Lot-et-Gar.	-0.015	0.013	0.018	0.010	0.012
Lozère	-0.054	-0.055	-0.037	0.013	-0.069
Maine-et-Loire	0.007	0.006	0.008	0.021	0.007
Manche	-0.063	-0.046	-0.046	-0.020	-0.074
Marne	-0.003	0.007	0.039	0.029	0.012
Marne(Haute-)	-0.005	-0.020	0.008	0.002	-0.077
Mayenne	-0.004	-0.024	-0.016	-0.005	-0.031
Meurthe	-0.054	-0.023	.	.	.
Meurthe-et-mos.	.	.	.	-0.066	-0.122
Meuse	-0.080	-0.047	-0.027	-0.031	-0.025
Morbihan	-0.012	-0.018	0.002	-0.018	-0.038
Moselle	-0.075	-0.043	.	.	.
Nièvre	-0.053	-0.041	-0.031	-0.019	-0.041

Table C.26 Net migration from [20-24] to [25-29] years old.

département	period				
	81-85	86-90	91-95	96-00	01-05
Gard	-0.006	-0.000	-0.032	-0.032	0.008
Garonne(Hte-)	-0.002	-0.018	-0.049	-0.052	0.006
Gers	-0.009	-0.021	-0.066	-0.083	-0.036
Gironde	0.049	0.062	0.037	0.027	0.011
Hérault	0.083	0.041	0.048	0.039	-0.012
Ille-et-Vilaine	-0.050	-0.048	-0.088	-0.140	-0.066
Indre	-0.041	-0.047	-0.049	-0.069	-0.040
Indre-et-Loire	0.016	0.008	0.012	-0.016	-0.001
Isère	-0.056	-0.096	-0.031	-0.007	-0.026
Jura	-0.028	-0.033	-0.053	-0.086	-0.034
Landes	-0.092	-0.075	-0.071	-0.140	-0.056
Loire-et-Cher	-0.036	-0.055	-0.030	-0.066	-0.035
Loire	0.015	-0.007	-0.024	-0.015	-0.018
Loire(Haute-)	-0.055	-0.074	-0.074	-0.104	-0.062
Loire-Infér.	-0.025	-0.031	-0.020	-0.060	-0.006
Loiret	-0.025	-0.024	-0.042	-0.074	-0.040
Lot	-0.029	-0.050	-0.107	-0.274	-0.082
Lot-et-Gar.	-0.009	-0.001	-0.024	-0.040	-0.006
Lozère	-0.094	-0.120	-0.161	-0.193	-0.076
Maine-et-Loire	-0.012	-0.010	-0.008	-0.007	-0.006
Manche	-0.041	-0.030	-0.058	-0.035	-0.034
Marne	0.005	0.000	-0.004	-0.038	-0.019
Marne(Haute-)	-0.029	-0.009	-0.079	-0.084	-0.047
Mayenne	-0.047	-0.073	-0.067	-0.115	-0.047
Meurthe	.	.	.	.	.
Meurthe-et-mos.	-0.060	-0.051	-0.002	-0.023	0.032
Meuse	-0.030	-0.039	-0.023	-0.068	-0.062
Morbihan	-0.052	-0.043	-0.083	-0.142	-0.068
Moselle	.	.	.	.	.
Nièvre	-0.069	-0.095	-0.108	-0.181	-0.096

Table C.27 Net migration from [20-24] to [25-29] years old.

département	period				
	1856-60	61-65	66-70	71-75	76-80
Nord	0.001	0.014	0.018	0.030	0.013
Oise	-0.012	-0.009	-0.003	0.001	-0.005
Orne	0.006	0.009	0.001	-0.017	-0.028
Pas-de-Calais	-0.023	-0.006	-0.002	-0.000	-0.007
Puy-de-Dome	-0.030	-0.022	-0.006	0.007	-0.034
Pyr.(Basses-)	-0.045	-0.044	-0.032	-0.007	-0.047
Pyr.(Hautes-)	-0.036	-0.027	-0.036	-0.006	-0.048
Pyrénées-Or.	0.012	0.027	0.027	0.016	0.003
Rhin(Bas-)	-0.072	-0.046	.	.	.
Rhin(Haut-)	-0.080	-0.035	.	.	.
Rhône	0.071	0.077	0.088	0.091	0.071
Saône(Haute-)	-0.042	-0.049	-0.053	-0.032	-0.083
Saône-et-Loire	-0.025	-0.021	-0.033	-0.007	-0.023
Sarthe	-0.033	-0.017	-0.015	-0.003	-0.033
Savoie	.	-0.096	-0.081	-0.031	-0.056
Savoie(Haute-)	.	-0.027	-0.089	-0.035	-0.044
Seine	0.258	0.294	0.063	0.184	0.140
Seine-Infér.	0.048	0.060	0.009	0.033	-0.003
Seine-et-Marne	-0.018	-0.012	-0.021	-0.009	-0.019
Seine-et-Oise	0.038	0.047	0.034	0.059	0.016
Sèvres(Deux-)	-0.006	0.002	0.001	0.019	-0.009
Somme	-0.009	-0.015	-0.008	-0.013	-0.024
Tarn	-0.023	-0.034	-0.018	0.001	-0.033
Tarn-et-Gar.	-0.006	-0.001	0.003	0.006	0.003
Var	0.078	0.045	-0.020	0.036	0.029
Vaucluse	-0.028	0.001	-0.013	-0.003	-0.037
Vendée	-0.010	-0.020	-0.008	-0.005	-0.015
Vienne	0.006	0.011	0.002	0.016	-0.004
Vienne(Haute-)	0.008	0.002	0.009	0.009	-0.014
Vosges	-0.040	-0.041	-0.031	-0.010	-0.046
Yonne	-0.069	-0.042	-0.034	-0.028	-0.046
Terr. de Belfort	.	.	.	-0.516	-0.318

Table C.28 Net migration from [20-24] to [25-29] years old.

département	period				
	1881-85	86-90	91-95	96-00	01-05
Nord	0.004	0.002	-0.023	-0.017	-0.035
Oise	-0.000	0.005	0.000	-0.022	-0.006
Orne	-0.032	-0.038	-0.081	-0.075	-0.049
Pas-de-Calais	-0.021	-0.047	-0.068	-0.082	0.041
Puy-de-Dome	-0.021	-0.027	-0.038	-0.060	-0.028
Pyr.(Basses-)	-0.041	-0.086	-0.097	-0.144	-0.075
Pyr.(Hautes-)	-0.062	-0.106	-0.136	-0.125	-0.063
Pyrénées-Or.	-0.008	-0.013	-0.031	-0.022	-0.036
Rhin(Bas-)	.	.	.	.	.
Rhin(Haut-)	.	.	.	.	.
Rhône	0.088	0.092	0.097	0.047	0.054
Saône(Haute-)	-0.054	-0.046	-0.070	-0.086	-0.038
Saône-et-Loire	-0.058	-0.036	-0.069	-0.040	-0.058
Sarthe	-0.035	-0.023	-0.019	-0.036	-0.015
Savoie	-0.052	-0.064	-0.056	-0.136	-0.054
Savoie(Haute-)	-0.047	-0.066	-0.074	-0.130	-0.050
Seine	0.173	0.181	0.198	0.193	0.151
Seine-Infér.	0.007	-0.006	0.006	-0.027	-0.024
Seine-et-Marne	-0.004	-0.016	-0.016	-0.030	0.025
Seine-et-Oise	0.050	0.030	0.053	0.072	0.090
Sèvres(Deux-)	-0.016	-0.022	-0.056	-0.030	-0.061
Somme	-0.014	-0.022	-0.001	-0.038	-0.040
Tarn	-0.046	-0.048	-0.054	-0.102	-0.026
Tarn-et-Gar.	-0.012	-0.004	-0.018	-0.057	-0.052
Var	0.062	0.064	0.074	0.064	0.074
Vaucluse	-0.017	-0.003	0.007	0.026	0.004
Vendée	-0.028	-0.004	-0.015	-0.020	-0.062
Vienne	-0.014	-0.050	-0.052	-0.086	-0.049
Vienne(Haute-)	-0.019	-0.032	-0.045	-0.095	-0.048
Vosges	-0.022	-0.014	-0.020	-0.017	-0.020
Yonne	-0.047	-0.068	-0.076	-0.109	-0.052
Terr. de Belfort	-0.199	-0.050	-0.123	-0.057	-0.024

References

Abeysinghe, T., 'Time Cost, relative income and fertility in Canada', *Journal of Population Economics* (1993), 189–98.

Akaike, H., 'Canonical Correlations Analysis of Time Series and the Use of an Information Criterion', in R. Mehra and G. Lainiotis (edd.), *Advances and Case Studies in System Identification* (New York, Academic Press, 1976).

Akima, H., 'A new method of interpolation and smooth curve fitting based on local procedures', *Journal of the ACM*, 17 (1970), 589–602.

Aoki, M., *State Space Modeling of Time Series* (New York, Springer Verlag, 1990).

Ariès, P., *Histoire des populations françaises et leurs attitudes devant la vie* (Paris, Self, 1948; Le Seuil, 1971).

——, *Deux motivations successives du déclin de la fécondité en Occident* (Liège, UIESP, 1980).

Bartels Richard, H., Beaty, John C., and Barsky, Brian A., *An introduction to Splines for use in Computer Graphics and Geometric Modeling* (Morgan Kaufman Publishers, 1987).

Bean, L. L., Mineau G. P., and Anderton D. L., *Fertility Change on the American Frontier, Adaptation and Innovation* (University of California Press, 1990).

Biraben, J. N., 'La statistique de la population sous le Consulat et l'Empire', *Revue d'histoire moderne et contemporaine*, XVII, juillet–septembre (1970), 359–72.

Bonneuil, N., 'Cohérence comptable des tableaux de la SGF', *Population* 4–5 (1989), 809–40.

——, 'Turbulent Dynamics in a 17th century population', *Mathematical Population Studies*, 2–4 (1990), 289-311.

——, 'Non-identifiabilité et cohérence démographique de la rétro-projection', in *Modèles de la Démographie Historique* (PUF INED, Congrès et Colloques 11, 1992), 99–108.

——, 'Démographie de la nuptialité au XIXe siècle', in *La Société française au XIXe siècle* (Fayard, 1992), 82–120.

de Boor, C., *A practical guide to splines* (Springer-Verlag, New York, 1978).

Blum, A., Houdaille, J., and Tugault, Y., 'Baisse de la fécondité dans la vallée de la Garonne (1740–1860)', *Population*, 3 (1987), 503–26.

Bourgeois-Pichat, J., 'Evolution générale de la population française depuis le XVIIIe siècle', *Population*, 6 (1951), 635–62.

——, 'Note sur l'évolution générale de la population française depuis le XVIIe siècle', *Population*, 7 (1952), 319–29.

——, 'The General Development of the Population of France since the Eighteenth Century', in D. V. Glass and D. E. C. Eversley (edd.), *Population in History* (Chicago, Aldine, 1965), 474–506 (translation of Bourgeois-Pichat, 1951 and 1952).

Brouard, N., 'Une modélisation de l'enquête sur la mortalité infantile et juvénile à Yaoundé', *INSERM*, 145 (1986), 385–406.

Brown, L., 'A review and version of the quantitative theory of the spatial diffusion of innovations', *Diffusion Dynamics, Lund Studies in Geography* B–29 (1968).

Brunet, R., *La Carte Mode d'Emploi* (Fayard, 1987).

Carlsson, G., 'The decline of fertility: innovation or adjustment process', *Population Studies*, 20 (1969), 149–74.

Chiang Chin Long, 'Introduction to Stochastic Processes in Biostatistics' (New York, John Wiley and Sons, Inc., 1968).

——, 'An introduction to Stochastic Processes and their applications' (New York, Robert E. Krieger Publishing Company Huttington, 1980).

Cleland, J., and Wilson, C., 'Demand theories of the fertility transition: an iconoclastic view', *Population Studies*, March, XLI, 2 (1987), 5–30.

Cliff, A. D., and Hagett, P., *Atlas of disease distributions, Analytic Approaches to epidemiological data* (Oxford, Blackwell, 1988).

Coale, A. J., 'The decline of fertility in Europe from the French revolution to World War II', in S. J. Behrman et al. (edd.), *Fertility and Family Planning: A World View* (Ann Arbor, University of Michigan Press, 1969).

——, and Demeny, P., *Regional life tables and stable populations* (Princeton N.J., Princeton University Press, 1966).

——, and Trussel, T. J., 'Model fertility schedules in the age structure of childbearing in human populations', *Population Index*, 40 (2) (1974), 185–258, *Erratum in Population Index*, 41 (1974), 572.

——, and Wattkins, S. C. (edd.), *The decline of fertility in Europe: the revised proceedings of a conference on the Princeton European fertility project* (Princeton N.J., Princeton University Press, 1986).

——, and Zelnik, M., *New Estimates of Fertility and Populations in the United States: A study of Annual White Births from 1855 to 1960 and of completeness of Enumeration in the censuses from 1880–1960* (Princeton N.J., Princeton University Press, 1968).

Cressie, N., *Statistics for Spatial Data* (New York, John Wiley & Sons, Inc., 1991).

Dahmen, W., and Micheli, C. A., 'Multivariate splines. A new constructive approach', in R. E. Barnhill and W. Boehm (edd.), *Surfaces in CAGD* (North Holland, 1983).

Davidson J. E. H., Hendry D., Srba F., and Yeo S., 'Econometric Modelling of the Agregate Time-Series Relationship Between Consumers' Expenditures and Income in the United Kingdom', *The Econometric Journal*, 88 (1978), 661–92.

Deloche, G., and Seron, X., *Mathematical Disabilities* (Lawrence Erlbaum Associates, 1987).

——, 'Numerical Transcoding: A General Production Model', in *Mathematical Disabilities* (Lawrence Erlbaum Associates, 1987b).

Del Panta, L., and Rettaroli, R., *Introduzione alla demograofia storica* (Editori Laterza, 1994).

Demeny, P., and Shorter, F., 'A general method of correcting age misrepresenting in census populations', *Demography*, 12 (1975), 303–12.

Dickey, D. A., and Fuller, W. A., 'Distribution of the estimators for Autoregressive Time Series with a Unit Root', *JASA*, 74 (1979), 427–31.

Doz, C., Malgrange, P., 'Modèles VAR et prévisions à court terme', *Economie et Prévision*, 106 (1992), 109–118.

Dumont, A., *Dépopulation et Civilisation* (Economica, 1990).

Dupâquier, J. (ed.) *Histoire de la Population Française* (PUF, 1988b).

——, and Kessler, D. (edd.), *La société française au XIXe siècle* (Fayard, 1992).

——, and Le Mée, R., 'La connaissance des faits démographiques de 1789 à 1914', in J. Dupâquier (ed.), *Histoire de la Population Française* (PUF, 1988).

Dyson, T., and Murphy, M., 'The onset of fertility transition', *Population and Development Review*, 11 (1985), 399–440.

Eckstein, Z., Schultz, T. P., and Wolpin, K. I., 'Short-run fluctuations in fertility and mortality in pre-industrial Sweden', *European Demographic Review*, 26 (1985), 295–317.

Engle, R. F., and Granger, C. W. J., 'Co-integration and Error Correction: representation, Estimation and Testing', *Econometrica*, 55 (1987), 251–76.

Fine, A., and Sangoï, 'La population française au XIXe siècle', *Que sais-je?* (PUF, 1991).

Fisher, L. D., and van Belle G., 'Biostatitics: a methodology for the health sciences' (New York, John Wiley & Sons, 1993).

Freedman, R., 'The contribution of social science research to population policy and family planning program effectiveness', *Studies in Family Planning*, 18 (1987), 57–82.

Fuller, W. A., *Introduction to Statistical Time series* (New York, John Wiley & Sons, Inc., 1976).

Galloway, P., 'Basic patterns in annual variations in fertility, nuptiality, mortality and prices in preindustrial Europe', *Population Studies*, 42 (1988), 275–303.

——, 'Changements séculaires des freins à court terme à la croissance démographique en Europe: frein positif, frein préventif et frein de température', in *Modèles de la Démographie Historique* Congrès et Colloques 11 (PUF INED, 1992), 193–240.

Geweke, J., Meese, R., and Dent, W., 'Comparing alternative tests of causality in temporal systems', *Journal of Econometry*, 21 (1983), 161–94.

Grafman, J., *Handbook of Neuropsychology, Acalculia*, (New York, Elsevier Science Publishers B.V., 1988).

Guérin-Pace, F., *Deux siècles de croissance urbaine* (Paris, Anthropos-Economica, 1993).

Gonzalez, E. G., and Kolers, P. A., 'Mental Manipulation of Arithmetic Symbols', *Journal of Experimental Psychology: Learning, Memory and Cognition*, 8 (1982).

——, 'Notational Constraints on Mental Operations' in *Mathematical Disabilities* (Hillsdale, Lawrence Erlbaum Associates, 1987).

Greville, T.N., 'Mortality tables analyzed by cause of death', *Record of the American institute of Actuaries*, 37 (1948), 283–94.

Guinnane, T., Okun, B. S., and Trussel, J., *What do we know about the timing of fertility transitions in Europe?*, Princeton University, Working Paper 92–11 (1992).

Hägerstrand, T., 'The propagation of innovation waves', *Lund Studies in Geography* B–4 (1952).

——, *Innovation Diffusion as a spatial process*, (Chicago, University of Chicago Press, 1953), (translation 1967).

Hamilton, J. D., *Time Series Analysis*, (Princeton, N.J., Princeton University Press, 1994)..

Henry, L., 'Fécondité dans le sud-ouest de la France (1)', *Annales ESC*, 3 (1972), 612–39 and 4–5 (1972), 977–1023.

——, 'Fécondité dans le sud-est de la France de 1670 à 1829, *Population*, 4–5 (1978), 855–84.

Henry, L., and Blayo, Y., 'La population de la France de 1740 à 1860', *Population*, 4–5 (1975), 905–14.

Henry, L., and Houdaille, J., 'Fécondité dans le nord-ouest de la France de 1670 à 1829', *Population*, 4–5 (1973), 873–924.

Hollender, D., and Peereman, R., 'Differential Processing of Phonographic and Logographic Single-Digit Numbers by the two Hemispheres', in *Mathematical Disabilities* (Hillsdale, Lawrence Erlbaum Associates, 1987).

Houdaille, J., 'La fécondité des mariages de 1670 à 1829 dans le quart nord-est de la France', *Annales de démographie historique* (1976), 342–91.

Johansen, S., 'Statistical Analysis of Co-Integration Vectors', *Journal of Economic Dynamics and Control*, 12 (1988), 231–54.

——, 'Estimation and hypothesis testing of co-integration vectors in Gaussian vector autoregressive models', *Econometrica*, 59 (1991), 1551–80.

——, and Juselius, K., 'Maximum Likelihood Estimation and Inference on Cointegration, with Applications to the Demand for Money', *Oxford Bulletin of Economics and Statistics*, 52 (1990), 169–210.

Judge, G. G., Griffiths, W. E., Hill R. C., Lötkepohl, H., and Lee, T. C., *The Theory and Practice of Econometrics*, Second Edition (New York, John Wiley & Sons, Inc., 1985).

Keyfitz, N., *Introduction to the mathematics of population* (Reading, Massachussets, Addison-Wesley, 1968).

Kuagbenou, K., *Les causes de décès à Paris, 1832–1849* (Paris, mémoire de DEA EHESS, 1992).

Knodel, J. E., *The Decline of Fertility in Germany, 1871–1939*, (Princeton, N.J., Princeton University Press, 1974).

——, 'Age patterns of fertility and the fertility transition: evidence from Europe and Asia', *Population Studies*, 31 (1977), 219–50.

——, *Demographic behavior in the past* (Cambridge, Cambridge University Press, 1988).

Le Bras, H., *Les Trois France* (Paris, Odile Jacob, 1986).

——, 'La chute de la fécondité', in J. Dupâquier (ed.), *Histoire de la Population Française* (PUF, 1988).

Ledent, J., 'Multistate life tables: movement versus transition perspectives', *Environment and Planning*, 12 (1980), 5–33.

Lee, R. D., 'Estimating Series of Vital Rates and Ages Structures from Baptisms and Burials: A New Technique with Applications to Pre-Industrial England', *Population Studies* 28 (1974), 495–512.

——, 'Short-term fluctuations of vital rates, prices and weather in England, 1539 to 1840', in E.A. Wrigley and R. S. Schofield (edd.), *The Population History of England, 1541–1871: a reconstruction* (Cambridge Mass, Harvard University Press, 1981).

——, 'Inverse Projection and Back Projection: A Critical Appraisal and Comparative Results for England, 1539 to 1871', *Population Studies*, 39 (1985), 233–48.

Ledermann, S., and Bréas, J., 'Les dimensions de la mortalité', *Population*, 4 (1959), 637–82.

Lepetit, B., 'Les dénivellations de l'espace économique en France', *Annales E.S.C.*, 6 (1986), 1243–72.

Lesthaeghe, R., *The decline of Belgian fertility, 1800–1970* (Princeton N.J., Princeton University Press, 1977).

——, 'A century of demographic and cultural changes: an exploration of underlying dimensions', *Population and Development Review*, 9 (1983), 411–35.

——, 'Motivation et Légitimation : conditions de vie et régimes de fécondité en Belgique et en France du XVIe au XIXe siècle', in *Modèles de la Démographie Historique*, Congrès et Colloques 11 (Paris, PUF INED, 1992), 275–318.

McCaa, R., 'The female population of Chile, 1855–1964: a microcomputer balance sheet method', *Latin American Population History*, 15 (1989), 9–14.

Meslé, F., and Vallin, J., 'Reconstitution de tables annuelles de mortalité pour la France au XIXe siècle', *Population*, 6 (1989), 1121–58.

Notestein, F. W., 'Population: the long view', in T. W. Schultz (ed.), Food for the World (Chicago, Ill., Chicago University Press, 1945), 36–57.

Oeppen, J., 'La projection inverse généralisée et le problème des crises de mortalitè', in *Modèles de la Démographie Historique*, Congrès et Colloques 11 (PUF INED, 1992), 109–28.

Park, H., 'Essays on the Application of Time Series Analysis to Regional Growth', PhD Thesis (University of Southern California, 1996).

Perron, P., and Campbell, J. Y., 'Racines unitaires en macro-économie : le cas multidimensionnel', *Annales d'Economie et de Statistique*, 27 (1992), 1-50.

Phillips, P. C. B., and Perron, P., 'Testing for a unit root in time series regression', *Biometrika*, 75 (1988), 335-346.

Pollak, R., A., and Watkins, S. C., 'Cultural and Economic Approaches to Fertility: Proper Marriage or Mésalliance?', *Population and Development Review*, 19 (1993), 467–96.

Poussou, J. P., Courgeau, D., and Dupâquier, J., 'Les Migrations intérieures', in *Histoire de la Population Française*, 3 (Paris, PUF, 1988), 177–97.

Pressat, R., 'L'analyse démographique' (Paris, PUF, 1983).

Racine, J. B., and Raffestin, C., 'Contribution de l'analyse géographique à l'histoire de l'art : une approche des phénomènes de concentration et de diffusion', in *Schweizerische Archeologie une Kunstgeschichte* (Band 41, 1984), 67–75.

Rogers, A., 'Introduction to Multiregional Mathematical Demography' (New York, John Wiley & Sons, 1975).

——, (ed.), 'Essays in Multistate Demography', *Environment and planning*, 12–5 (1980), 33.

——, Raquillet, R., and Castro, L. J., 'Model Migration Schedules and their Applications', *Environment and Planning*, A 10(5) (1978), 475–502.

Rosero-Bixby, L., and Casterline, J. B., 'Modelling Diffusion Effects in Fertility Transition', *Population Studies*, 47–1 (1993), 147–67.

Saint-Julien, T., 'La diffusion spatiale des innovations', *GIP Reclus* (Montpelier, 1985).

Saporta, G., *Probabilités, Analyse des Données et Statistique* (Paris, Editions Technip, 1990).

Schoen, R., *Modeling Multigroup Populations* (New York, Plenum Press, 1988).

Shryock, H., and Siegel, J., 'The Methods and Materials of Demography' (Washington D.C., Government Printing Office, 1973).

Spiers, P. A., 'Acalculia revisited: current issues', in *Mathematical Disabilities* (Hillsdale, Lawrence Erlbaum Associates, 1987).

Tabah, L., 'La répartition par âges de la population française en 1851', *Population*, 2 (1947), 349–54.

Taylor, P. J., *Quantitative Methods in Geography, An Introduction to Spatial Analysis* (Boston, Houghton Mifflin, 1977).

Tugault, Y., *La mesure de la mobilité*, Cahier INED 67 (Paris, PUF, 1973).

——, *Fécondité et urbanisation*, Cahier INED 74 (Paris, PUF, 1975).

van de Walle, E., *The Female Population of France in the Nineteenth Century* (Princeton, Princeton University Press, 1974).

Wachter, K. W., 'Ergodicity and Inverse Projection', *Population Studies*, 40 (1986), 275–87.

Watkins, S. C., 'The fertility transition: Europe and the Third World compared', *Sociological Forum*, 2–4 (1987), 645–73.

Wattelar, C., *Perspectives démographiques par sexe et par âge: les indices de mortalité et le calcul des survivants*, Collection Recherches démographiques, cahier 2 (Cabay, Louvain-la-Neuve, Université Catholique de Louvain, 1983).

Weir, D. R., *Fertility Transition in Rural France 1740–1829*, PhD Thesis (Stanford University, 1982).

——, 'New estimates of nuptiality and marital fertility in France, 1740–1911', *Population Studies*, 48 (1994), 307–31.

Woods, R. 'The spatial dynamics of the demographic transition in the West', in Woods R. and Rees P. (edd.), *Population, Structures and Models* (London, Allen and Unwin, 1986), 21–44.

Wrigley, E. A., 'The Fall of Marital Fertility in Nineteenth-Century France: Exemplar or Exception?', *European Journal of Population*, 1–1 (1985), 31–60 and 2 (1985), 141–77.

——, and Schofield, R. S., *The Population History of England 1541–1871, A Reconstruction* (London, Edward Arnold, 1981).

Zellner, 'An efficient method of estimating seemingly unrelated regressions and tests for aggregation bias', *JASA*, 57 (1962), 348–68.

Index